Practicing Midrash

Practicing Midrash

Reading the Bible's Arguments as
an Invitation to Conversation

F. Timothy Moore

WIPF & STOCK · Eugene, Oregon

PRACTICING MIDRASH
Reading the Bible's Arguments as an Invitation to Conversation

Wipf & Stock
An Imprint of Wipf and Stock Publishers
199 W. 8th Ave., Suite 3
Eugene, OR 97401

www.wipfandstock.com

PAPERBACK ISBN: 978-1-5326-4546-4
HARDCOVER ISBN: 978-1-5326-4547-1
EBOOK ISBN: 978-1-5326-4548-8

Manufactured in the U.S.A.

Dedicated to the congregation at Sardis Baptist Meetinghouse, Charlotte, North Carolina, which for two decades encouraged me to explore the Scriptures with them along unconventional paths toward unknown horizons.

May the peace of God, which passes all understanding, guard your hearts and minds in Christ Jesus, our Lord (Phil 4:7).

Amen.

Contents

Preface

THE SEEDS OF THIS book began several years ago when the deacons at Sardis Baptist Church decided the congregation should take a year to read and study the Bible. In preparing a study guide I organized the schedule so that passages about the same event could be read one after another. For instance, during the Babylonian conquest of Jerusalem the daily readings would interchange between Jeremiah, Habakkuk, Ezekiel, 2 Kings, and 2 Chronicles. In attempting to help my congregation read the Bible as a continuous story, I inadvertently paired Bible passages so that their contrasts and disagreements could be as easily seen as their similarities. I was no less amazed than my congregation that we found recurring dynamics. The consistent and frequent disagreements that Chronicles and Kings had when telling the same story, or how Acts told events in Paul's life differently than the apostle spoke of them, or the characteristic ways Matthew and Luke kept changing how Mark told a story about Jesus were some of the contrasts apparent to all of us. During that year repeatedly I found myself saying, "How is it that I've never noticed this before?"

I had grown up in the church, read the Bible regularly since my teens, earned two seminary degrees, and served churches for a couple of decades. Professors taught me about J, E, P, and D along with the synoptic problem, and yet I was still surprised. Perhaps I wasn't such a good student. But I think it was because for a long time the church has been working hard to assimilate passages so that we see similarity rather than difference. And as with many things, we see what we expect to see in the Bible.

Since that year further reading and study has helped me to see the Bible in a new way—as a dialogue of competing voices, which forced me to rethink the revelation of God's word. This became a new hermeneutic—what scholars call a way of interpreting—for me. It is not just that the four gospels have different versions of the Jesus story, or the Torah was compiled from different sources. Something more is going on. Earlier texts influenced later writers. Ways of thinking about God were passed onto new adherents, or rejected and countered by reactionary writings. Intertextual studies are opening up new understandings in the way that biblical books were formed. Some of these will be wrong turns, or dead ends, but in time stronger theories will surface and endure. This exploration has taught me that the divergent voices in Scripture intentionally speak from different vantage points. It happens so regularly that if God truly inspired the Bible, then there must be some divine purpose to these arguments.

This quest began as a congregational journey to read the Bible, and so this study is offered in thanksgiving back to the church in hopes that congregations and people of faith will enter divine conversations. Churches may download a free study guide to use in small groups and Sunday school classes. They can access the Practicing Midrash Study Guide at https://ftimothymoore.wordpress.com.

Regarding the text, inclusive language for God has been used throughout. Where pronoun use makes the text read better I have interchangeably used male and female pronouns for God. Likewise, I have alternately used female and male pronouns for unidentified persons or biblical characters. For instance, regarding the farmer in Mark's Parable of the Growing Seed, whose gender is unidentified, I used the pronouns she, her, hers.

Traveling mercies,

Tim Moore
Lent 2018

Acknowledgments

I AM INDEBTED TO a number of friends and colleagues who have assisted me in the creation of this book. Tillie Duncan, who before she became a partner pastor with me for fifteen years at Sardis Baptist Church was an English teacher, proofread my text and talked me through a challenging chapter. I am grateful for advice from Gail O'Day and Rodney Sadler, which gave me the insight to change an unruly and unfocused manuscript. To a host of readers, many of them pastors, of earlier drafts—Wayne Wike, Jack Causey, Joanne Brannon, Layne Smith, Mandy England Cole, Mike Jamison, Jim Mitchell, Mike Queen, Tillie Duncan, Darrin Bird, Mahan Siler, Larry Hovis, and Amy and Russ Dean along with the late Jack Bracey who talked this out of me—your recommendations and encouragements were invaluable.

This would never have been possible without the saints at Sardis Baptist who let me work out my ideas in sermons and studies with them and whose feedback and support shaped my thinking. Close to my heart was the suggestion by my Aunt Bernice Lemley to dig further into James Sanders's writings—she was one of his students at Colgate Rochester in the 1950s.

I am thankful for all of you.

It has been easy to work with the folks at Wipf and Stock Publishers, who have laid out every step along the way for this first-time author. My editor, Matthew Wimer, is quick to answer emails, whether early or late. I appreciate their willingness to publish this book, and make it available to readers such as you.

Finally, to my wife, Magay, who made it possible for me to have the time to work on this study, thank you for always being at my side—all my love to you.

Abbreviations

IDB	The Interpreter's Dictionary of the Bible
NIB	The New Interpreter's Bible
JBL	Journal of Biblical Literature
SBL	Society of Biblical Literature

Introduction

"IN THE DAY THE LORD God made the earth and the heavens" (Gen 2:4b) could have been the first words of the Bible. As a child makes sandcastles at the beach, the God of creation knelt down on hands and knees and fashioned the first human being from the dirt of the earth. Then, the LORD cradled the human like a loving mother and breathed into the human's nostrils and it became a living being. As the story continues the LORD also molds animals from dirt and breathes life into them. The LORD places all the living creatures in a place called enjoyment, where plants and trees provide every food they need. Finally, this God creates a second human, so that the two will be partners for each other. The Bible once began with an intimate portrait of how the LORD loved the world into existence.[1]

"In the day the LORD God made the earth and the heavens" are not the first words of the Bible, today. A different story became the beginning. An editor thought there was a better story. Another writer told an alternative creation story in which God spoke words from an unknown location. "Let there be light" (1:3), God says, and there was light. God speaks the universe into existence. There is not one day of creation, but six days. At the end of six days of work, God rests on the Sabbath. With Sabbath rest creation is complete. This story is nothing like the other story. This God did not act like the God in the other story.

Thus, the Bible begins with an argument—two competing creation stories with Gods that have different names and who bring the world into existence in contradictory ways. Ancient Israel kept both stories. Instead of selecting one story and erasing the other from the history of time, it decided both stories were sacred and passed them down through the generations. Despite their contradictions, despite their arguments about creation and

---

1. Bloom and Rosenberg, *Book of J*, 17–48; Friedman, *Hidden Book*, 3–32. Each claim that the earliest collection of biblical writings came from an author called the Yahwist by scholars, who compiled an early theological history of Israel. This was standard scholarship through the twentieth century, though current scholarship questions this theory.

God, they were placed back-to-back on the scroll of Genesis. "In the beginning when God created the heavens and the earth . . ." (1:1) became the first words of the Bible when the Priests decided to place their creation story before the other one.

This argument between two competing creation stories is not an anomaly in the Bible. What happens in the beginning happens throughout. Time and again ancient writers of what became biblical texts changed and rewrote earlier passages. They paired competing stories next to each other, or kept scrolls that argued against other scrolls.

Someone rewrote the Ten Commandments and reversed the most important statement about God's character in the Bible. Multiple and contradictory tales about Abraham, Jacob, and Joseph were written and kept side-by-side. A scribe took an earlier scroll about King David's life and Israel's history and wrote a second version of the story, removing any questionable acts from David's life. In every crisis of ancient Israel's history, they kept the prophecies of at least two prophets who approached the crisis from different theological perspectives. Hosea and Amos, Isaiah and Micah, Jeremiah and Ezekiel, each pair had different messages for the people. Israel kept them all.

In the New Testament, Matthew and Luke changed many of Jesus' teachings and events in his life from how the Gospel of Mark first reported them. John's gospel deviates from the other three and sees Jesus' ministry in a totally new light. Paul's letters to several Christian churches were some of the first written parts of the New Testament. Later, Luke retold Paul's story in the book of Acts, sometimes in ways that Paul would not recognize himself. Subsequent letters to churches by other authors challenged Paul's theology and questioned how people read Paul because his letters were "hard to understand, which the ignorant and unstable twist to their own destruction" (2 Pet 3:16).

Almost every section of the Bible is written by multiple authors who encountered God's Spirit in diverse and sundry ways. They disagreed about how God created the world, and made promises to Abraham, Moses, and David. Prophets spoke divergent messages to the people at times of crisis. Jesus' teachings were remembered in contrary ways. Is it, for instance, the poor who are blessed, or will the poor in spirit be the recipients of the kingdom of God? The Bible begins with an argument about how God created the world and the arguments continue throughout.

When the Christian church started to standardize orthodox beliefs it was rarely comfortable with these contradictions and for most of its centuries minimized the differences and synthesized the contradictions. In the case of the two creations stories, it stopped talking about them as two separate stories and taught the second story—the Adam and Eve story—as a complementary ending to the first. Though to do so, the church had to ignore many details in both stories.

The inherent arguments and contradictions in Scripture did not seem to bother the Jewish faith. A practice called *midrash* developed in Judaism sometime before the days of Jesus. The word derived from *darash*, which meant to investigate, to seek.[2] Rabbis and scholars sparred over opposing passages, developed theological arguments, and filled gaps in biblical stories with their own understandings. The way Jesus taught could have been understood as midrash by the rabbis of the day. Matthew's recording of the Sermon on the Mount was structurally arranged as midrash. Jesus recalled a teaching from the Scriptures, "You have heard that it was said to those of ancient times" (Matt 5:21), and then offered a commentary for his contemporary times, "but I say unto you" (5:22). In simple terms that was midrash.[3] While midrash was a Jewish practice of studying the Scriptures, it was brought into early Christianity. Matthew and Luke's version of Jesus' temptations may have been a Christian midrash of the brief mention of his wilderness temptations in Mark 1:12–13. It was a longer story that filled in the gaps of what was first said.[4]

The practice of midrash developed a few written texts. Rabbis wrote the *Mishnah* during the second century at the same time Christians were beginning to determine their New Testament. This collection of midrashim, or oral teachings, of the rabbis created a Jewish *new testament* to the Hebrew Scriptures, though it only occasionally quoted the Bible. The *Mishnah* provided a new guide for living an ancient faith under new challenges. In the fifth and sixth centuries two versions of the *Talmud* were written, one in Palestine and the other in Persia. The *Talmud* was a commentary on the *Mishnah*, in which the Bible was regularly quoted to ground the oral teachings of the rabbis in the written word of the Torah. The Persian version, called the *Bavli*, organized the practice of midrash. It provided written commentary—interpretations, arguments, suggestions on what the original authors should have said, which structured a debate across the centuries. It also provided

---

2. Armstrong, *Bible*, 81.

3. Hays warns scholars about being too loose with the term midrash. "The term *midrash* can serve as a convenient cover for a multitude of exegetical sins" (*Echoes of Scripture in Paul*, 13). His warning noted, he does think it is worth exploring Paul's letters through the rabbis' work. "Rabbinic midrash and the letters of Paul are natural analogies because both are paradigmatic instances of intertextual discourse, both wrestling with the same great precursor" (*Echoes of Scripture in Paul*, 14).

4. Gerhardsson, *Testing of God's Son*, offers an analysis of the temptation narrative as an example of early Christian midrash.

space for the new student to enter the conversation by recording his own understandings. Karen Armstrong in her history on the Bible explained it this way: "The Bavli gave no definitive answers. If an argument ended in impasse, the students had to sort it out to their own satisfaction with their teachers. . . . When studying the Bible through the Bavli, the student learned that nobody had the last word, that truth was constantly changing, and . . . was aware that both he and his opponent were in some way participating in a conversation that stretched back to Moses and would continue into the future."[5] Debating the Scriptures kept Judaism alive, kept the stories alive. Biblical texts that could not be reinterpreted would become obsolete and die of old age. "Turn it and turn it again," the *Talmud* said of the Scriptures, "for everything is contained therein."[6] If one interpretation did not satisfy, the practice of midrash kept turning the text, circulating the discussion until a meaning became clear. Midrash is an enemy of fundamentalism, which believes there is one correct, orthodox interpretation of Scripture.[7] It never assumes that there is "a single authoritative reading of scripture," explains Armstrong. "As events unfolded on earth, even God had to keep studying his own Torah in order to discover its full significance."[8] Midrash rejuvenated the faith from one generation to the next as new societal challenges sought wisdom from an old religion. Midrash did not end with the writing of the *Mishnah* and the *Talmud*. Students of the Torah used them as tools to examine, debate, and comprehend the meaning of Scripture. Jewish synagogues still use the term midrash as a way of studying the Scriptures.

This book will not be a historical study of Jewish midrash. Instead, it allows Scripture passages to midrash each other. This study brings contrasting biblical texts together and gives them a voice to speak to one another. Overhearing the dialogue invites the reader to join the conversation. This book recognizes that there are arguments, contradictions, and gaps in both the Hebrew Bible and the Christian New Testament. Instead of being a problem that needs to be fixed, divergent texts in the Bible serve a purpose that midrash reveals. They invite every generation to reenter divine conversations and decide how the revelation of the Bible will guide them to face new challenges for their day. In this way the Bible remains a living word.

In recent years there has been a lot of publicity about translations of gospels that did not make it into the New Testament. The gospels of Thomas

---

5. Armstrong, *Bible*, 99–101.

6. Rabbi Ben Bag Bag, *Talmud, Pirkei Avot*; as quoted in Kunst, *Burning Word*, 4.

7. Hammer explains, "Its very method is itself a message of importance. . . . Midrash is the very enemy of fundamentalism. Simplistic, literalistic interpretation and reading of a text can be its death knell. That is where the letter kills" (*Classic Midrash*, 42).

8. Armstrong, *Bible*, 81.

and Mary Magdelene, among others, hit the religious section in bookstores, in part, because of the best-selling success of Dan Brown's novel *The Da Vinci Code*.[9] Elaine Pagels wrote an informative book on many of these writings thirty years ago in *The Gnostic Gospels*, but it did not garner the popular success that Brown's novel did. Pagels said that the noncanonical gospels found and translated in the last two generations revealed "a more diverse and complicated world than any of us could have imagined."[10] Maybe we should have had better imaginations.

The diversity that many seek in the books that did not make it into the New Testament is already in the Bible. This book will examine examples of divergent texts in the Bible following the example of Jewish midrash. Its aim will not declare an orthodox winner. Rather, its purpose will allow each of the contrasting passages to speak for themselves, reveal their disagreements, and thereby invite the reader to join divine conversations.

Practicing Midrash

In the sixteenth century, St. John of the Cross developed a threefold habit of praying that may help us to listen to the various voices of God in the Scriptures.[11] John called this layered way of praying *via purgativa, via illuminativa*, and *via unitiva*. The way of purgation (*via purgativa*) is a practice of letting go, of purging things that hinder your soul. Brian McLaren likened this to cleaning the windows of your soul so God's light can shine through.[12] The way of enlightenment (*via illuminativa*) is a practice of opening your soul to the light of God. The way of union with God (*via unitiva*) is a practice of becoming one with the Spirit of God. The second half of each chapter will use this contemplative prayer as a modified way to practice midrash.

9. Brown's wildly popular novel (and movie) claimed that the Roman Catholic Church excluded several reliable gospels from the New Testament for political reasons. While it made for good fiction, none of the noncanonical gospels could in any serious way be considered on par with the canonical gospels. With the possible exception of Thomas, all the noncanonical gospels were written more than a century after Jesus' death. The interest in the Gospels—canonical and noncanonical—caused by Brown's novel was generated by misinformation.

10. Pagels, *Beyond Belief*, 34.

11. St. John of the Cross wrote, "God produces striking effects in the soul, for by purging and illuminating it, He prepares it for the union of love with God" (*Dark Night*, 100). Though these ideas about prayer preceded him in the sixth-century writings of Pseudo-Dionysius, St. John of the Cross developed them in *Dark Night of the Soul*.

12. McLaren, *Finding Our Way*, 151.

(1) Free the Stories to Speak for Themselves

The theological belief that all Bible stories and passages must harmonize and complement one another places a layer of doctrine on top of the narrative. It alters how we read the Bible and shuts down our curiosity. Modeling the practice of *via purgativa* we let go of this need to fix Scripture and hide its contradictions. We are free to explore rather than follow another's lead. We are free to curiously question rather than memorize another's teaching.

Freed from the dogma of forcing biblical texts to synchronize with other passages, we may read them as they are. We do not care if they offer contradictory information about God, or the faith that sustains us. Where there are differences we are not compelled to smooth them out, or create elaborate theories to explain them away. Without the pressure of trying to make the stories conform to theological presuppositions, we are free to note the differences and similarities of the stories, and to look at them with wonder. When comparing the contrasts and lining up the parallels in the stories we are free to ask questions that lead to further understanding of the passages. Where perplexed, we do not feel compelled to create a solution. We remain open to the mystery and resist packaging it into a neat little answer. Understanding that there may be two opposing tales requires the reader to accept that some contradictions will remain unresolved. This practice of midrash allows opposing voices to speak for themselves and invites the reader to be open to what each has to say.

(2) Listen to the Stories as Contrasting Voices within God

When reading two or more contradictory expressions of a biblical event or a theological concept, hear them as contrasting voices in the word of God. Resist the temptation to assimilate them into one narrative. Let them independently speak their truths about God, the world, faith and you. Imagine that the wisdom of God is working through dialogue, debate, or civil argument. Rather than try to declare what *the* truth is, hear the truths that each story speaks. Let the light (*via illuminativa*) shine forth from each story.

Some of the divergent stories in the Bible were written independently of one another. There is no way to know, for instance, if the Priests of Judah knew the creation story in Genesis 2. We cannot know if the Priests purposely wrote their version of creation to correct, or to compete with the other story, or vice versa. Nevertheless, an editor thought it was divine wisdom to bring them together and put them side-by-side. This created a debate, a conversation of differing points of view, even if one did not exist when the passages were written.

Sometimes, however, one text was written with another text precisely in mind. In cases where a biblical writer used previously written material and changed the earlier version, it is important for the reader to listen to both voices. One tendency is to give greater weight to the later writing. Rather than uncritically accept Luke or Matthew's changes to Mark's gospel, it is important to read Mark's version of Jesus' ministry as an equal debater opposing Luke or Matthew's version of events. Imagine Mark talking back to either Matthew or Luke, "No, I wrote it like this for a reason." Another tendency is that when one writer removes a passage from an earlier text the silent testimony is ignored. Chronicles removed the story of David raping Bathsheba and murdering her husband from 2 Samuel. Both testimonies have something of value for the reader. Unless the writer of Chronicles thought the scrolls of Samuel and Kings would be destroyed, he knew the tale of how David took Bathsheba and killed Uriah would continue to be known. What does it mean to tell this tragic tale about Israel's great king, and what does it mean to not tell it? What theological ideas may be at work in both the telling and in the silence? There is a reason stories were removed from earlier texts. Listen to the silent testimony as well.

The divergent stories in the Bible are competing against each other to inform the faith of its readers and hearers. Our task as readers is to first listen to these competing voices. Can we describe their point of view, and name their theological concepts? Can we hear the divine conversation, and be enlightened by the debate?

(3) Find Where You Want to Join the Divine Conversation

St. John of the Cross believed that the purpose of deep prayer was to unite the believer in the Spirit of God (*via unitiva*). John desired to be one with God. Our purposes are a bit more modest. Modifying John's third level of prayer, we seek to join the divine conversation. Part of the divine wisdom for the pluralism of Scripture is to make it a living word. Reading Scripture as a threefold midrash leads us to the point where we enter divine conversations. Here, it is time to start asking where the stories speak more deeply to our hearts.

The divergent stories of the Bible will always be in tension, unrelenting, and unresolved. This is an ongoing conversation, a conversation that includes you, your house of worship, and your community. You may resolve the tension. You may choose to give greater weight to one story over the other, or find yourself at home somewhere in between. Just as Paul disregarded the Priestly accounts in Genesis, you may choose to disregard them as well. Or following James, you may choose to debate Paul's use of Genesis. The importance is finding where you fit in the divine conversation, so that your voice becomes part of the whole. There, your voice will influence your church and community.

With each chapter in this book we will encounter an argument in the Bible and enter a divine conversation. The foolishness of God, which offers contradictory stories in the Bible, is a wisdom that provides the dialogue to face new generational challenges.

Excurses

Near the beginning of each chapter an excursus will supply a brief excursion into the biblical scholarship that provides a foundation for understanding the passages that will be compared. This study will rely on the scholarship that in the past two centuries created a *historical-critical* approach to the Bible. Pastors and devoted Bible readers may be familiar with the terms and concepts used in this study, but others may not. Think of the excurses not as something necessary, but like a historical roadside marker that gives you more information about the place you are traveling. When possible they will provide information on the time period, authors/editors, and key components of their context.

Finally, I come to this task from the perspective of a pastor who has a great love for the Bible and a desire that more people would treasure its revelation. This work is approached from the assumption that the Bible is the word of God. All the fingerprints left from the hands that have shaped it are examples of Christianity's incarnational faith. I assume the contradictory stories of the Bible have a divine purpose. My hope is that you, the reader, on your own or in a group study, will reengage the Bible and enter an ongoing conversation among the faithful, whereby each generation decides anew how the biblical faith of Abraham, Isaac, Jacob and the gospel of Jesus Christ will address the challenges we all face.

CHAPTER 1

Which God Created the World?

The test of a first-rate intelligence is the ability to hold two opposed ideas in mind at the same time, and still retain the ability to function.[1]

—F. Scott Fitzgerald

THE BIBLE BEGINS WITH an argument, a disagreement between friends, who agree to disagree. You do not have to be a biblical scholar to see this. All you have to do is pretend you have never read the beginning of the Bible, remove any preconceived notions about the first two stories and read them plainly as would a child.

A plain reading of the stories reveals a break at Genesis 2:4. The creation process starts over again. It is apparent that there are two stories, and that they have few things in common. In the first story God creates the world in six days, seven, if you include the Sabbath rest. In the second story, God pulls an all-nighter and finishes the work in a single day. In the first story God ends by creating human beings. In the second story God begins with a human being. In the first story God creates with methodical precision. In the second God creates by trial and error. The two stories read as polar opposites.

This is a curious beginning to the Bible, which should lead one to wonder. Why does the Bible begin with two *contrasting* creation stories? This question is worth pondering throughout this chapter, indeed, throughout this whole book. The first two pages of the Bible are the first impressions of God's written word. If you believe that God is the inspiration of the Scriptures, then what purpose would God have in beginning the Bible with contradictory tales? If this were an anomaly, it would be easy to toss it aside as an inconsequential mystery. Rather than being an exception, what happens on the first two pages of the Bible continues throughout, where dueling

1. Fitzgerald, "Crack Up," 41.

*either OR — BothAnd*9

stories give conflicting accounts of Abraham's blessing, the Ten Commandments, King David's life and Jesus' ministry.

Given the regularity with which Bible stories are told through multiple
versions, it is rather surprising that the church has not taught the faithful
how to read comparative stories in order to form their faith. The task of this
book will be to highlight the differences in contrasting stories of the Bible
and to encourage readers to work out their own faithful understanding of
dueling texts. We will begin with the beginning.

EXCURSUS 1.1

Two Creation Stories

The first two chapters of the Bible tell competing stories on the
creation of the world. The first story was part of the Priestly writings in Genesis. The second story was written by the Yahwist, a
storyteller of a number of tales in Genesis, Exodus and possibly
elsewhere. This examination of the two creation stories will assume
an editor put these two contrasting stories together sometime after
the Babylonian exile—sixth to fifth century BC.

There is nothing in either story that suggests one was dependent on the other. It is possible neither author knew of the other's
work. An editor brought them together to be read side-by-side. He
did not mind the disagreement, since he could have easily changed
the first words of the second story to remove some of the contradictions. Rather than keep, "In the day that the LORD God made
the earth and the heavens," he could have written, "In the day that
the LORD God made human beings," then removed vv. 5–6, and it
would have been less obvious that these were originally two different stories.

The Torah (the first five books of the Bible) is a collection
of numerous stories that were passed down and compiled by the
Priests of the Second Temple period (sixth to fifth century BC).[2]
The Priests (P) wrote major portions of the Torah in addition to

2. De Pury, "Jacob Story," 70. De Pury dates the writing of the Priestly document to
the late sixth century BC, specifically between 535 and 530 BC. He does not think the
Priestly work is possible before the Babylonian exile. Brueggemann, *Theology of the Old
Testament*, 74. He states that more recent scholarship points to a postexilic, late sixth
century BC, date for a completion of the Torah.

gathering other texts. Their tradition claimed a heritage to the
Zadokite priests of Solomon's temple.

Another author, whom scholars have called the *Yahwist* for
the past one hundred fifty years because he always referred to God
as Yahweh, compiled a collection of stories about Israel's early
history and prehistory. A generation ago scholars typically dated
the Yahwist as early as the tenth century BC, possibly writing as a
scribe for King Solomon.[3] Yahwist theory has been substantially
questioned in more recent scholarship; some reasoning that there
never was a Yahwist. John Van Seters thinks a Yahwist did write an
Israelite history. However, he shows that it was dependent on Deuteronomy and was an exilic text (sixth century BC).[4] If Van Seters
is correct, then the Yahwist's stories of God's steadfast love would
have been a challenge to Deuteronomy's emphasis on God's justice
and offered Jewish exiles a different understanding of their loss. In
this book the Yahwist will be regularly identified as the Storyteller.

This examination of the two creation stories will be read from
the perspective that an editor put these opposing tales together—
one by the Priests of Judah and the other by a Storyteller—sometime after the Babylonian exile.

In the Beginning or In the Day

The creation stories on the first pages of the Bible begin with similar first
sentences. "In the beginning when God created the heavens and the earth"
is how the first story begins. "In the day that the LORD God made the earth
and the heavens" is almost an echo of the first. There is one main difference
between the initial sentences. They use different names for God. This is the
case throughout both stories. In the first creation story the name for God
is *Elohim*, which was a common name for God in the ancient world and
used by Israelites and other peoples.[5] The second creation story calls God

3. Friedman, *Hidden Book*, and Bloom, *Book of J*, propose that the Yahwist's work
goes back to Solomon's temple. Whereas Dozeman and Schmid's book, *Farewell to the
Yahwist*, contains several articles questioning Yahwist theory.

4. Van Seters, "Report of the Yahwist's Demise," 153–54. See also Van Seters, *Prologue to History*, 332.

5. Anderson notes that the word *Elohim* is in plural form, and is closely related to
a generic term for God, *El*. The word, however, is used in a singular sense. "This use is
often called the 'plural of majesty.' . . . Elohim includes all gods; the fullness of deity is
comprehended in him. Thus the word is equivalent to 'deity' or 'Godhead'" ("Names of

by the specific name *Yahweh*, which is translated LORD in the Bible using all uppercase letters to signify that this is a translation of the divine name. Throughout the second creation story the divine references are always LORD God (*Yahweh Elohim*), a practice that is dropped by the Storyteller in the fourth chapter of Genesis where the name *Yahweh* stands alone.[6] The two names for God used in these creation stories suggest that there are two different authors with two different theologies about God operating in these stories. They are both speaking of the God of Israel. In using different names for God they offer a clue that invites us to explore the ways in which they uniquely experienced God.

With the first words in Genesis 1:1 God created order out of chaos: "The earth was a formless void and darkness covered the face of the deep. . . . Then God said, 'Let there be light'; and there was light." This God creates by a methodical, detached manner, bringing ever-increasing levels of order into being. As the light so created by God's word drives out the darkness, so the order of God's creation drives out the chaos of pre-creation. In successive order God creates light, sky, dry land, vegetation, sun, moon, stars, the animal kingdom, and finally, human beings. God creates by words. God speaks a thing and it comes into being. At the end of each day God looks upon what has been created and saw that it was good. Before moving onto the next step, God evaluated what had been created and declared divine satisfaction.

You may find it helpful to read the first chapter of Genesis. If you have the option, read it from a traditional translation (NRSV, RSV, NIV or KJV) instead of a paraphrase. The text has a rhythmic stiffness to it, which gives it dramatic authority. Power is embodied in these words. This is a powerful God, a God who speaks a word from a distance and instantaneously things come into being. This God is precise. This God does not make mistakes. Everything has been placed where it should be. God looked upon all that was made and saw that it was good.

This powerful God is also distant, which may be a good thing. How close do you want to be to a God that causes mountains to be built and sets the sun in the sky with just a word? It is not surprising that this God creates the heavens *and then* the earth. This is a holy God, a God that is other, not

---

God," 2:413).

6. Friedman explains, "In Genesis 2 and 3 the word 'God' appears each time after the name YHWH. But this double identification, 'YHWH God,' occurs only in these introductory chapters and nowhere else in the Pentateuch. It therefore appears to be an effort by the Redactor (R) to soften the transition from the P creation, which uses only 'God' (thirty-five times), to the coming J stories, which will use only the name YHWH" (*The Bible*, 35).

like us. And yet, we have been created in this God's image. We are not like this God, but we are a reflection of this God.

The Priests of Judah wrote the first creation story. You can see elements of their theology in this story. They emphasized God's holiness. In the Priestly writings of the Torah, the word *holy* is used at least one hundred twenty times. In contrast Deuteronomy uses it only ten times. The first creation story is a depiction of a holy God. Holy means not-like-others. It is set apart. The opposite of holy is common, or ordinary. God is not like us. God is wholly other.

The holiness theology of the priests loved order. Things remained holy by remaining in their place. This is clear in the book of Leviticus where diet, gender roles, and worship rituals had a particular order. Mixing up God's order is prohibited. In creation everything is good because God placed it where it is supposed to be. To be holy is to keep things—and people—in their place. God created order out of chaos and the Priestly tradition of holiness continued the practice of creating order and expelling chaos.

The second creation story (Gen 2–3) is far from orderly. Take a few minutes to read at least the first half of this story, beginning with Genesis 2:4b through the end of the chapter. Notice how differently the narrative flows. The methodical rhythm is gone. It feels like a folktale as many of the Storyteller's tales do. The LORD got down on hands and knees and molded the first earth creature out of the ground. The Hebrew word *human* means *earthling*, or *earth creature*. In English, we might say that God created humans from the humus.[7] Like a kid making sandcastles at the seashore, God gets down in the dirt to create a human being. Having molded a human, the LORD "breathed into his nostrils the breath of life; and the man became a living being" (2:7).[8] This God has human qualities and wants to be near humans. Like a mother the LORD cradles her newborn baby. This is not a holy depiction of God.

7. Trible, *Rhetoric of Sexuality*, 76.

8. Trible translates *nephesh* as "the totality of the 'self'" (*Rhetoric of Sexuality*, 140n5).

EXCURSUS 1.2

Differences in the Two Creation Stories of Genesis 1 and 2

	First Story—Genesis 1	**Second Story—Genesis 2–3**
Name for God	*Elohim*	*Yahweh Elohim*
Period of creation	Six days, plus Sabbath.	One day.
Order of creation	Light, sky, dry land, vegetation, sun, moon, animals, and humans.	Earth, a human, vegetation, animals, and a second human.
Mode of creation	God spoke things into existence with words.	God planted vegetation and formed a human and animals.
Process of creation	Methodically planned.	Trial and error.
Humans	Made in God's image.	Became living souls with God's breath.
	Given dominion over the earth.	Made caretakers of the garden.
	Given every plant upon the earth.	Given the fruit of every tree, except one.
Evaluation	It was very good.	Some things were not good.
Conclusion	God rested on Sabbath.	Paradise was lost.

In contrast to the first story this God made the earth *and then* the heavens (2:4b). Earth is where this God resides. Aside from the initial sentence, the heavens are never mentioned in this creation story. Instead of creating from far away with words that echo throughout the universe, the Lord gets hands dirty being playful and intimate. Instead of looking at things from afar and declaring it all good, this God notices that something is not-so-good. The earth creature is alone. The Lord decided to correct the problem by creating a suitable partner. Once again digging with hands, God began forming animals and bringing them to the earth creature. God invited the human to name them, one by one, and then listened to the human to see if one would make a suitable partner. If Gary Larson, the *Far Side* cartoonist, would draw this picture, he might draw a chubby, child-like

God molding animals, lining them up—giraffe, lobster, donkey, polar bear, snake, dog—to meet the human, but the human just keeps shaking his head for no suitable partner is found. According to the Storyteller, the animal kingdom was created by mistake, a series of failed attempts to find a partner for the earth creature.

Finally, the LORD gave up on this method and tried a different procedure. Soon, male and female were created from the one earth creature. Still, all was not good. God created male and female naked, or vulnerable, in a world where God also created sly serpents.[9] This God, the LORD, does not act like the God in chapter 1.

The second creation story is clearly not written with a theology of holiness in mind. This God is intimate and immanent. The author describes the LORD with human characteristics: planting vegetation like a farmer, forming things with hands like a potter, and even walking in the cool of the evening with human companionship. This God partners with humans in creation, giving the first earth creature the privilege of naming the animals and determining if one would be a suitable partner. It is hard to imagine the God of the first creation story asking for human input on creation. Yet, human interaction seems to be important to this God from the beginning of the creation of the world. This God puts choices before humans. They are prohibited from eating the fruit of the tree that is in the middle of the garden. "You may freely eat of every tree of the garden; but of the tree of knowledge of good and evil you shall not eat, for in the day that you eat of it you shall die" (2:16–17). Eve and Adam soon tested that warning and disobeyed God. However, they did not die *that* day—as the text said—or the story would have been over. Instead, beginning that day, their days are numbered. Soon God outfits the couple, which at first was naked and unashamed, in fur coats after banishing them from paradise.

This creation story describes the world as a complex and wondrous place. Everything needed is here, but some things are prohibited. Friendship alleviates loneliness, but betrayal divides. God's loving presence is near, but at a key moment absent. Companionship covers nakedness, or vulnerability, but that may still be exposed. There are consequences, both good and bad, to human actions. While it is difficult to summarize the theology behind this story, it is clearly not the holiness theology of the Priests. It could be read as an anti-holiness creation story. The mistakes that this God makes reveal what this Storyteller believes. It is more important that God be close and caring, than perfect and powerful. Even when the

---

9. Trible, *Rhetoric of Sexuality*, 108. Trible points out that there is a Hebrew pun on nakedness and the slyness of the serpent.

humans must be removed from the garden of Eden, God makes fur coats for them, covering their nakedness and their vulnerability for the challenge ahead. Like a parent frustrated by the bad choices of her children, this God still offers a bit of grace in a compromised moment. Phyllis Trible called the second creation story "A Love Story Gone Awry."[10] It is in a literary sense a tragedy. With all the imperfections of creation, when Eve and Adam stand together at the close of act 1 naked and not ashamed, the reader knows this paradise will not last.

In disobeying God, however, Eve and Adam realize their nakedness. While the humans reached for the immortality of the Tree of Life, "they must settle for the collective immortality of generational succession—the human family tree."[11] Something good comes out of something bad. There is life even in the midst of death. Adam and Eve do not die that day, despite God's warning, but their days are numbered. Yet, in their numbered days they bring life into the world.

The Priestly theology of holiness points to the ideals of the way things should be. The Storyteller's theology finds grace even in the tragic way things are.

Practicing Midrash

Most people are taught to read the two creation stories of the Bible as complementary parts of a single creation story. By plainly reading the two stories, however, we have seen that they are two independent stories of how God created the world. They are irreconcilable stories. They cannot be blended into one long story without changing the details of one or the other. To read these contradictory stories let us walk through a threefold practice of midrash.

(1) Free the Stories to Speak for Themselves

We begin by allowing the stories to speak for themselves. We do not care if they offer contradictory information in their depiction of God, or make conflicting reports on how God created the universe. If we find their differences to be disconcerting we will resist trying to fix them. Understanding that there are two opposing tales means to accept that some contradictions will remain unresolved.

---

10. Trible, *Rhetoric of Sexuality*, 72–143.

11. Meeks, *HarperCollins Study Bible*, 10, footnote at Gen 3:22.

While the differences in the stories raise a number of questions, their similarities provide a base upon which the conversation may begin. Both stories speak of God as the one who initiates all creative activity. No other being is at work in creating the universe. There is no dualism here. Both stories describe a connection between God and human beings. In the first story, humans are created in God's image. In the second story, God intimately forms them and breathes the breath of life in them. Both stories place humans in relation to their world. In the first they are given authority over it. In the second they are to be caretakers of it. Both stories speak of the equality of male and female. In the first, they are both created in God's image. In the second, gender is created at the time of the second human's creation. She is to be an equal partner with him, and when they cling to each other they are one flesh. Both stories share these values, which were developed from independent viewpoints.

Combining the two stories compromises the second one. When we let it stand alone and speak for itself a number of interesting points stand out. When compared to the first story, this God intimately engages the creation process—planting, forming, breathing life, and fixing problems—all of which give the LORD very human characteristics. Furthermore, the LORD relates closely with humans. God molds them out of the ground and breathes the breath of life into them. God speaks to them, instructs them, and enjoys their company on walks through the garden.

Second, this God makes mistakes. Or at least this God does not create with the same precision as the God of the first story. The LORD uses a trial and error method to create a suitable partner for the human. Finally, after numerous failures, God decides to try another method and a second human is created. This is not usually how we picture God. Why did it take the LORD so long to try another method? Apparently God creates the whole animal kingdom before giving up on the first method. Was God stubborn? Lacking innovative thinking? Most importantly, what does it mean that the LORD fails to be successful in the first place?

Other things are not as they should be. Only after the human is created from the earth does the LORD realize that it is not good for the human to be alone. Why did God not know this beforehand? Even after God creates a partner and makes human gender, here again, problems remain. The humans are naked and vulnerable, though not ashamed. Unfortunately, the LORD creates a sly and crafty animal while unsuccessfully trying to create a human partner—just the kind of creature that would prey on naked and vulnerable humans.[12] Finally, God places them in a garden that provides

12. Trible, *Rhetoric of Sexuality*, 108.

every thing they need, as well as something that they are prohibited from having. They may eat from every tree in the garden, except for the tree that is in the middle of the garden. If they eat from the tree of the knowledge of good and evil, in that day they will die. God places it in the middle of the garden, where the humans would regularly pass by it. Why does God create a tree whose fruit will kill the humans? Furthermore, why is it placed in-the-way, instead of out-of-the-way? Everyday they face temptation to have the one thing they are restricted from having. Everyday they live they face the consequence of death. Furthermore, when the humans eat the forbidden fruit, they do not die that day as warned. Instead, they become like God, knowing good and evil. Did God lie to them? By the end of the story, God banishes them from the garden and their days are numbered. It was an inevitable tragic ending.

These details in the story raise a number of questions for individual readers to ponder and church communities to discuss. What kind of God creates the world in this manner? What attributes does this God display? What would a God like this want in a relationship with human beings? Do God's imperfections in the process of creation foreshadow the imperfections of the humans' ability to obey God?

The first story is better known as a creation story, so allowing it to stand alone may not immediately bring new thoughts to mind. Comparing it to the second story, however, makes things taken for granted stand out. This portrays a powerful God in complete control. This God speaks a word and it comes into being. God says, "Let there be light," and there was light, and so goes the rest of creation. Creation is a methodical process where God repeats a rubric of speaking (which executes the command), observing, and evaluating. It is hard to imagine anything standing in this God's way. The sovereignty of God over all creation is apparent in the first story. This God does not stumble trying to make two humans, male and female, and the animals certainly are not mistakes. God executes everything commanded. "For he spoke, and it came to be; he commanded, and it stood forth" (Ps 33:9).

The implementation of God's spoken words separated one thing from another. Light is separated from darkness, day from night, and dry land from the water covering earth's surface. Even humans are separated as male and female. Finally, God separates one day of creation from the other six days, blessed and made sacred as a day of rest. While these separations describe what we experience in nature, this description is different from the second story where God creates the first human and the animals out of the ground. The humans, while created one out of the other, were also to be one flesh. The first creation story sees difference by separation, whereas the second sees difference through connection.

At each phase of creation, God looked back on all that God made and declared it good. On the final working day of creation, God declared that it was very good. This is not a dualistic world where good and evil are balanced in some shape or form. The material world as created is good. Everything has been put in its place. "All creatures function perfectly in a marvelous whole that is without fault or blemish," says Bernhard Anderson. "The essential goodness of God's creation is a recurring theme in Israel's praises."[13] Whereas creation in the second story has inherent problems, this story described creation as a perfect process.

Human beings were given a mandate to create generationally as well as have dominion over all life on earth. God commanded them to "fill the earth and subdue it" (Gen 1:28). God gave every plant and tree to humans and dominion over the animals. There is a hierarchy in creation. One part of creation serves another part. Among created beings, humans are given authority over all. In the second creation story, the earth creature was put in "the garden of Eden to till it and keep it" (2:15).

Finally, God rests on the Sabbath at the end of creation. Sabbath is therefore declared an essential part of creation. The Exodus 20 version of the Ten Commandments confesses this, "For in six days the LORD made heaven and earth, the sea, and all that is in them, but rested the seventh day; therefore the LORD blessed the Sabbath day and consecrated it" (Exod 20:11). Sabbath rest is woven into the natural world. Without it things would be out of place.

The details of this story take us in different directions from the earlier questions. What kind of God creates the world in this manner? What attributes would you give the God of the first creation story? What would a God like this want in a relationship with human beings? And specifically, does God's dominion over the universe mirror the dominion given humans over the animals?

Reading these stories comparatively reveals similarities and differences. They create a dialogue in Scripture about the God who created the universe. The reader is an observer to this dialogue, comparable to a person sitting in the audience of a theatrical play. The unique details of each story form distinct voices within the word of God. These are not simply stories with contradictory details. They are voices with different viewpoints.

The second movement of prayer according to St. John of the Cross is enlightenment, a way to receive light from God. Using this model for reading the comparative stories of the Bible, let us listen to them as contrasting voices.

13. Anderson, *From Creation to New Creation*, 31.

(2) Listen to the Stories as Contrasting Voices of God

We have already highlighted differences and similarities in the two creation stories at the beginning of the Bible. Their distinctions raise theological questions. The differences are not simply factual disagreements, random mistakes, or minor variances. They form a consistent narrative framework and theological perspective. They represent different voices of God within the Bible. So, what are they uniquely trying to say about God?

The first creation story speaks of a transcendent God. This God creates the world from outside the universe. This God operates beyond our material capacities, a holy God, completely different from humanity and the material world. The interchange between God and the world is therefore limited. God speaks creation into existence. God does not appear in any form; God engages only through non-corporeal words. God, who is separate from creation, creates by separating things from one another. This separation comes without judgment.[14] Nevertheless, it establishes difference. Light is not dark. Land is not water. Sun is not moon. Male is not female, and vice versa. While God declares all of creation good, difference is created. The Priests of Judah will make judgments about difference. For people whose religious life focused on boundaries of holy and unholy, clean and unclean, righteous and unrighteous, the separations of the first creation story corresponded to those holiness boundaries. The first story portrays a holy and transcendent God.

God's transcendence cannot be limited by the physical world, making God's power beyond human imagination. God builds mountains and oceans with just a word. Transcendence gives God unlimited power. When calling upon this kind of God for aid against one's enemies, this is greatly desired. However, when realizing that you have disobeyed this God, such a trait is greatly to be feared.

The second creation story speaks of an immanent God. This God dwells in the created universe with human capabilities. Creation is literally a hands-on experience. God plants vegetation like a farmer, forms the first human and the animals from soil of the earth, and breathes life into them. While this God is certainly powerful, having the ability to make creation, God's power is not unlimited. In making a second human, for instance, God must use a different method because the old one failed to provide a

---

14. Neville, "Differentiation in Genesis 1," 226. Neville concludes that the differences in kinds mentioned in the first creation story emphasize the comprehensiveness of God's creative work. He does not believe it anticipates Priestly distinctions between clean and unclean.

satisfactory result. Accordingly, the animal kingdom was a futile effort to create a suitable partner for the human.

The imperfections do not ruin this creation story, because the writer is not trying to describe an all-powerful, transcendent God. That God creates a sly serpent that preys on naked, vulnerable humans does not diminish the story, but in fact adds to its complexity. What matters is that God enjoys the company of humans for walks in the cool of the evening. The Storyteller is comfortable with an imperfect world, even with an imperfect relationship with God (After all, where was God when the serpent was tempting Eve and Adam to eat the forbidden fruit?), because she imagines that God cares deeply for humans, even when they disobey God. This story believes God's love is more important than God's power. While it ends with Adam and Eve's banishment from the garden, this does not end their relationship with God. Disobedience has consequences, but the relationship does not end. Rather than portray God creating an ideal world with everything in place, this story describes a flawed world, in which God's love and grace is nonetheless present. The theology in this brief tale is consistent with the steadfast love of the LORD described in Exodus 34.

Immanence and transcendence are two exclusive terms. You are either one or the other. Yet, Christian theology has tried to keep both descriptive terms for God, because we have experienced God as transcendent and as immanent. With two creation stories, the believer does not have to choose. The reader can hold onto God's transcendence in one hand through the first story and God's immanence in the other hand through the second story. The Christian doctrine of the Trinity achieves the same purpose. It does not matter that this is a logical paradox. Without trying to solve this mystery, or being forced to choose one or the other (though this may be a personal option), the reader is free to explore the possible meaning of both God's transcendence and immanence through these stories. This is an old Jewish and Christian tradition. Daniel Migliore in summarizing the attributes of God wrote that Christianity "has tried to synthesize the confession that God is compassionate, suffering, victorious love revealed decisively in Jesus Christ with a number of speculative ideas about what constitutes true divinity, such as immutability, impassibility, and apathy."[15] People like Augustine, Anselm, and Calvin clung so tightly to transcendent descriptions of God that they could only get to the compassionate and suffering part of God through the divinity of Jesus Christ.[16] Maybe they should have spent more time reading the second creation story. These contrasting stories about God

---

15. Migliore, *Faith Seeking Understanding*, 72.

16. Migliore, *Faith Seeking Understanding*, 72–73.

hold onto two seemingly contradictory ideals about God—transcendence and immanence. They hold in tension God's holiness and God's love.

Hearing their truths separately leaves the hearer with choices. Do you decide to try and synthesize both ideals, reject one outright, or favor one while still listening to the other?

(3) Find Where You Want to Join the Divine Conversation

The conversation between these stories continues in Scripture. The ideas of God as transcendent or as immanent interact with Israel's lived history. The Priests of Judah see God's creative work as a model for the work of Moses and the priests. Moses creates Israel's sanctuary in the book of Exodus similarly to the way God created the world. Compare the Priests' creation story ending, "Thus the heavens and the earth were finished. . . . God finished his work which he had done" (Gen 2:1–2), with "Thus all the work of the tabernacle of the tent of meeting was finished . . . so Moses finished the work" (Exod 39:32; 40:33). Just as all the elements of the universe did as God commanded at creation, so Moses "did everything just as the LORD had commanded him" (40:16) in the creation of the tabernacle sanctuary. Just as God saw what was made and blessed each phase of creation, so "when Moses saw that they had done all the work just as the LORD had commanded, he blessed them" (39:43). When creation was completed, God rested on the Sabbath. When the sanctuary was completed, God found a place to rest. "Then the cloud covered the tent of meeting, and the glory of the LORD filled the tabernacle" (40:34).[17] This distant, transcendent God, who has no form, but whose presence is made known by a murky cloud, is present among mortals in the tabernacle's sanctuary. The Priests make this powerful, transcendent God known through the rituals of the temple, becoming the mediators of God's presence. In comparing the first creation story with the other Priestly writings in the Torah, Albert de Pury wrote, "In the world of humans the sons of Israel are not meant to be just another nation but that they will have a mission of their own within the community of nations. Israel's fundamental and perhaps only mission is to build and keep the sanctuary (25:8a, 9) that will allow YHWH to reside among the sons of Israel and through them, among humankind."[18] The Priests believed God's perfectly ordered world could still be known in God's perfectly ordered

17. Boorer, "Envisioning of the Land," 106–11. She compares the Priestly creation story, the Priestly stories of the tabernacle, and the receiving of the promised land. See also De Pury, "Jacob Story," 67–72.

18. De Pury, "Jacob Story," 67–68.

sanctuary. From God's point of view the ideal of the world always exists, from a human point of view the holy space of the temple opens a portal to commune with a holy God.[19] In the Priestly world God acts in systematic, knowable ways. Though distant, people can know God through predictable, reliable rituals. There is right and wrong, good and evil, common and holy—and never the two should meet.

The first creation story tells more than how God created the world. It creates a foundation for how to worship and relate to this holy God of creation. Given that the consensus among biblical scholars is that the first creation story was written during the Babylonian exile or just following it, the story tells exiled Jews, robbed of everything they had, that they still had a unique and treasured place in God's world. The first creation story gave the Priests hope in a time of ruin. Despite their circumstances, they still worshiped a powerful God who created the world, and who had a purpose for them. If they practiced the rituals of the faith, they again would find their place in God's creation, a sanctuary from the rest of the world.

The second creation story never acknowledges the ideal world portrayed by the Priests. It describes a world that has problems right from the start. This does not seem to be a concern for the Storyteller. She does not seek a perfect place to commune with God. From her perspective God is somehow present, even though absent as well. The ending of the second creation story foreshadows exile. Adam and Eve, having failed to keep God's single command, must leave the garden of Eden and go out into the world, "to till the ground from which he was taken" (Gen 3:23). The next tale continues this theme with Cain banished to be a fugitive and wanderer as punishment for murdering Abel. Later, Jacob must flee his homeland after stealing his brother Esau's birthright and blessing. Years after he returns his son Joseph is sold into slavery and lands in Egypt. Each of these stories, written by the same Storyteller, carries this exilic theme. For Jews exiled in Babylon, they were not simply stories that explained how God created the world, or how the nation of Israel began. These narratives revealed how to live through exile and how to have faith in the LORD even when God's absence obscures God's presence.[20] In the Adam and Eve ending, as well as in Cain's story, God provides some means of protection, before they have to go out and live with the consequences of their actions. In Jacob and Joseph's

19. Lohfink clarifies, "After all, the readers of the priestly document did not live within the glorious and peaceful order that had been planned by God and that could be theirs. . . . The ideal shape of the world is known, it has already existed before. From the point of view of God it is always present, and all that is necessary is to return to it" (*Theology of the Pentateuch*, 172).

20. See Edenburg, "From Eden to Babylon," 155–67.

stories, these faith heroes, who had lost everything, overcame their exiled losses. Jacob returns to his homeland, a rich and prosperous man with a large family and household. Joseph remains in his exiled land, but rises to prominence in his foreign home. The exiles of Babylon could see images of hope in each of these stories. These exiles accepted a world where an immanent God cares deeply for them, but who did not (or could not?) create a perfect world, and who would not be perfectly present—the sly serpent seems to always approach when God is not around. While these stories each point to the consequences of failed actions, God never severs the relationship. Both the Priestly and Deuteronomy traditions assign the blame of the Jewish exile upon the people's sin against God. The Storyteller's exilic theme from Adam and Eve to Joseph is more complex.[21] Adam and Eve's nakedness makes them sitting prey for the sly serpent. Cain's anger comes from God's arbitrary rejection of Cain's offering. Jacob may have taken what did not belong to him, but his mother, like the sly serpent, set him up. Finally, slavery and exile is an extreme and unfair punishment for Joseph's arrogant boasting. Each exile character has a different level of culpability.

The second creation story begins a series of exile tales where mitigating factors refract the blame from solely resting upon the fallen heroes as well as portray God with a more nuanced perspective. God cares for humans, but has arbitrary rules with stiff consequences. God creates, but not without flaws. God rescues, but takes a long time. God protects, but in the midst of exile, not from it. The conversation of the two creation stories turns out to be much more than what you believe about creation. They both carry on a conversation about what kind of faith in God you will live into during exile and trouble and heartache. Which creation story, in other words, gives you hope?

The third movement in St. John of the Cross's way of prayer is to unite (*via unitiva*) with the presence of God. When reading comparative stories in the Bible begin with a simple question: Which portrait of God speaks more deeply to your heart? Give yourself permission to be formed by *that* story. Ignore the other, if you wish.

Our goal is not simply to find out which story we believe in most, or if we believe in both, or neither. Our aim is to somehow unite with God in the process of exploring these stories. To ask, which portrait of God speaks

---

21. Van Seters convincingly shows that the stories of Adam and Eve, Cain and Abel, Jacob and Joseph all carry exilic themes. "These literary, historiographic, and theological characteristics of the Yahwist are not unique to the paradise narrative. What I hope to show in what follows is that they are typical of his writing about the primeval history as a whole" (*Prologue to History*, 129).

most deeply to your heart, is to ask a question beyond belief. It is to invite you to explore through contrasting images what you already experience.

Whether in your own spiritual discernment, or in conversations with a small group, take time to review these divergent voices in God's word with regards to the creation of the world.

First Creation Story	Second Creation Story
A transcendent God.	An immanent God.
God is a non-corporeal being.	God has human characteristics.
God creates with distant words.	God creates with intimate formation.
God creates methodically.	God creates by trial and error.
God's power seems unlimited.	God's power has limits.
God perfectly carries out intentions.	God makes mistakes.
God's creation is very good.	Not everything is good in God's creation.
God is holy.	God is loving.
God is distant.	God is present, but not continuously.
Humans are made in God's image.	Humans come alive with God's breath.
In times of trouble the faithful find hope in a powerful God who carries out intentions.	In times of trouble the faithful find hope in God's grace which imparts good into the struggles of life.

There is purpose in the Bible's habit of providing contrasting stories. In providing a conversation between two theological concepts, the Bible invites us into a deeper experience with God than indoctrination. Looking back over these two creation stories, their differences and similarities, we see the description of a transcendent God commanding creation into a specific order in the first story, and in the second the description of an immanent God that draws near creation even though it has flaws from the beginning. Both stories brought hope in different ways to the Jewish people living in exile.

The question as to which God created the universe is unanswerable in the past tense. The two stories will always remain side-by-side debating that issue. It is an ongoing conversation, a conversation that includes you, and your house of worship, and your community.

- Does one of the stories connect more deeply with you? In what way?

- Does one caricature of God strike you as strong or caring, productive or collaborative, or any other positive way? How so?

- Does one caricature of God strike you as cold or weak, heartless or impotent, or any other negative way? How so?

- How might each story provide hope and perseverance in times of struggle or fear?

- In what way, if any, do you see God still creating in one or both of these ways?

- Which story guides you most on how the church should impact the world?

- In what ways does one story or both strengthen your faith?

CHAPTER 2

How Deep and Wide Is the Love of God?

Perhaps the most important finding that came out of our
research on the spoiled syndrome was that kids recognize
that their parents are often too soft on them—that we let
them get away with more than they should.[1]

—DAN KINDLON

ONE SHELF IN MY library is devoted to parenting. As the parents of triplets, my wife and I do not have the luxury of a learning curve. If we make one mistake, we multiply it by three. So we have sought the wisdom of friends, family, and lots of books as they have grown. Nearly every parenting book we have—from toddlers to teens—stresses the importance for parents to unconditionally love their children while also providing discipline to guide behavior. The definition of what is age appropriate varies. The techniques of time-out, grounding, contracts, removal of privileges, or even old-fashioned paddling will be explained, debated, championed, and rejected by experts as to their success, or lack thereof, for guiding childhood behavior. Through all the debating one thing will be clear—the parent who does not provide boundaries, as well as love, is robbing her child of the self-discipline and self-confidence needed for a healthy and successful life.

In trying to understand God's relationship to humans, biblical writers sometimes portrayed God in a parenting role. Like the parenting books on my shelf, they talked about love and discipline. Deuteronomy thought God's discipline was the most important attribute of God's character and imagined this from a parent's perspective, "Know then in your heart that as a parent disciplines a child so the LORD your God disciplines you" (Deut 8:5). The prophet Hosea preferred to imagine God through parental love, "When Israel was a child, I loved him. . . . The more I called them, the more they went from me. . . . How can I give you up, Ephraim? How can I hand you over O

---

1. Kindlon, *Too Much of a Good Thing*, 176.

Israel?" (Hos 11:1–2, 8). These two images from Deuteronomy and Hosea identify a debate within the Bible about God's character. What is God's most important parenting characteristic—love or discipline? This question was at the heart of Israel's early understanding of God, and its debate influenced the rest of the Bible.

EXCURSUS 2.1

Three Versions of the Ten Commandments

There are three versions of the Ten Commandments in the Torah. Two are familiar. The Levites from the northern kingdom of Israel wrote the set in Deuteronomy 5. The Priests of Judah wrote an almost identical set in Exodus 20. The only change is found in the fourth commandment—keeping Sabbath. Here, the purpose of Sabbath is tied to the rest God took after creating for six days. The Priests' version ties the Ten Commandments to their creation story. In the Levites version, Sabbath rest is a matter of justice built on the remembrance of how God liberated them from slavery.[2] This single discrepancy highlights a key difference between the holiness theology of the Priests and the justice theology of the Deuteronomists.

The third set of Ten Commandments is unfamiliar to most people. Found in Exodus 34:14–26, it is a different set of commandments, but the only set identified in Exodus as the Ten Commandments (34:28). This version shares only three commands with the familiar ten. They are all cultic related.[3] They are about worship, sacrifice and devotion to the LORD. Walter Harrelson proposed that they were the ritual Ten Commandments. They regulated "sacred time and sacred rites of a sort we might suppose was characteristic of Israel early in her life in the land

---

2. Brueggemann, *Theology of the Old Testament*, 187–88. Brueggemann mentions that the two versions of the Sabbath commandment exemplify the twin trajectories of social justice and purity from the Deuteronomistic and Priestly traditions.

3. Rowley writes, "Within these verses we find twelve, or perhaps thirteen, commandments, however, instead of ten, and scholars differ in their views as to which were the original ten and which were the additions. . . . For this Decalogue, however we delimit its ten terms, appears to be a much more primitive document than the other Decalogue which we are considering. . . . There is the insistence that Yahweh alone shall be served, and that idols must not be tolerated. . . . But here we find none of the ethical commandments which are characteristic of the other Decalogue. . . . Instead we find purely ritual commands" (*Moses and the Decalogue*, 89–92).

of Canaan."[4] Van Seters considers it to be from the Storyteller.[5] In our study, we will focus on the preamble to these commandments, where the LORD makes a self-description of God. The familiar sets of the Ten Commandments reversed this description and embedded it in the second commandment. All three versions write a self-description of God.

This chapter will compare two passages in which the second rewrote the first version. It does not matter for our study which self-description of God was first. What matters is that contrasting versions were created and that editors kept all versions in the Torah.

Additionally, we will also look at David's covenant in 2 Samuel 7. The Deuteronomistic Historian (hereafter called the Historian) picked it up and made changes to it later on in the narrative.[6] He wrote in concert with those who edited Deuteronomy in the period preceding the Babylonian invasion—600 BC. He/they edited a history of Israel that covered Samuel and Kings and possibly Joshua and Judges. A couple of centuries later the Chronicler rewrote the Historian's work and changed the 2 Samuel covenant in other ways.

Are There Limits to God's Love?

The debate over God's love and discipline can be found in one of the Bible's core documents: the Ten Commandments. Israel collected the stories of how God gave the Ten Commandments and the Mosaic law over a long period of time. The number of duplications and the disorganized way that the commands are compiled provide the evidence for this. There are three sets of Ten Commandments. Many commands in Exodus 21–23 were rewritten in Deuteronomy 12–26. Had Moses brought all these commands

---

4. Harrelson, *Ten Commandments and Human Rights*, 34.

5. Van Seters, *Life of Moses*, 345–60.

6. While Fretheim notes, "It has been suggested that certain passages, particularly 1 Kgs 2:4; 8:25; and 9:4–5, make the unconditional promise to David into a conditional one," and he does concede that the promise becomes more limited in scope, nonetheless he believes the Historian still thought the promise depended on God's faithfulness (*Deuteronomic History*, 112). See also Geoghegan, "Redaction of Kings and Priestly Authority," 118. Geoghegan concludes that the Historian is a "mediator of competing ideologies." While he acknowledges David's covenant, he promotes the "northern priestly/prophetic" criticism of monarchy's abuse of power.

down from the mountain at one time, the Mosaic law would have been more orderly. Furthermore, the stories cannot agree about the name of the mountain on which Moses received the commandments. In Deuteronomy the mountain is either called Mount Horeb or the mountain of God. The Storyteller and the Priestly writings—Leviticus and parts of Exodus and Numbers—always call it Mount Sinai.

The preamble to the Exodus 34 version of the Ten Commandments contains the most explicit description of God's nature written in the Bible. Portions of it are repeated in the other two versions of the Decalogue as well as in the books of Numbers, Jeremiah, Jonah, Nahum, Joel, Nehemiah, and in several Psalms. This list of the Ten Commandments, however, is not familiar. It was not the version Judge Roy Moore encased on a stone slab outside an Alabama courthouse in defiance of the Supreme Court. It has never been hung in American schools, nor been the subject of lawsuits during the culture wars of the past generation. Yet, it is the only Decalogue to be called the Ten Commandments in Exodus (Exod 34:27–28). As Moses climbs Mount Sinai a cloud descends around him. The LORD passes before him and speaks:

> The LORD, the LORD,
>
> > a God merciful and gracious, slow to anger,
> >
> > > and abounding in steadfast love and faithfulness,
> >
> > keeping steadfast love for the thousandth generation,
> >
> > > forgiving iniquity and transgression and sin,
> > >
> > > yet by no means clearing the guilty,
> >
> > but visiting the iniquity of the parents upon the children
> >
> > > and the children's children,
> > >
> > > to the third and the fourth generation. (34:6–7)

This defining statement about God sounds like a creed.[7] Biblical writers reference it more than any other passage in the Bible.

The term translated as steadfast love comes from the Hebrew word *hesed*. This word has also been translated as grace, loving kindness, compassion and mercy. Paul Hanson described *hesed* as "utterly trustworthy"

---

7. Brueggemann explains, "Scholars believe this is an exceedingly important, stylized, quite self-conscious characterization of Yahweh, a formulation so studied that it may be reckoned to be something of a classic, normative statement to which Israel regularly returned, meriting the label 'credo'" (*Theology of the Old Testament*, 216).

and it became a model for all relationships.[8] The term assures us of God's loyalty in keeping a promise. The LORD sticks by human beings who constantly break God's heart. Walter Brueggemann suggested that *hesed* may be the notion that holds all the other characteristics of God together. Each characteristic in Exodus 34:6–7 does not matter as much as "the cumulative effect of all of these terms together, which bespeak Yahweh's intense solidarity with and commitment to those to whom Yahweh is bound. . . . Yahweh abides for Israel in complete fidelity, even among those who enact 'iniquity, transgression, and sin.'"[9]

A few stories reveal the LORD's own struggle to be faithful to people who would not be faithful. In Exodus 32 the LORD decides to consume the Israelites for creating and worshipping a golden calf. Moses responds by reminding God of the divine covenant with Abraham. In Numbers 14 the LORD was frustrated by Israel's disbelief and decides to abandon them. Shocked, Moses reminds the LORD of the divine promise of steadfast love, quoting Exodus 34:6–7. In both stories God repents and chooses to remain faithful in steadfast love.

The theology behind the credo of Exodus 34 does not look like the justice theology of Deuteronomy, or the holiness theology of the Priests. This theology emphasizes God's steadfast love. This Mount Sinai story declared that God keeps promises: "I hereby make a covenant. Before all your people I will perform marvels, such as have not been performed in all the earth . . . for this is an awesome thing that I will do with you. Observe what I command you today. See, I will drive out before you the [inhabitants of the land]" (Exod 34:10–11). Notice that God initiates and makes the covenant. God will perform marvels and do an awesome thing for Israel. God will drive out the inhabitants of the land for Israel. Rather than warn the people of dire consequences if they do not obey the commandments, this theology is based on God's grace. The LORD is going to do an awesome thing for Israel, something that will send them running to God in appreciation. Therefore, the people must observe God's command in thanksgiving for God's graciousness. This set of commands instructs Israel to worship the LORD alone.

The two familiar versions of the Decalogue reverse the statement about God's steadfast love and God's discipline (Exod 20; Deut 5). Embedded in the second commandment of each are these words:

8. Hanson, *People Called*, 27.

9. Brueggemann, *Theology of the Old Testament*, 217.

For I the LORD your God am a jealous God,

   punishing children for the iniquity of parents,

      to the third and the fourth generation of those who reject me,

but showing steadfast love to the thousandth generation

   of those who love me and keep my commandments.
   (Exod 20:5–6; Deut 5:9–10)

This description restates the preamble of Exodus 34. Here, the two sides of God are more obviously in tension with one another–what Trible calls "God the lover" and the "God the punisher."[10] The writer introduces the LORD as jealous, one who punishes people who reject him. Not only will this rejected God punish the guilty, but will also punish their children and grandchildren to the third and fourth generation. To reject this God is to condemn your descendants for a century.

The statement secondarily claims that this is a loving God. Those who keep God's commandments receive God's steadfast love for a thousand generations. Additionally, the shadow side of love, jealousy—which is a desire to possess what you love and sparks anger when what you love cannot or will not be possessed—is attached to God's love. While God's love and jealousy are held in tension by the statement, the Deuteronomist chooses to begin with jealousy. If the Israelites would reject God, then the LORD would severely punish them out of jealousy. God reserves steadfast love only for those that keep the commandments. This love is conditional. It is contingent upon obedience. The Deuteronomist does not entice the hearer by potential reward, as the Storyteller did when discussing how God formed a covenant with Israel. No, he begins his description of God's nature with a warning. This is a jealous God, so beware.

Justice is one focus in the book of Deuteronomy. The book requires God's justice to be practiced on a horizontal human plane—where the poor are not oppressed and the widow protected—and also on a vertical divine plane—where humans and God each have promises to keep. There are rewards for keeping covenant with God. There are retributions for breaking covenant with God. Justice on the horizontal plane is tethered to justice on the vertical plane. In justice-based theology you cannot speak of one without the other. Deuteronomy 5 shapes the creedal statement about God in a way consistent with everything else the book of Deuteronomy says about God's relationship with the people Israel.

We have two ideas about the character of God's love. One is a love that never ends and forgives even when betrayed. The other is a love that is

10. Trible, *Rhetoric of Sexuality*, 1.

bound by a covenant of justice; while God will be faithful, Israel's faithfulness determines the relationship.

Practicing Midrash

The preamble to the Ten Commandments in Exodus 34, and the statement on God in the second commandment in Exodus 20 and Deuteronomy 5 share many of the same words, even ordering the words in the same sequence in places. Let us allow these two texts—so closely related—to practice midrash with the other. First, we want to let their differences speak and resist the temptation to smooth out their disagreements.

(1) Free the Stories to Speak for Themselves

Someone has switched the two main parts of God's self-description. The Deuteronomistic version begins with God's jealousy and ends with God's love. The Storyteller's account starts by speaking of God's steadfast love, clarifying that God is merciful, gracious, slow to anger, and abounding in steadfast love—words that are not in the other description—and then ends by speaking of God's judgment. Jealousy does not come up until the First Commandment.

EXCURSUS 2.2

The LORD's Self-Descriptions in the Ten Commandments

Deuteronomy 5:9–10 and Exodus 20:5–6	Exodus 34:6–7
[9/5] I the LORD am a jealous God,	[6] The LORD, the LORD, a God merciful and gracious, slow to anger, and abounding in steadfast love and faithfulness,
punishing children for the iniquity of parents, to the third and fourth generation of those who reject me.	[7] Keeping steadfast love for the thousandth generation, forgiving iniquity and transgression and sin,
[10/6] But showing steadfast love to the thousandth generation of those who love me and keep my commandments.	Yet by no means clearing the guilty, but *visiting the iniquity of the parents upon the children and the children's children to the third and fourth generation.*

The Storyteller described God by several adjectives—merciful, gracious, slow to anger, steadfast love, and faithfulness. The Deuteronomist removed all those qualities and instead stated the LORD is a jealous God. God's jealousy was not unknown to the Storyteller (Exod 34:14), but it was not the first thing you should know about the LORD. Notice the breadth of God's love. Despite iniquity, transgression, and sin, God forgives. The guilty will not be cleared—and punishment transfers to their children—but the guilty are undefined. We do not know who they are. Thus, the credo leaves it to the interpreter of God's mercy or God's judgment to make the charge.

The Deuteronomist begins with God's jealousy. The breadth of God's steadfast love is narrow, restricted to only those who keep God's commandments. As Phyllis Trible notes, "Reversing the order of emphasis, the Deuteronomic decalogue appropriated the text to distinguish between those who hate and those who love the deity."[11] The guilty are now named. They are the ones who reject the LORD, the ones who do not keep the commandments.

One of these statements grew out of the other, and for our purposes it really does not matter which one was first. Either the Exodus 34 passage was shortened and rearranged to minimize the breadth of God's steadfast love while emphasizing God's command of obedience as a requirement to receive God's love, or the Deuteronomistic version was expanded to minimize God's judgment while showering descriptive praise for God's enduring steadfast love. Both possibilities reveal a theological debate in ancient Israel, a debate that continued through the biblical period.

Phyllis Trible showed in a brief study how phrases from these statements are used elsewhere in the Hebrew Bible to emphasize either God's steadfast love, or God's judgment.[12] The prophet Nahum removed any references to God's mercy in order to describe the LORD as a God of judgment and destruction (Nah 1:2–3). He reversed the meaning of "slow to anger" from an element of divine mercy to portray the LORD's wrath as slow and sure—like a slow boil. The prophet Joel did the exact opposite, removing any references to God's wrath in order to encourage his people to return to the LORD, because God's mercy could be trusted (Joel 2:13). The prophet Jonah quoted the merciful parts of the credo almost the exact same way as Joel did, but he did it in anger. He wished for the destruction

11. Trible, *Rhetoric of Sexuality*, 2.
12. Trible, *Rhetoric of Sexuality*, 1–5.

of Nineveh. God's mercy for those who did not deserve it made him furious (Jonah 4:2). When Nehemiah went to God in a confessional prayer on behalf of his people, he chose the Exodus 20 version of the creed, praying, "O LORD God of heaven, the great and awesome God who keeps covenant and steadfast love with those who love him and keep his commandments" (Neh 1:5). The prayer speaks of God's conditional love as an enticement to encourage repentance and obedience.

Trible believes that the interpretative use of these statements illustrates the way Scripture is used by other people in biblical times. "These passages illustrate the hermeneutics at work within the Bible. . . . A single text appears in different versions with different functions in different contexts. Through application, it confesses, challenges, comforts, and condemns. What it says on one occasion, it denies on another. Thus, Scripture in itself yields multiple interpretations of itself."[13] In her study, Trible failed to find any set of interpretive principles in the way the credo from Exodus is referenced and reinterpreted throughout the Hebrew Bible. Thus, it is somewhat unpredictable how future generations and contexts may reinterpret a text. Though future generations will predictably continue to debate the ways to interpret these statements about God.

There is a clear contrast between these descriptive statements of God and the contrast is verified in the way the passages are quoted elsewhere in the Bible. Is the LORD first and foremost a God of steadfast love, who forgives sin and iniquity even to the thousandth generation, and secondarily a God whose slow anger judges the guilty? Alternatively, is the LORD first and foremost a God of justice who punishes those who reject the LORD and secondarily a God of love *for only those* who keep the commandments? These contrasting questions are not simply rearranged semantics. They describe two very different portraits of God. They influenced other biblical authors for hundreds of years. They affect the way people understand, worship, and follow God still today.

The preamble in Exodus 34 explains that God's love overcomes the unfaithfulness of God's people with forgiveness for sin, transgression and iniquity. God remains faithful even when the people are unfaithful. In this way, God's love may be described as unconditional. This Storyteller's perspective would be in line with the understanding that the LORD's covenants with Israel were unconditional promises, everlasting and without end.

The statements embedded in the second commandment declare that God's justice must be satisfied before God's love is shared. If the people break God's commands and reject God, then God is not obligated to remain

---

13. Trible, *Rhetoric of Sexuality*, 4.

faithful. The LORD, in fact, will punish those who reject God. This Deuter-onomistic perspective made God's covenants conditional, contingent upon the Israelites upholding the commandments of the Mosaic law.

(2) Listen to the Stories as Contrasting Voices of God

According to the stories of Israel's history the LORD made three great promises, or covenants, with Israel: (1) a covenant with Abraham, which promised a land for him and his descendants; (2) a covenant with Moses, which gave a law to guide the people to live in the land; and (3) a covenant with David, which promised that his descendants would rule the land from the throne in Jerusalem. God promised land, law and leadership to Israel, and furthermore promised God's presence. There are multiple stories about each of these covenants. In each case, some stories depict each covenant as an unconditional, everlasting promise, while other stories claim the opposite, that God's covenant is conditional only as good as Israel's commitment to keeping God's commandments.[14] The covenant stories—with their duplications—reveal that the two versions of God's self-description in the Decalogue affect the way Israel remembers God's promises.

The Storyteller's version of the Ten Commandments gives no hint that God placed any conditions upon Israel in validating a covenant with them. This God kept steadfast love for a thousand generations, forgiving iniquity, transgressions and sin. When Moses warned God that Israel was a stiff-necked people, the LORD showed no hesitation, "I hereby make a covenant. Before all your people I will perform marvels, such as have not been performed in all the earth or in any nation; and all the people among whom you live shall see the work of the LORD; for it is an awesome thing that I will do with you" (Exod 34:10). God's generosity is astonishing. Forewarned about Israel's stubbornness, God nevertheless moves forward, makes a covenant with Israel, and promises to do amazing things to win the people over to the LORD. There are commandments to follow and God warns that to break them will "become a snare among you" (34:12), but there are no threats.

When God makes a covenant with David a similar theme develops. David had begun making plans to build a house for God, in which to place the ark of the covenant. The LORD will have none of it. God provides for Israel, not the other way around. "The LORD declares to you that the LORD

14. This chapter will not examine Abraham's covenant. The Storyteller's version is found in Genesis 12 and partially in 15. The Priestly version is in Genesis 17 and tethers the covenant to circumcision. Another version is found at the end of the story of sacrificing Isaac in Genesis 22. Two stories are unconditional; two have conditions.

will make you a house. When your days are fulfilled and you lie down with your ancestors, I will raise up your offspring after you, who shall come forth from your body, and I will establish his kingdom. He shall build a house for my name, and I will establish the throne of his kingdom forever" (2 Sam 7:11b–13).[15] God anticipates that David's descendants will not be perfect. Like a father correcting a son, God will punish them, but will not take away God's steadfast love. "Your house and your kingdom shall be made sure forever before me; your throne shall be established forever" (7:16). David responds in prayer, "Is there another nation on earth whose God went to redeem it as a people, and to make a name for himself, doing great and awesome things for them" (7:23). Brueggemann declares that this "sweeping assurance" overrides the conditional *if* found in the Priestly and Deuteronomistic writings.[16]

This idea that God had made unconditional, everlasting promises to Israel was deeply entrenched in the minds of some of Israel's people and leaders. There is plenty of evidence in the Bible to confirm that people did believe God made such outlandish covenants. A number of psalms speak of the everlasting covenant God made with David and how God's steadfast love endures forever (2 Sam 23; Ps 77; 89; 105; 136). Psalm 89 is particularly interesting. The first half speaks confidently of God's steadfast love and everlasting covenant with David. Originally, the psalm likely ended with v. 37 with the moon serving as a memorable metaphor for God's covenant. Later another poet added a new ending to the old psalm, after the terrible destruction of Jerusalem and the subsequent exile to Babylon. This poet questioned God in a very Job-like manner.

> But now you have spurned and rejected [David];
>
> you are full of wrath against your anointed.
>
> You have renounced the covenant with your servant;

---

15. See Friedman, *Hidden Book*, 248–49. There is considerable debate about this passage, because it shows a mix of writers, nevertheless the general sentiment follows a theology based on God's steadfast love. The Historian did not override this Yahwistic notion of an unconditional covenant until 1 Kings. Friedman includes vv. 9–12, but not 13–16, as original. Brueggemann points out that "there is no doubt that this passage has had redactional work done on it and that some parts are later than other parts. The specific distinctions are very difficult to make, but none of that detracts from its main claims" (*David's Truth*, 74). See also von Rad, *Old Testament Theology*, 1:310. He thought the oldest verses in this section were 11b and 16—that God would establish David's house forever. What was originally promised to David, von Rad believes, was later transferred to David's descendants and then to the whole people of Israel.

16. Brueggemann, *Theology of the Old Testament*, 605.

you have defiled his crown in the dust.

You have broken through all his walls;

you have laid his strongholds in ruins. . . .

How long, O LORD? Will you hide yourself forever?

How long will your wrath burn like fire? . . .

LORD, where is your steadfast love of old,

which by your faithfulness you swore to David? (89:38–49)

The psalm testifies about how God broke the everlasting covenant. The fault lies with God, not Israel. The poet is shattered. He does not understand why this has happened because he formerly believed in God's everlasting, unconditional covenants.[17]

When Isaiah prophesied in Jerusalem while the Assyrian army besieged the holy city in 701 BC, he counted on God's unconditional promises. "The LORD of hosts will protect Jerusalem; he will protect and deliver it, he will spare and rescue it. . . . Then the Assyrian shall fall by a sword, not of mortals; and a sword, not of humans, shall devour him" (Isa 31:5, 8). One dawn the sunlight revealed dead bodies scattered among the Assyrian siege lines while the rest of the army had vanished. In the people's minds this miraculous event confirmed that God truly protected Jerusalem without fail. When Jeremiah preached on the temple steps a little over a century later, he mocked the people for believing that God's temple and the holy city were like home base in a game of tag—if you are there, you are always safe! If people did not believe that God unconditionally protected Jerusalem, Jeremiah's temple sermon would have been meaningless (Jer 7:1–15).

Jeremiah, among others, did not think God made unconditional promises. His temple sermon rebuked those who did. He was a prophet molded by the Levites who wrote Deuteronomy, and they believed that God's promises, like God's love, were conditionally shared with Israel. They believed that the gift of the land was tied to keeping the law. The focus of their theology can be captured in a single, two-letter word: *if*. The Levites understood God's promises in the context of exile. The idea of being conquered and exiled from the land was in direct contradiction with the idea that God unconditionally gave the land forever. Deuteronomy had a solution to that dilemma with that short word. "If you obey the commandments

17. Fretheim notes, "Did not history, through the Exile, contradict this promise (of God) to David? Psalm 89 may well be a lament focusing on this question in that context" (*Deuteronomic History*, 121).

of the LORD your God . . . then you shall live and become numerous . . . in the land. . . . But if your heart turns away . . . I declare . . . that you shall perish; you shall not live long in the land" (Deut 30:16–18).

If the people keep God's covenant, *then* the promises of God's protection will be sustained. Deuteronomy had no tolerance for those who believed God's promises were unconditional and everlasting. What people did mattered. If the people were conquered and exiled, it would be because of their disobedience, not because of God's lack of protection. God waits for a faithful response—or disobedience—before acting. Deuteronomy emphasized that the covenant with Moses was a two-way street between God and the Israelites. This was made clear by the way the covenant was presented at Mount Horeb (5–6), reaffirmed in the Transjordan (26–28), amended and reaffirmed in Moab (29–31), and then finally renewed by Joshua at Shechem (Josh 8 and 24)—at least four and maybe five separate events![18] The Israelites were told that if they did not keep their promise to God, there would be dreadful consequences. In each case, they promised to keep the covenant through the Mosaic law.

> See, I am setting before you today a blessing and a curse; the blessing, *if* you obey the commandments of the LORD your God that I am commanding you today; and the curse, *if* you do not obey the commandments of the LORD your God, but turn from the way that I am commanding you today, to follow other gods that you have not known. (Deut 11:26–28)

> See, I have set before you today life and prosperity, death and adversity. *If* you obey the commandments of the LORD your God . . . the LORD your God will bless you in the land that you are entering to possess. But *if* your heart turns away and you do not hear, but are led astray to bow down to other gods and serve them, I declare to you today that you shall perish. . . . I have set before you life and death, blessings and curses. Choose life so that you and your descendants may live. (30:15–19; cf. 4:26; Josh 24:19–21)

The Deuteronomistic writers sent an unmistakable and threatening message. If the hearer became worried and afraid that was not a bad effect. They wanted to change people's behavior with dire warnings. To covenant with the LORD and then to break it was to place your life in peril. Now, to be fair, Deuteronomy spoke of great blessings for those who kept the

18. See Mendenhall, "Covenant," 1:721; and Rast, "Joshua," 243. Some scholars speculate that the multiple covenant renewals are actually separate traditions that have been brought together by Deuteronomy.

commandments. Time and again the Israelites were made aware of the benefits of this covenant—liberation from slavery and presentation of a new land along with promises of prosperity (Deut 7:12–15). Later the Israelites were told that even rain from the heavens would be showered on them as long as they heeded the LORD's commandments (11:13–17). Blessings and curses of the LORD were contingent upon Israel's commitment to keeping God's covenant. God was beholden to Israel only as long as Israel kept the covenant. If Israel broke the covenant, not only would God remove the promised blessings, but in addition would actively curse Israel.

To make their case the Deuteronomistic writers reworked the Davidic covenant as well. At the end of his life David offered a last word to Solomon encouraging him to follow the LORD's ways and commandments and then stating that *if* he followed them, the royal line would always rule the throne. "Be strong, be courageous, and keep the charge of the LORD your God, walking in his ways and keeping his statutes, his commandments . . . as is written in the law of Moses. . . . Then the LORD will establish his word that he spoke concerning me: 'If your heirs . . . walk before me in faithfulness with all their heart and with all their soul, there shall not fail you a successor on the throne of Isreal'" (1 Kgs 2:2–4).

Compare that version of David's covenant with the original one written in 2 Samuel 7. "I will raise up your offspring after you . . . and I will establish the throne of his kingdom forever. I will be a father to him, and he shall be a son to me. When he commits iniquity, I will punish him . . . but I will not take my steadfast love from him. . . . Your house and your kingdom shall be made sure forever before me; your throne shall be established forever" (2 Sam 7:12–16). With that one simple two-letter word—if—the Historian changed the Davidic covenant from an unconditional promise to a conditional one. In the 2 Samuel passage, God establishes David's kingdom without condition. Even if his heirs commit iniquity God will not take away steadfast love, or the throne, from them. David's throne shall be established forever. Conversely, the 1 Kings passage says that God will only establish the promise *if* his heirs walk before God in faithfulness with all their heart and soul. Notice that in the 2 Samuel passage God is the subject who makes the promise and speaks to unbreakable qualities, whereas in the 1 Kings passage the focus is on Solomon and his heirs, upon whom the promise rests by their behavior.

In the chapters that followed, the Historian further explained that God promised to dwell in the temple only if Solomon walked in the way of God's commandments (1 Kgs 6:12–13) and to protect Israel in the land only if he walked after the LORD as did his father, David (9:4–9). Solomon is warned that if he strays from the LORD's commandments that David's dynasty will become a heap of ruins. Readers can see the connection with Deuteronomy, because 1 Kings 9:8–9 and Deuteronomy 29:24–27 are nearly identical.

The argument about the character of God's steadfast love determined how Israel understood the promises God made with them. The Storyteller's description of the LORD as a God abounding in steadfast love (Exod 34) encouraged many in Israel to believe that when God made promises they were unconditional and everlasting. Nothing Israel could do would change God's faithfulness.

Conversely, the Levites who wrote the Deuteronomy tradition (as well as the Priests who wrote the Priestly tradition) explained that the steadfast love of the LORD had limits. All of God's gifts and promises to Israel were contingent upon the kings and the people keeping the commandments of the Mosaic law. The covenantal theology could be summed up in a single verse, "If you seek him, he will be found by you; but if you forsake him, he will abandon you forever" (1 Chr 28:9).

(3) Find Where You Want to Join the Divine Conversation

How do you hold onto the idea that the LORD is a "God merciful and gracious, slow to anger, and abounding in steadfast love and faithfulness, keeping steadfast love for the thousandth generation, forgiving iniquity and transgression and sin" (Exod 34:6–7), and also ascribe to the idea that "if you seek [God], he will be found by you; but if you forsake him, he will abandon you forever" (1 Chr 28:9)?

In this chapter, we have looked at two opposing ideas concerning God's love. On one side is the idea that God's steadfast love is amazingly wide and generous, forgiving sins for a thousand generations. This view supported a theology that believed God's covenants with Abraham (land), Moses (law), and David (leadership) were unconditional, everlasting gifts from God. Should Israel stray from God's covenant, the LORD would do amazing things to keep drawing the Israelites near. God would not take away steadfast love even if they committed sin and iniquity.

On the other side is the idea that God's justice tempers God's love. Those who reject God's gifts will not continue to receive God's love and protection. God's justice will not allow God's love to be abused by those who would take advantage of it—which is the reason Jonah angrily protested when God forgave the people of Ninevah (Jonah 4:1–3). All of God's covenants are based on faithfulness of keeping the commandments of the Mosaic law. God is faithful to Israel. The question is whether the people will be faithful to God.

This debate about God's love continues throughout the Bible. As noted above, Phyllis Trible found a dozen instances in which the Exodus 34 passage was quoted and/or reinterpreted as a statement about God's love or God's wrath. Jesus' willingness to meet with sinners carried the discussion about the wideness of God's love into the New Testament—under the same continuum. The nature of God's love affects theological beliefs about sin, repentance, salvation, the church, ordination, and even eschatology (end times). The reversal of the statements about God's love and judgment in the three versions of the Ten Commandments represents a conversation that will scatter into numerous arguments in the Bible and today in the church.

I cannot help but wonder if it would be the case that what a person believes about God's love shows up in his or her parenting style. Or, how a person supervises workers on her or his staff? Or, maybe where a person falls on the continuum of law and order issues? The beliefs about God's love and judgment may be less likely theologically articulated and more often lived out in how we embody that love and judgment in our relationships and experiences. It may be fair to question which comes first: our conscious beliefs about God's love and judgment, or our practice of love and judgment in relationships (as modeled to us). These questions about God's steadfast love are as much about human capacity as they are about God's nature. Is it possible, in other words, for human beings to become self-disciplined in an environment with no boundaries? Or, does such an environment lead to permissiveness and instability? Or, could it be that the biblical debate over God's love and judgment operate under the same mystery as fraternal twins who grow up in the same household of parental love and discipline (whatever those are), yet one becomes a model citizen and the other a moral reprobate?

It should be no surprise that the great, defining statements about God in Exodus 34, and in Deuteronomy 5 and Exodus 20, were reversed, reworked, repeated, reinterpreted numerous times, nor that all three of God's covenants with Israel—land, law, and leadership—were repeated multiple times with different versions because they dealt with matters more personal than just what people believed about God. These beliefs touched on how people experience love and life at home with family and out in the world.

- So, what do you want to believe about God's love and judgment? The Bible, as you have now seen, gives you a wide berth. Consider, how do you want to love your children, work with people on the job or in the community? How do you think law and order should operate in our nation, or between nations of the world? How does all of that translate into what God's love looks like?

- When you name the strengths of a faith based on a God who is merciful and gracious, slow to anger and abounding in steadfast love, forgiving iniquity and sins for a thousand generations, what comes to mind? What might be some weaknesses to such a faith?

- When you name the strengths of a faith based on a God who jealously guards covenant—showering steadfast love for a thousand generations upon those who love God and keep God's commandments, but punishing those who reject God—what comes to mind? What might be some weaknesses to such a faith?

- Could you imagine a faith based on a God whose love and judgment are in perfect balance? If so, what does that look like to you?

- Maybe the most important question is: How deep and wide do you want the love of God to be for you . . . and for your enemies?

CHAPTER 3

Do You Want the Whole Truth?

What you don't read is often as important as what you do read. . . . The misery, woe, and treachery contained in the pages of this book are so dreadful that it is important that you don't read any more of it than you already have.[1]

—LEMONY SNICKET

RATHER THAN BE SCARED away by the warnings Lemony Snicket placed on his first pages of the thirteen books in A Series of Unfortunate Events, a curious third grader will immediately plow into its pages in the hunt for misery, woe, and treachery. Daniel Handler—Lemony Snicket's real name—knows how to get children hooked into a story. Both frightened and fascinated by misery, woe, and treachery, children want to explore such things from the safety of a story—books first, because what you see is only as scary as your imagination, movies after they are a bit braver.

This does not change much as we grow older. Human nature wants to hear the gossip, watch the gore, read about the dirt—as long as we are not experiencing it firsthand. It's why negative politics are effective, and why actors and actresses like to play the villain. Though parents often teach children, "If you can't say something nice, don't say anything at all," many people want to know the whole truth—the good, the bad, and the ugly.

When it comes to bad news about somebody, when should you say nothing at all and when should something be said? What should you read and not read? As for historical figures, if none of their mistakes is told, then we do not get the whole truth about the person. It can be the case that a regret, an error in judgment, or a scandal may be the catalyst that inspires a person to change her character and attempt great things. To hear only about a person's accomplishments, but not his doubts, or her struggles, may cause us to miss the very thing that made a person reach greatness. Then, again,

---

1. Snicket, *Vile Village*, 1–2.

sometimes it is just dirt with no redeeming value. As Lemony Snicket said, "What you don't read is often as important as what you do read." So, how much of the misery and woe about someone do you tell in order to tell the truth about him or her? This was a question in the minds of people who wrote portions of the Bible.

EXCURSUS 3.1

Two Versions of Jacob & David's Stories

For this chapter we will explore two versions of Jacob's story and King David's life. Jacob's story of stealing his brother's blessing belongs to the Storyteller, and exhibits his typical style: flawed hero, life consequences, and the grace of God's steadfast love. A Priestly version of why he left home frames the original story at its beginning and ending. The Storyteller's version is found in Genesis 27:1–45. The Priests' story begins in Genesis 26:34–35, just before the other tale. Link it to Genesis 27:46—28:9 and it becomes a seamless separate story. "When Esau was forty years old, he married Judith daughter of Beeri the Hittite, and Basemath daughter of Elon the Hittite; and they made life bitter for Isaac and Rebekah. Then Rebekah said to Isaac, 'I am weary of my life because of these Hittite women. If Jacob marries one of these Hittite women such as these . . . what good will my life be to me?' Then Isaac called Jacob and blessed him." The Priests' version displays some of its common traits as well: hero as role model, clear right and wrong, and exclusion of the other.

David's story was originally written in the Succession Narrative that began in 2 Samuel 9, which may go back to Solomon's kingdom.[2] Friedman lists a number of a curious links between the Succession Narrative and the Storyteller's work in Genesis.[3] One was possibly dependent on the other. The Historian picked

---

2. The Succession Narrative is generally considered an independent court history that was later brought into the Historian's work. Friedman offers a minority position that the Yahwist wrote the Succession Narrative, possibly as a scribe in Solomon's court (*Who Wrote the Bible*, 33–69). Fretheim holds to a more common position that the Succession Narrative was an earlier composition, not connected with the Yahwist, but which is hard to date (*Deuteronomic History*, 122–23). See also Auld, *Life in Kings*, 11–12. He provides another view that the Succession Narrative was a supplement to the Historian's work, not a source for it.

3. Friedman, *Hidden Book*, 33–44.

up the Succession Narrative along with other stories about David when creating Samuel and Kings just before the Babylonian exile. Later the Chronicler, who was part of the Priestly tradition, re-wrote David's story.

Flawed Hero or Role Model?

King David was the quintessential hero in Israel's remembered history. A mighty warrior, he slew the giant Goliath while yet a teenage boy. He killed "ten thousands" (1 Sam 18:7), conquered Jerusalem, and established it as Israel's royal capital and holy city. He was also a sensitive soul who played the harp and wrote psalms. He showed kindness to his enemies; spared Saul's life, forgave the loudmouth Shimei, and kept his promise to protect Saul's only surviving heir, Jonathan's son, the crippled Mephibosheth. Above all, he was a man after God's own heart, who danced when the Levites brought the ark into Jerusalem. David was a renaissance man—brave, kind, shrewd and devout.

The writers in 1 and 2 Samuel obviously admire David a great deal. That is what makes the rest of the stories about him so fascinating. One writer exposed the scandal of how David raped Bathsheba and conspired to have her husband murdered. Later, he revealed how David's shortcomings as a father nearly cost him his kingdom. Samuel and the first couple of chapters of 1 Kings portray David in perplexing ways. His flaws are flaunted as much as his feats. This makes the way Chronicles describes David even more interesting. Chronicles does not repeat any of David's sins or flaws. After all, if you can't say something nice, don't say anything at all. Where David was tainted, the Chronicler said nothing at all.

EXCURSUS 3.2

To Tell or Not to Tell, That Is the Question

2 Samuel 11:1–4	**1 Chronicles 20:1–3**
[1] *In the spring of the year, the time when kings go out to battle,* David sent *Joab* with his officers and all Israel with him; they *ravaged* *the Ammonites, and besieged Rabbah. But David remained at Jerusalem.*	[1] *In the spring of the year, the time when kings go out to battle, Joab* led out the army, *ravaged* the country of *the Ammonites,* and came *and besieged Rabbah. But David remained at Jerusalem.*
[2] It happened, late one afternoon, when David rose from his couch and was walking about on the roof of the king's house, that he saw from the roof a woman bathing; the woman was very beautiful. [3] David sent someone to inquire about the woman. It was reported, "This is Bathsheba, daughter of Eliam, the wife of Uriah the Hittite." [4] So David sent messengers to get her, and she came to him, and he lay with her. . . . Then she returned to her house.	Joab attacked Rabbah, and overthrew it. [2] David took the crown of Milcom from his head; he found that it weighed a talent of gold, and in it was a precious stone; and it was placed on David's head. He also brought out the booty of the city, a very great amount. [3] He brought out the people who were in it, and set them to work with saws and iron picks and axes. Thus David did to all the cities of the Ammonites. Then David and all the people returned to Jerusalem.

The Chronicler started the David and Bathsheba story and then intentionally diverted from it. The words in italics above show that v. 1 in 2 Samuel 11 and 1 Chronicles 20 are nearly identical. The Chronicler, who rewrote Samuel and Kings to fit his own theological agenda, changed the first verse only slightly. Then he skipped ahead in the Samuel narrative and rewrote 2 Samuel 12:26–31.

The Chronicler had closely followed Samuel's narrative until this point, except for the verses listed above he leaves out the next ten chapters where Samuel tells the dark side of David's life. Curiously, he returns to Samuel's narrative just in time to save one of David's most remembered accomplishments. In an otherwise forgettable passage the 2 Samuel text says, "Then there was another battle with the Philistines at Gob; and Elhanan son of Jaareoregim, the Bethlehemite, killed Goliath the Gittite, the shaft of whose spear was like a weaver's beam" (21:19). The sentence seems to indicate that someone other than David killed Goliath—who as in the story in 1 Samuel 17 had a spear shaft the size of a weaver's beam.

Had David's fame taken the achievement of another person from Bethlehem, as his desire had taken another man's wife, to make his own story better? Or could Elhanan once been a local name for David? The Chronicler did not quibble with such questions. He saw the problem and changed the story, "There was war with the Philistines; and Elhanan son of Jair killed Lahmi the brother of Goliath the Gittite, the shaft of whose spear was like a weaver's beam" (1 Chr 20:5). The Chronicler makes this change even though he does not include the Goliath story in his narrative because he picks up King David's life with his coronation. Nevertheless, he is mindful of the larger Samuel and Kings narrative even when he does not choose to follow it. So, just in case you were confused, it was Goliath's *brother* who was killed in this later battle.

This contrast between Samuel/Kings and Chronicles is not a one-time occurrence. Chronicles never speaks of David or Solomon's sins, or errors, with one exception, where Satan catches the blame (21:1). In Chronicles David and Solomon are perfect kings, role models for all aspiring leaders. All the good things about David are repeated in Chronicles without any of the problems that were also shared in Samuel. Furthermore, Chronicles never questions the people's support for David. Israel was "of a single mind to make David king" (12:38). Chronicles removes any indication that the people ever turned against David and supported Absalom's coup. The transfer of power from David to Solomon was an easy, peaceful process in Chronicles (29), whereas in Kings it was a bloodbath (1 Kgs 1–2). Chronicles made David a role model for others to follow, as all Priestly heroes were.

Samuel made David a flawed hero. Uriah ends up being murdered because his character is more commendable than David's. As soon as the king learns that Bathsheba is pregnant, he sends for Uriah to come home from the front. David assumes this furloughed soldier would have sex with his wife the first night home. Then, he hoped in eight month's time Uriah would believe he is the father of a pre-mature baby. The plan falls apart when Uriah would not betray solidarity with his fellow troops and sleep with his wife. He would not enjoy her company when his fellow soldiers were missing their wives while facing the horrors of war. When David realizes Uriah would not betray his solidarity with the troops, he decides to have him killed. Uriah's high principles make him dangerous to David's deceptions. So, David issues a military order to put Uriah on the front line. In the heat of battle, the other troops would be ordered to fallback leaving Uriah exposed and doomed. The king hands Uriah a sealed note, knowing that he could count on Uriah's good character to hand over his own unopened death sentence to the commanding officer (2 Sam 11). Hollywood could not write a better murder mystery!

Rape and murder are just the first of a series of troubling events. This writer reveals David's failures as a father. When Amnon follows his father's lead and rapes his half-sister, Tamar, David shrugs his shoulders over the incident. Absalom, Tamar's outraged brother, eventually kills Amnon, undercuts his father's authority, and then leads a successful, but short-lived, coup against his father (13–18). As if this is not enough, the first and last stories about David depict him as a pitiful character. The story about his secret coronation characterizes him as a leftover son (1 Sam 16).[4] Told that God would choose the next king from among Jesse's sons, Samuel travels to Bethlehem to anoint the one who would be king. When Jesse brings his sons to meet Samuel he leaves David at home to tend sheep, which explains how important David was in his own family! Even at his first moment of greatness, when he slayed Goliath, the story begins by showing that he came to the front lines only to bring his older brothers' lunches to them. When David spoke up, his older brothers told him to shut up and go back where he belonged. He was not even big enough to wear a man's armor (17).[5]

At the end, David is portrayed as a pathetic, dying, old man. His officers find a beautiful virgin Abishag to wait on him and lie with him in hopes of arousing the king. Mocking him by his worst sin, the king's impotency keeps him from raping another woman. Meanwhile, Bathsheba, a survivor, pushes him around like a pawn to grab power for her son by guaranteeing that Solomon would be anointed king (1 Kgs 1). What a surprising way to portray a hero!

This extreme contrast between Samuel/Kings and Chronicles is repeated elsewhere. There are a number of stories in the Torah where the flaws of heroes are readily confessed, and then contrasted by Priestly versions of the person's life that either provide alternative explanations, or ignore the flaws altogether. In the Storyteller's tales there seems to be a need to reveal the shadow side of heroes, whereas in the Priestly writings of the Torah and for Chronicles, almost nothing bad is ever said about a hero. The contrast is clear and intentional. According to the Storyteller Abraham lied about his wife, Sarah, and married her off to another man to save his

4. It was thought that the number seven was a true blessing from God. David was the eighth son. He was outside the true blessing—a leftover.

5. Brueggemann, *David's Truth*, 27–35. Here Brueggemann points out that the "trustful truth of the tribe" relishes the fact that David is nobody, because they are nobodies.

own skin. Jacob, who became the father of the twelve tribes of Israel, was a conniving con artist. Joseph was vain and arrogant. Judah had sex with his daughter-in-law, and then condemned her afterwards. Moses murdered a man, then ran for his life. In contrast the Priestly writings show these heroes to be role models for the community. We only see Abraham, Jacob, and Moses at their best in the Priestly texts.

The duplications in explaining how Jacob received his father's blessing and why he traveled to his uncle's house provide a comparison of two versions. In the longer and more familiar version, Jacob lies to his father (with his mother's help) and steals his brother's blessing. When Esau starts planning to kill Jacob their mother overhears and warns Jacob: "Your brother Esau is consoling himself by planning to kill you. Now, therefore, my son, obey my voice; flee at once to my brother Laban in Haran, and stay with him a while, until your brother's fury turns away" (Gen 27:42–44). The Priestly version, however, does not mention Jacob's deceit, and offers another explanation for Jacob's visit to his uncle: "Then Rebekah said to Isaac, 'I am weary of my life because of the Hittite women. If Jacob marries . . . one of the women of the land, what good will my life be to me?' Then Isaac called Jacob and blessed him and charged him, 'You shall not marry one of the Canaanite women. Go at once to Paddan-aram to the house of Bethuel, your mother's father; and take as wife from there one of the daughters of Laban, your mother's brother'" (27:46—28:2).

EXCURSUS 3.3

Bad Jacob / Good Jacob

Genesis 27:1–45	**Genesis 26:34–35; 27:46—28:9**

A Mother's Intervention

"Now Rebekah was listening when Isaac spoke to his son Esau. So when Esau went to the field to hunt for game and bring it, Rebekah said to her son Jacob . . ." (27:5–6). Rebekah then schemes to help Jacob steal Esau's firstborn blessing.	Esau's Hittite wives made "life bitter for Isaac and Rebekah. . . . Then Rebekah said to Isaac, 'I am weary of my life because of these Hittite women. If Jacob marries . . . one of the women of the land, what good will my life be to me?'" (26:34–35; 27:46).

| Genesis 27:1–45 | Genesis 26:34–35; 27:46—28:9 |

A Father's Blessing

After tricking his father into thinking he was Esau, Isaac said, "May God give you the dew of heaven, and of the fatness of the earth. . . . Let peoples serve you, and nations bow down to you. . . . Cursed be everyone who curses you, and blessed be everyone who blesses you!" (27:28–29). Isaac's blessing of Jacob emphasizes fertility and dominion. There is no mention of Abraham's covenant with God.

After Rebekah's complaint, Isaac calls Jacob, charges him not to marry one of the Canaanite women and blessed him, "May God Almighty bless you and make you fruitful and numerous. . . . May he give you the blessing of Abraham . . . so that you may take possession of the land where you now live as an alien—land that God gave Abraham" (28:3–4). Isaac's blessing recalls the covenant with Abraham—progeny and land.

Jacob travels to his Uncle Laban's home

With Esau determined to kill Jacob, Rebekah told him to "flee at once to my brother Laban in Haran, and stay will him a while, until your brother's fury turns away" (27:43–44). Jacob received his father's blessing, but is forced into exile as a consequence.

Instructed not to marry a local Canaanite (Hittite) woman, Jacob is told to "go at once to Paddan-aram to the house of Bethuel, your mother's father; and take as a wife from there one of the daughters of Laban, your mother's brother" (28:2). Jacob leaves with his parents' well wishes.

These were once two separate stories about Jacob that have been merged in Genesis 26:34—28:9 with the Priestly version framing the other story at its beginning and ending with comments about Esau's wives. The same dynamic that was at play with David's story is operating here. One writer reveals the flaws in an Israelite hero, and then a Priestly version of the story cleans him up.

The Priests make Jacob the good son, the one who listens to his parents, refuses to marry a girl outside the tribe, and who dutifully leaves home to seek the wife his parents wished for him. They make Esau the bad son, because he married local Canaanite women, which made life for his parents bitter. Marrying people of the land was consistently condemned by the holiness-based theology of the Priests. Later, Esau took a wife acceptable to his parents, but he did not divorce his other wives. Therefore, blessing did not come. The Priests claim Jacob as the child of God's promise and his actions prove him to be so.

The Storyteller portrays Jacob as the bad son—the one who schemed and lied to his father to steal his brother's blessing—and makes Esau the good son, his father's favorite. Years later, when word reached Esau that Jacob was returning to the home country, Esau greets him with open arms, and forgives him for all that he had done. Jacob then used Esau's forgiveness as an opportunity to deceive him once again. Esau begged his brother to come home with him to their father, but Jacob deferred. Frederick Buechner pictured Jacob talking about their encounter: "'My lord, my lord,' [Esau] said. He was grinning. He made as if to do battle with me. He circled me, bobbing and feinting. He jabbed at the air all around me with his fists. Once or twice he slapped at my cheeks lightly, like a girl, with his open palms. 'You'll have your way, won't you darling?' he said. 'Nobody ever got the better of you yet. Nobody is ever going to get the better of [ol' Jacob].'"[6] Jacob and Esau provide a dramatic contrast in this version of their lives. One was shrewd and dishonest, the other dim-witted and forgiving. In this case, shrewdness won out over forgiveness. It is hardly the moral folks teach children in Sunday school. Yet, despite all his flaws, the Storyteller also claims Jacob as the chosen child of God's promise. Go figure!

Practicing Midrash

Just as the Bible offered two versions of the creation of the universe it gave us two versions of King David's life and Jacob's decision to leave home. In both cases writers from different eras of the Priestly tradition remove any sign that David or Jacob broke any of God's commandments. In the other stories, the authors seemed intent on revealing the sins and flaws of David and Jacob. This contrast is consistent throughout the historical narrative from Genesis through Chronicles. It represents an argument that some writers— who had similarities with the stories of Genesis 2 and Exodus 34—made with the holiness theology of the Priests of Judah.

When the Chronicler rewrote Israel's faith history, it is hard to imagine that he thought the version in Samuel and Kings would be destroyed. What, then, is the purpose in silencing part of a character's story? Surely he did not believe that if he remained silent about Bathsheba's rape and Uriah's murder that people would one day forget King David did such terrible things. This was not an attempt to cover up sin. This argument is about different approaches to righteousness.

6. Buechner, *Son of Laughter*, 167–68.

(1) Free the Stories to Speak for Themselves

If we let go of a desire to combine these stories in hopes of creating one true composite narrative of David or Jacob and instead let these contrasting stories speak for themselves, we begin to see that theological truth, not factual truth, drove the agendas. In the dark stories about David and Jacob there is a common theme that is shared with other such stories in the Torah and the narrative in Samuel and Kings. Their heroes are flawed. It is not simply a case of human fallibility naturally showing up in the course of a story. The authors selected these stories about David and Jacob for the purpose of showing these heroes at their worst. The Priestly tales showed that their lives could be told without those stories, but these aforementioned writers thought them necessary.

The author in Samuel did not just report David's sins; she colored the narrative to describe a troubled man. "In the spring of the year, the time when kings go out to battle," the tale began, "David sent Joab with his officers and all Israel with him. . . . But David remained at Jerusalem" (2 Sam 11:1). The author suggests something had changed in David. This great warrior king remained behind while his general and officers took his troops into battle. Maybe, he was weary of battle or had gotten a little thick in the waist. Maybe he was having a mid-life crisis. Whatever it was, it gave him idle time at the palace. He soon sees the beautiful Bathsheba. As king he had been introduced to many beautiful women. Now, however, he looked at her as a belittled warrior king who stayed behind while other men led the battle in his place. He would have a conquest one way or another.

Shortly thereafter the writer juxtaposed the loyal Uriah with the tarnished king. David was a child of Judah, Uriah a Hittite, one of the peoples of the land. David could not control his lust for another man's wife. While the king's troops were sacrificing their lives for his kingdom, he was raping one of their wives. On the other hand, Uriah controlled his sexual desires for his own wife to honor his fellow troops stationed on the front lines. David dishonestly covered up his rape and conspiracy to murder, whereas Uriah honestly carried his own death sentence to his general.[7] The chosen one, David the king, the one with whom God had made an everlasting covenant, is the one who sinks to moral depravity. Yet, he remains God's chosen. Uriah the Hittite, a descendant of the people of the land, is the one who displays the LORD's high moral standards. David's sins have consequences, ones that included the death of the infant and nearly cost him the kingdom when Absalom's coup temporarily succeeded, but they do not

7. Brueggemann, *David's Truth*, 56–61, provides an insightful discussion on the interplay between David and Uriah.

revoke his status with God. Uriah's morality actually costs him his life and as far as we know does not earn him any rewards of righteousness. Thus the story depicts David's moral failings, as well as the high moral standards of one of the Canaanite peoples, and therefore it challenged the holiness theology of the Priests on two fronts.

The Storyteller who tells Jacob's dark side is not the writer who told David's tale, but the stories have similarities. From the beginning Jacob is portrayed as a mama's boy, which has never been a compliment in patriarchal cultures, while Esau is his father's favorite and a man's man. Sibling rivalry stems from parental favoritism. Esau is good-natured, though dim-witted. Jacob is a scheming charlatan. His theft of Esau's blessing is told in agonizing detail, in which he must consciously deceive his father several times. Later, he prospers at his father-in-law's expense (Gen 30:25–43), cowardly puts his wives and children in danger to save his own skin (32:22–24), and even when Esau forgives him he uses that kindness to deceive him once more (33:12–17). Even God does not escape Jacob's selfishness. The first night after he escaped Esau's wrath he slept under the stars at Bethel and God came to him in a dream. But upon waking from the dream, instead of praying to God in thanksgiving, Jacob strikes a bargain, "If God will be with me, and will keep me in this way that I go, and will give me bread to eat and clothing to wear, so that I come again to my father's house in peace, then the LORD shall be my God" (28:20–21). Jacob's prayer turns Deuteronomy's idea about divine covenants upside down. In Deuteronomy, it is the LORD who lays down conditions. If Israel obeys God's commandments, then the LORD will prosper and protect Israel. Jacob's vow reversed this. If the LORD brings prosperity to Jacob and brings him home to his father's house in peace, then Jacob will make the LORD his God! Jacob's audacity is only matched by God's willingness to grant Jacob's vow by the end of the story. This Storyteller stood Deuteronomy's ideas of a conditional covenant on its head. Not only do these stories reveal God's steadfast love for Jacob despite his appalling character, but additionally Jacob is the one who places conditions upon God in their relationship! Truly, he is one who "wrestled with God . . . and prevailed" (32:28).

Jacob, whom God renamed Israel, became the father of the twelve tribes of Israel. David became Israel's greatest king. Along with Abraham and Moses, they are the most important persons in the Hebrew Bible, which is why their confessional stories are so significant. These stories did not simply tell the hearer that even faith heroes are flawed. They revealed that righteousness is given through God's steadfast love to people that could not earn it.

The Priests did not write with the same flair as these writers who were willing to show the dark side of their heroes. Like a 1950s, black and white television sitcom, Priestly heroes were shown without blemishes. They are portrayed as models of the faith for which hearers should strive. The narrative in the Priestly texts is stilted. The Priests—trying so hard to avoid taboos, be ritually correct, and make every hero a faithful example—create stories that sound methodical, overworked, and distant. Readers who may smile at the Storyteller's characters are left cold by the Priestly characters. Take for example the Jacob and Esau story. The Storyteller draws readers into his story with betrayal and desire, intrigue and longing. Jacob is a shallow, selfish man, yet nonetheless God has a heart for him. Esau, the loser, is dim-witted and passionate. He threatens to kill his brother, but later forgives him. It is a fascinating story. However, in the Priestly version of the story, they portray Jacob as a dutiful son, who loyally listens to his parents. Jacob doesn't have to steal Esau's blessing, because according to the Priestly version Isaac willingly blesses Jacob (28:1–5).[8] The sole conflict in the story is that Esau disobeys his parents' wishes and marries women from among the local Hittite people (Uriah's ancestors, an odd fact that connects it with David's story), while Jacob obediently leaves home to marry a girl from among his mother's people. Frankly, it's boring (27:46—28:9). It has all been sanitized. With no conflict to resolve, the story fizzles.

The Chronicler treats the negative aspects of David's life in a similar fashion. He consciously never mentions any of David's errors. The Chronicler copied the first verse of the David and Bathsheba story and then veered in another direction, thereby avoiding not only Bathsheba's rape and Uriah's murder, but also David's failings as a father and the temporary loss of his kingdom during Absalom's coup. Chronicles adds stories about David's concern for the ark of the covenant (1 Chr 13:1–5; 15:1–14) and for the building of the temple (21:28—22:19; 28:1—29:22). Not only does David remain free from moral depravity in Chronicles, he championed the temple and the cultic rituals that sustained it. Here, the warrior king becomes a holy and devout worshipper of the LORD.

In the holiness theology of the Priests, righteousness before God is received through the rituals of the faith and by obedience to God's commands. They show Jacob and David's righteousness by the lives they lived. The Priests portrayed their heroes as role models for the faithful.

---

8. Lohfink, *Theology of the Pentateuch*, 155. Lohfink believes the Priestly text avoided Jacob's sin because the Priests did not deal with the topic of sin until the people turned from God and the wilderness wandering began. Therefore, the Priests "found a different reason for Jacob's journey to the East."

(2) Listen to the Stories as Contrasting Voices of God

These contrasting stories about David and Jacob easily arrange arguments for midrash. Why did Jacob leave for his Uncle Laban's home? Was it because he stole his brother's blessing and had to flee his wrath, or because his parents sent him there to marry in the family? Only in the most convoluted of tales could it have been both. The Chronicler's erasure of David's sins raises deeper theological debates. The point of the stories that reveal Jacob and David's sins was not simply to show that they were flawed people, that king and patriarch can be as imperfect as peasant and carpenter. The Deuteronomy tradition did not mind telling the sordid truth about any number of Israelites, either. However, the Deuteronomistic writers did so in order to condemn individuals in particular, or all Israel in general, for breaking God's commandments and bringing God's judgment down upon them. In 1 Kings a very similar tale to the taking of Uriah's wife is told (1 Kgs 21). The Israelite king, Ahab, looked out from his summer palace and saw a vineyard belonging to Naboth that he wished to have for himself. King Ahab kills Naboth and takes the vineyard as David killed Uriah in order to take Bathsheba. Elijah the prophet confronts Ahab, as Nathan confronted David. However, Elijah condemns Ahab's dynasty because of what he did, whereas David's kingdom was never in jeopardy. Ahab's sinful deeds were one of many parts of the Historian's prosecution of Israel for breaking the Mosaic Covenant. Whether it was to call out the Israelites for doing "what was evil in the sight of the LORD" (Judg 2:11–12), or place the guilt of the exile upon the sins of King Manasseh (2 Kgs 23:26), Deuteronomistic writers compiled prosecutorial stories about the sins of the people and their leaders to document the conviction that God sent Israel into exile because they had broken the Mosaic covenant.

While the Deuteronomists told stories of sin to convict Israel, these tales about David raping Bathsheba and murdering her husband, and of Jacob lying to steal his brother's blessings, along with the other confessions about Abraham, Judah, or Moses were not told to condemn them for sin, or blame them for exile. Instead, they testified to the amazing love of God, who was merciful and gracious and slow to anger and who forgives iniquity, transgression and sin for a thousand generations to a people who did not deserve such grace. The theology of these stories matches the description of God found in Exodus 34. While there are natural consequences for sin—Jacob spends two decades exiled from his family, David's family is shattered by violence and death, Moses spends years of exile in Midian—nothing any of these persons does breaks their relationship or covenant with God.

This is not so in the Priestly writings. Sin, as defined by the Priests, brought harsh consequences and ended any relationship with the LORD. God took the lives of Aaron's sons Nadab and Abihu because they improperly handled sacred rituals—offering "unholy fire" before the LORD (Lev 10). During the exodus journey, when a man was discovered working on the Sabbath, the LORD commanded Moses to have the people stone him to death (Num 15:32–41). Aaron's grandson Phinehas takes a spear and executes Zimri and his wife, Cozbi, because he had married her—a Midianite woman—and taken her to the sacred place of worship. The LORD praises Phinehas for his zealous execution (25:6–18).[9] The theology of these stories matches the description of God found in the traditional Decalogue of Exodus 20. The Priests were consistent in how they wrote about those who broke God's commandments. This is why they were silent about Jacob's misdeeds. Not only is Jacob a thief and a liar, but also he is unrepentant. Yet, he remains the LORD's chosen. It is why the Chronicler could not talk about the terrible things David did. The king enters into the worst of depravity, yet he remains God's chosen and his kingdom is protected. The tales of their sins contradicted the Priests' theology about sin and God's punishment. The Priests wanted to show that all people could choose to be righteous and follow God's commands, so they needed new stories about Jacob and David.

Both the Deuteronomistic and Priestly traditions blamed the Israelite kings and the general population for their nation's destruction and subsequent exile at the hands of the Babylonians. It was their sins, their rejection of God, which led to their demise. The alternative grace stories refute the idea that sin leads to God's abandonment of his people. They were a direct challenge to both the Priestly and Deuteronomistic traditions regarding the exile in particular, and the understanding of sin and God's judgment in general. Without saying a word about doctrines, these tales simultaneously spoke to humanity's fallible nature and God's steadfast love. There is as much grace in these tales as anywhere in the New Testament.

In the stories about David and Jacob we hear two different approaches to righteousness in God's word—one earned, one given. In thinking about both of these approaches what are their strengths and weaknesses on how to follow God? What do they say to Christians about sin and forgiveness? Perhaps you could imagine a parent trying to guide their teenagers. What are the strengths and weaknesses of each approach?

---

9. Friedman, *Who Wrote the Bible*, 203–4. This passage may have been critically aimed at Moses, who according to non-P stories of the Torah married a Midianite woman, in order to elevate Aaron's family among the Israelites.

(3) Find Where You Want to Join the Divine Conversation

This argument about Jacob and David grows out of last chapter's disagreement about God's character. The grace stories about Jacob and David show the LORD as a God of steadfast love, forgiving iniquity and sin (Exod 34). No matter how many times they tried God's patience, the LORD refuses to abandon them. Alternatively, the LORD as a jealous God, who will punish those who break the commandments (20), seems to be the God operating in the background of the Priestly stories in the Torah and Chronicles. Jacob and David's sins vanish in those accounts, sparing them God's wrath. When others commit sins, they are swiftly and harshly punished. More importantly, the LORD cuts off their relationship.

Christians love a good conversion story—where the sinner becomes saint. If King David's story had ended with a teary-eyed repentance after Absalom's army had driven him out the palace and the capital city, it could have been the Damascus Road story of the first testament. However, God had already made a covenant with David, in which God promised that his descendants would always rule from the throne in Jerusalem. The long narrative from 2 Samuel 11–20 is about the saint becoming a sinner. It is a tale the Priestly tradition did not think worthy to be told.

This divine conversation over how to tell David and Jacob's stories is not simply an academic issue. Every week the question about the relationship of God's grace and love in regards to the sins of the faithful is answered in countless ways in Christian congregations. What is the degree of openness with which people speak of their differences, mistakes, regrets, or sins? Is their congregation a safe place to be unburdened from carrying regrets and mistakes? Or is it a place to keep silent about such matters, lest you face judgment?

Try to imagine a particular situation. Would a drug addict, or an alcoholic with a DUI conviction, continue to be welcomed in a congregation you know? Or would she be shunned? In what ways is she able to let others know of her struggle? Or does she have to keep her addiction a secret? Must she publicly repent and recommit herself to the LORD in order to be fully embraced by the congregation? If this person were a teenager, would other families let her and her siblings continue to hang out with their children?

Imagine other sins, regrets, errors, or simply differences upon which shame and guilt may ostracize a person. Does a fear of exposure in the congregation cower people into silence? Or is the congregation recognized as a safe place where such shame and guilt may be released? Can the whole truth about our lives be told, or must our lives be whitewashed and a smile painted on our faces?

Biblical stories had a pedagogical purpose for instructing the next generation on how to live within the community. Congregations continue to use Bible stories for educational and formative purposes with children and teenagers today. The decision to tell the whole truth about David, Jacob and others, or to be silent concerning their faults, had to include the instructional value for teaching young people. The Priests may have had a pedagogical as well as a theological reason for remaining silent as to the sins of their heroes. Would that be so different from the way we think? I cannot imagine the David and Bathsheba story ever being the central passage of a Vacation Bible School. Competent leaders carefully select which Bible stories are age appropriate, and that story should never be selected for children. Like the Priests of Judah such leaders would choose to be silent with a number of passages well into the teenage years.

When lives have been struck by moral failings, how the faith community around them receives or excludes them is the way it demonstrates redemption, both to the persons involved and to the community at large, and especially to the next generation. Both sides have persuasive arguments. Human beings are flawed. Sooner or later, we will find ourselves bitten by remorse, either by our own shortcomings, or by those close to us. At such times there is little we desire more than to receive the good news that neither God, nor our community, will abandon us. And yet, sometimes this grace can actually enable such behavior to multiply. When expected consequences do not materialize, some people return to their sins rather than utilize grace as an opportunity for recovery; whereas, the stiffer response can sometimes produce a change in habit. There is a reason the Deuteronomists repeatedly warned the Israelites not to break God's commandments. Sometimes it takes the warnings and even the impact of severe consequences to guide certain persons toward a righteous path.

If you emphasize the grace and love of God, as displayed in the stories of Jacob and David, you offer that grace to untold numbers of persons whose own lives have been burdened by regrets and sins. But at the same time, you risk encouraging others to remain in their destructive habits, or give a new generation the idea that it does not matter if you keep or break God's commandments.

If you emphasize the righteous lives of faith heroes, never speaking of their shortcomings and only portray sinners as outsiders, you set high moral standards and give a clear message to the next generation on how to live. But at the same time, you risk shoving people's sins into the shadows of their shame, creating a fear of being abandoned both by God and by the community of God's people.

Which side of this tug-of-war pulls at your heart the most? Which risk are you willing to take to secure the message that sings to your soul? Neither version comes without its perils. So you have to decide which version of David and Jacob's stories is worth the risk. In doing so you reveal your own theological leanings and you join this divine conversation.

CHAPTER 4

Dueling Prophets

*Both read the same Bible, and pray to the same God; and
each invokes His aid against the other. . . . The prayers of
both could not be answered; that of neither has been answered fully. The Almighty has his own purposes.*[1]

—ABRAHAM LINCOLN, SECOND INAUGURAL ADDRESS

THE CIVIL WAR OCCURRED during a deeply religious age in our nation's
history. Despite the religious fervor of many Americans, we entered into
four brutal years of war, which cost the lives of 600,000 to 750,000 soldiers.
The war was not split between religious factions. This was not a conflict
between Protestants and Catholics as Northern Ireland saw in the twentieth century, or between Sunni and Shiite Muslims today, or an interre-
ligious conflict between Christians and Muslims or Muslims and Hindus.
Christian Protestants were the dominant religious group in both South and
North. Despite their common religious heritage and passionate faith they
approached the issue of slavery from two opposite extremes. They found
Scripture passages that not only convinced them of the rightness of their
cause, but also justified their acts of war against the other. How is it that
people with such similar religious backgrounds could come to such radically different theological positions? As we consider pairs of prophets who
spoke when their nation—Israel and Judah—were under military threat,
remember this question.

---

1. Lincoln, "Second Inaugural Address," in *His Speeches and Writings*, 793.

EXCURSUS 4.1

Dueling Prophets of the Assyrian and Babylonian Crises

Another way the Bible includes contrasting texts occurs through the writing prophets in Israel's history. The Assyrian Empire attacked Israel and Judah during the late eighth century. (The united kingdom of Israel under David split into two kingdoms in 922 BC. Ten northern tribes became Israel and two southern tribes Judah.) In 722 BC it conquered the northern kingdom of Israel, making it a part of its empire. Assyria attacked the southern kingdom of Judah and besieged Jerusalem in 701 BC, but ultimately retreated. A little over a century later another empire expanded; in 596 BC the Babylonian army conquered Judah and Jerusalem, and made the king's brother, once he swore allegiance to Babylon, the new king. After a minor Jewish revolt the Babylonian army came back. This time it turned Jerusalem into a pile of rubble in 587 BC.

We know from these texts that many prophets spoke God's word for their particular time and the challenge before them. In each case their messages were far from identical. The three sets of prophets we will study are: Amos and Hosea preaching in the northern kingdom of Israel in the late eighth century BC; Micah and Isaiah speaking to the kingdom of Judah near the same time; and Jeremiah, Habakkuk, and Ezekiel to the Jerusalem community at the turn of the sixth century BC.

These prophets wrote independently of each other. The language and style of the writing in Amos and Hosea is unlike any of the major portions of the Hebrew Scriptures. Though most scholars date Amos a decade before Hosea, there is no sign that the latter prophet knew of Amos's work. Micah and Isaiah's books were also unique texts, which included substantial additions. Micah 1–3 may have been the extent of original prophet's scroll, though parts of chapters 6–7 may also be original. One famous passage—about how God will turn spears into pruning hooks and shields into plowshares—is also in Isaiah and connects the two dueling prophets. The book of Isaiah is the work of at least two prophets. Chapters 1–39 comprise the prophecy of the first Isaiah, who lived during the Assyrian siege of 701 BC.[2] The last

---

2. Conrad, *Reading Isaiah*, 155. There is a very clear break after chapter 39, which has its setting during Hezekiah's reign around 700 BC. Chapter 40 is set during or after

four chapters duplicate 2 Kings 18–20. Beginning with chapter 40 the writings in Isaiah shift to the events of the Babylonian exile in the mid-sixth century BC and were composed by an unnamed prophet influenced by the writings of first Isaiah. This chapter will only explore Isaiah 1–39.

The last set of prophets in this chapter are active around the Babylonian conquest and exile—around 600 BC. The language of Jeremiah's book shares many phrases with Deuteronomy, leading scholars to believe the prophet was close to the Deuteronomistic community. Jeremiah preaches about God's justice and for fidelity to the Mosaic law. Ezekiel began writing after he was exiled to Babylon. He preaches about God's holiness and with a background in the cultic practices of the temple priests of Jerusalem. It appears he was familiar with Jeremiah's work, and at several points challenges the former's preaching. Habakkuk quotes neither prophet, but his first chapter seems to indicate that he had heard Jeremiah's prophecy, or others who preached like him.

All the prophets agree trouble was coming. They all agree God's judgment was involved. After that they begin disagreeing. Those who edited and compiled the Hebrew Bible kept a dueling pair from each of these three crisis periods.

Hosea vs. Amos

Amos and Hosea brought messages of judgment to the northern kingdom of Israel during the latter half of the eighth century BC. The Assyrian Empire had begun to expand its influence into the region. Small principalities such as Israel and Judah could not help but notice. The Assyrian threat generated a theological crisis in addition to geopolitical one. The Hebrew people believed they lived in the land at the protection of the LORD. This threat questioned the potency of this protection. Amos and Hosea spoke about God as the subject, not the Assyrians. God was the one with ultimate power. To get a sense for Amos read chapters 3–5.

Amos was a shepherd in Judah, who heard the call of God to preach to his northern cousins. He believed that the LORD had a special relationship with Israel, "You only I have known of all the families of the earth"

the Babylonian exile 150 to 250 years later. Isaiah's first 39 chapters were also reedited by the later author(s). Conrad makes the case that the later vision in Isaiah was in response to the first Isaiah, which he regards as chapters 6–39.

(Amos 3:2). He mentioned that God had brought them up out of the land of Egypt and led them through forty years of wilderness in order to possess the land (2:10). Although Amos does not mention a covenant between God and Israel, he apparently believed that the gift of the land came with expectations. Since those were not being met, God's judgment would fall. Amos did not struggle with the message of judgment as Hosea did. God would "punish" Israel for all its "iniquities" (3:2).

Israel had robbed the poor and sold the weak into slavery. They took bribes instead of handing down justice. Retailers cheated customers with false scales. The rich feasted on luxuries without care for the poor. They could not wait for the Sabbath to be over so they could return to making money by dishonest means.[3] Amos focused on the way the poor were treated. He only had a couple of condemnations not related to justice issues.[4] He used the book of the covenant, an old law code found in Exodus 21–23, as prosecutorial material.[5]

Amos was the first of several prophets to declare that justice was more important to God than the rituals of worship: sacrifices, festivals and psalms (Amos 5:21–24). Remarkably, he did not rebuke Israel's worship because the Bethel and Dan temples deviated from the Jerusalem cult. This would be an accusation of later writers, but it was not Amos's concern. It did not matter how Israel worshiped God, if they oppressed the poor and crushed the needy, God would receive it as parody (4:1–5).

Amos believed the LORD's judgment had already been dispensed upon Israel as an inducement toward repentance, but to no avail. The LORD had withheld rain, diminished the wheat harvest, struck their crops with blight and locust, sent disease and armies that overthrew their towns "as when God overthrew Sodom and Gomarrah," yet Israel did not return to the LORD (4:6–12). These signs resemble the curses, described in Deuteronomy 28:15–25, though Amos does not directly quote any of them. Given

---

3. Amos condemned Israel for social injustice in the following: 2:6–8; 3:10; 4:1–5; 5:11–12, 21–24; 6:4–7; 8:4–6.

4. In 2:12, he said that Israel had commanded the prophets not to prophesy, and they made the Nazirites drink wine. The only reference to worshipping other gods is in 5:26 and its meaning is debatable. Amos refers to a father and son having sexual relations with the same woman, which would have been a matter of sexual purity. Except this could be a reference to a slave girl, which was a justice issue prohibited in the Book of the Covenant (Exod 21:8).

5. Hanson, *People Called*, 154. Here, Hanson points to four places where the prophet alludes to the Book of the Covenant in Amos 2:6–12: Exodus 21:8, 22:26–27, 23:6, 23:7. In addition Amos 5:12 recalls Exodus 23:8. Von Rad states that Amos's ethical elements "are to be found point by point in the older tradition of sacral law, especially in the Book of the Covenant" (*Old Testament Theology*, 2:136).

that Amos's scroll predated Deuteronomy, this could indicate that the idea of a blessing-and-curse theology was a part of northern theology before Deuteronomy was developed. Since Israel had not recognized and heeded God's earlier warnings, there was no escaping the coming judgment. It would be "as if someone fled from a lion, and was met by a bear; or [having escaped the bear] went into the house and rested a hand against the wall, and was bitten by a snake" (Amos 5:19). In the end Israel was going to lose her special status with God. "Are you not like the Ethiopians to me, O people of Israel? says the LORD. Did I not bring Israel up from the land of Egypt, and the Philistines from Caphtor and the Arameans from Kir?" (9:7). If Israel were going to be as unjust as any other nation, then God would judge her as any other nation.[6]

Whereas Amos spoke of God's coming destruction in a cold, matter-of-fact manner, Hosea spoke of God as a broken-hearted lover. God's love for Israel compared to Hosea's love for Gomer, his wife and mother of their three children. Gomer was depicted as an adulterous wife, who left husband and children for her lovers. At one point Hosea had to buy her back from her pimp to bring her home. The heartache that Hosea experienced in his love for unfaithful Gomer he believed mirrored God's love for Israel. Gomer made Hosea jealous and angry. Lovesick, he looked around at his fellow citizens and understood that they made God jealous and angry, too. God hated Israel because God loved Israel (Hos 9:15). Take time to read chapters 1–4 and 11 for your own impressions of Hosea.

Hosea spoke of love more than any other prophet—a word Amos never used. He described the LORD as the God of Exodus 34: merciful, forgiving, and abounding in steadfast love, but also jealous. God's jealousy had been crossed according to Hosea with the worship of other gods and the worship of idols. This was a God who brought Israel out of Egypt and now warned of returning her in a reverse exodus, because of her adultery (11:5). As the dangers of the growing Assyrian Empire loomed larger, this was how Hosea made theological sense of this threat. He vacillated back and forth. Would God save Israel out of steadfast love despite her infidelities, or would God abandon Israel and leave her with her lovers (other gods) and allow them (Assyria) to do what they would with her? Although at times Hosea seems to believe that God's protection of Israel in the land is conditional, based on how Israel returns God's love, at other times he seems convinced that God's love is so strong that God will save her no matter what—just as Hosea bought his wife back from her pimp.

---

6. Brueggemann, *Texts That Linger*, 92–103, provides an engaging discussion on this mysterious verse.

Whereas Amos completely focused on the injustices of Israel, Hosea has very little to say about such matters. He briefly recalls the traditional Ten Commandments (4:2), and condemns deceit, theft and oppression in a couple of brief verses, but it is clear he did not proclaim justice as Amos did. Hosea condemned the people for worshiping the LORD along with other gods, like a spouse who betrays through adultery. This rebuke was pervasive throughout his prophecy.

At the end of each of Hosea's main sections there was a passage on forgiveness and restoration. And yet, Hosea could not quite picture how things were going to turn out, since the people continued to break God's covenant by worshiping other gods and the Assyrian threat continued to grow. Chapter 11 drafts a haunting image. The metaphor switched from wife to son as God remembered, "When Israel was a child, I loved him. . . . The more I called them, the more they went from me. . . . How can I give you up, Ephraim? How can I hand you over O Israel?" (11:1–2, 8). It was as if Hosea depicted this loving, jealous God sitting on the side of a bed, sobbing with head in hands. You just don't know if in the background there was a closet emptied of clothing, or a body slumped on the floor. His own rocky marriage had shown him the power and heartache of love. Would God woo Israel back one more time, nurture her back to health, or remain with a broken and longing heart? God's last words through Hosea were, "It is I who answer and look after you. I am like an evergreen cypress; your faithfulness comes from me" (14:8). Was this where Hosea landed? Or did the Assyrian army kill him and his family before he wrote a last word?

Amos and Hosea preached to the same citizens of Israel, facing the same military threat. They both believed God's judgment was the source of this threat. Yet, they preached very different messages.

Isaiah vs. Micah

After witnessing the destruction of the northern kingdom of Israel, and listening to the stories of their northern cousins who flowed into Judah as refugees, when the Assyrians decided to expand their empire further south in 701 BC, it is hard to imagine a prophet preaching good news. Yet, Isaiah did exactly that, though another prophet, Micah, preached judgment and destruction. Neither prophet mentions the Mosaic covenant, so there is no acknowledgment that keeping the law was a requirement for possessing the land. Both operate from the perspective that the people and leaders believe the LORD will protect them. This confidence came from God's covenant with David according to Isaiah. Micah, however, believes this reliance is a falsehood perpetuated by deceitful priests and prophets.

Micah was a country boy, raised in the little town of Moresheth, a day's walk from Jerusalem in southwest Judah. The Assyrians would overrun his town on their way to besiege Jerusalem. He was more like the shepherd Amos than his aristocratic peer Isaiah, who received his call inside Solomon's splendid temple. Like Amos, he chastised the people for their sin of injustice. They used false scales and weights, practiced violence and deceit, and took bribes and perverted justice. False prophets preached, "Peace," to those with money, but raised hellfire on those who were hungry and homeless. They coveted and seized fields and homes; they oppressed people and stole their inheritance from the LORD. Reading chapters 2–3 and 6 will give you an overview of Micah's prophecy.

Micah was the first prophet to speak of the destruction of Jerusalem and the temple. To question Jerusalem's security questioned God's faithfulness. False prophets stood by this belief: "Surely the LORD is with us! No harm shall come upon us" (Mic 3:11). Micah declared that people's faithfulness was in question, not God's. He directly opposed Isaiah when he said, "Jerusalem shall become a heap of ruins" (3:12). It did not make him a popular man. A century later his words were still remembered, as was the surprise that the king did not kill him (Jer 26).

Micah reminded them that the LORD had brought them up from "the land of Egypt, and redeemed [them] from the house of slavery" (Mic 6:4–5). With this gift came expectations. "What does the LORD require of you?" Micah asked, a question also found in Deuteronomy. There it is answered, "Only to fear the LORD your God, to walk in all his ways, to love him, to serve the LORD you God with all your heart and with all your soul, and to keep the commandments of the LORD your God" (Deut 10:12–13). Micah had a similar, more succinct, sentiment, "To do justice, and to love kindness, and to walk humbly with your God" (Mic 6:8).

Micah's scroll ended with a word of hope (though many scholars believe this was added later). It sounds like the justice theology of the Deuteronomists, which seems fitting for Micah. God would save a remnant out of those who would be cast off. "Who is a God like you, pardoning iniquity and passing over the transgression of the *remnant* of your possession? He does not retain his anger forever, because he delights in showing clemency. He will again have compassion upon us; he will tread our iniquities under foot. You will cast all our sins into the depths of the sea. You will show faithfulness to Jacob and unswerving loyalty to Abraham, as you have sworn to our ancestors from the days of old" (7:18–20, italics added). Remove the word remnant and this vision would sound very much like Isaiah. However, the word remnant changes the meaning of the whole statement, from a God of love to a God of justice. According to this, God would only pardon the iniquity of the remnant. The rest would be lost to history and to God.

Isaiah could not disagree more. He believed that God would deliver Jerusalem from the Assyrians. The good and the bad would be saved; the righteous remnant would have to make room for the riffraff. Unlike Micah, Isaiah lived in Jerusalem and had connections to the royal court.[7] Read a minimum of chapters 1, 6, 9–10, 31–33 and 36–37 to understand Isaiah.

He received his call during an epiphany at the holy temple in the year 738 BC, sixteen years before the destruction of the northern kingdom. Isaiah joined Micah in warning that God's judgment was coming to Jerusalem. It would become a "besieged city" (Isa 1:8). If the LORD were to save Judah, the people would have to turn their full allegiance to God. Like Isaiah, they, too, must turn to God and be forgiven (6:5–7). Isaiah called the people to repentance, "Though your sins are like scarlet, they shall be like snow. . . . If you are willing and obedient you shall eat the good of the land; but if you refuse and rebel, you shall be devoured by the sword" (1:18–20). He criticized Judah's leaders for relying on military alliances rather than upon the LORD. "Alas for those who go down to Egypt for help and who rely on horses, who trust in chariots . . . but do not look to the Holy One of Israel or consult the LORD. . . . The Egyptians are human, and not God; their horses are flesh, and not spirit" (31:1–3). To be fair to Judah's king and advisors, Isaiah had extraordinary faith. With an overwhelming army on the march, Isaiah advised prayer and declared that military alliances would bring God's judgment.

God tired of people who as Isaiah said, "Draw near with their mouths and honor me with their lips, while their hearts are far from me, and their worship of me is a human commandment learned by rote" (29:13). Yet, rather than call them to justice as Amos did, or plead with them to love God as Hosea did, Isaiah told Jerusalem that God was really going to show them now, "I will again do amazing things with this people, shocking and amazing" (29:14). The phrase is reminiscent of what God said before giving the Ten Commandments in Exodus 34. In both cases God's amazing deeds were supposed to secure the loyalty, trust, and belief of the people. Isaiah understood God to be the giver in this relationship and the people's part of the covenant was to be devoted and loyal. So, now in the face of the people's disloyalty, what will God do? The LORD will do even more amazing things to win the people's hearts again. Whereas the Deuteronomists and their prophets believed God redirected behavior through punishment,

7. Von Rad, *Old Testament Theology*, 2:147.

Isaiah believed God acted in a different way. God seemed to be saying, "Just wait and see. Then, you'll realize why you should worship me, alone."

The Lord got the chance to amaze the people in the year 701 BC when the Assyrian army conquered much of Judah and besieged Jerusalem. Despite what happened to the northern kingdom, Isaiah steadfastly believed the Lord kept promises and would save Judah. He thought Jerusalem would be punished. "I will besiege you with towers and raise siegeworks against you . . . your voice shall come from the ground like the voice of a ghost" (Isa 29:3–4). Yet, Jerusalem will also be saved. "All that fight against her . . . shall be like a dream, a vision of the night" (29:7). Isaiah preached punishment and salvation. When God made the promise to David, God warned him that iniquity and sin would be punished, but nothing would remove God's presence from David's descendants (2 Sam 7:14–16). Assyria might be an instrument of God's anger, but "when the Lord has finished all his work on Mount Zion and on Jerusalem, he will punish the arrogant boasting of the king of Assyria and his haughty pride" (Isa 10:12). At a time when it must have been easy to give up hope and to switch beliefs about God in the face of pending doom, Isaiah was confident that the promises of God are forever. If Zion will "turn back to him whom you have deeply betrayed, O people of Israel . . . then the Assyrian shall fall by a sword, not of mortals; and a sword, not of humans, shall devour him" (31:6–8). The narrative conclusion at the end of Isaiah's work (36–39) reports that this is exactly what happened. One morning the inhabitants of Jerusalem awoke, looked over the fortified walls of the city, and found the Assyrian army had vanished during the night like a dream.[8] The Lord had saved them. Isaiah's confidence in the Lord was well placed.

By the end of 701 BC, it was clear that Isaiah was right, and Micah was wrong. Jerusalem was not a "heap of ruins." Despite the fact that Micah appeared to be a false prophet, his words were saved. They remained a testimony for another day.

8. See Gray, *I & II Kings*, 694, and Bright, *History of Israel*, 296–308. The reading from Isaiah, which duplicates the record in 2 Kings 18–20, claims that God struck down the Assyrian army. However, a note in 2 Kings 19:7 suggests that the Assyrian king had to return to his capital city to quell a rumor. It is also noted in 2 Kings 18:14–16, which was not copied in Isaiah, that Hezekiah paid a tribute to the Assyrian king. Was this the real reason for Assyria's withdrawal? Did the Assyrian king withdraw to put down a coup, or because Hezekiah bought his way out of destruction, or because of a plague, or a miracle angel? Those are historically impossible questions to answer. Nevertheless, it is important to stay with Isaiah's reading. His message was that God had delivered Israel again. In Isaiah's eyes (and in the eyes of his readers) a miracle happened and God was at the heart of it. Auld compares the two stories, "The book of Isaiah stresses the piety of Hezekiah, but the book of Kings emphasizes the efficacy of the prophet Isaiah" (*Life in Kings*, 187). See 182–89 for his discussion on Hezekiah's tribute to Assyria.

Jeremiah vs. Habakkuk vs. Ezekiel

Jeremiah's book reveals the diversity within ancient Jewish theology more than any other prophetic text. The times were precarious. The northern kingdom had been gone for a century. King Josiah reformed Judah, based on a book of the law (a core of Deuteronomy) that was found in the temple in 623 BC. These newly discovered teachings inspired a new prophetic voice.[9] Jeremiah was a student of the sacred texts available to him. He proved to be quite knowledgeable of Deuteronomy and the Torah, and also knew Psalms, Amos, Hosea, Micah, First Isaiah, as well as his peers, Zephaniah, Nahum and Habakkuk.[10] While he cited all the texts listed above, he relied on Deuteronomy the most. What had been a hopeful time after Josiah's Deuteronomistic reform came to an end when the great and blessed king was killed on the battlefield against Egypt's forces in 609 BC. The monarchy fell into unstable leadership just as Babylon rose to power. It should not be surprising that different voices were each trying to understand God in order to guide the people during those tumultuous days. Jeremiah is a long and rich text. Read chapters 1; 7; 14–15; 21; 28–29; and 31–32 for an overview of his message.

Jeremiah's opening act somersaulted him into the division and made him a marked man for the rest of his life. He walked up the temple steps as an eighteen-year-old boy and delivered a scathing sermon.[11] His assault on the unconditional promises of the Davidic covenant was as direct as anything throughout Deuteronomy's long scroll. His sermon took place just months after King Josiah's tragic death. The people had gathered to celebrate

---

9. Friedman, *Who Wrote the Bible*, 146–49; *The Bible*, 14; "Deuteronomistic School," 76–78. He notes that in Jeremiah's poetry, alone, there are at least forty-five occurrences of words and phrases that are characteristic of Deuteronomy or the Deuteronomistic history. He speculates that Baruch, Jeremiah's secretary, is the Deuteronomistic Historian. See also Holladay, *Jeremiah*, 2:53. He states that Jeremiah drew from "proto-Deuteronomy" (Deut 5–26; 32; and maybe 28) and then the exilic editors of Deuteronomy sometimes utilized Jeremiah's words. For his discussion on the connection between Deuteronomy, the Historian, and Jeremiah, read 2:40–44, 53–64.

10. Holladay, *Jeremiah*, 2:35–53.

11. Holladay, *Jeremiah*, 2:24–35. I follow Holladay's chronology for Jeremiah for several reasons, not the least of which is that he was my Old Testament professor, and I find it hard to believe he'd be wrong about anything Jeremiah. Holladay assigns Jeremiah's birth to the year 627 BC, based on the belief that his call "in the womb" (Jer 1:5) was not just a poetic device but actually was Jeremiah's self-awareness of a prophetic call at birth. This makes Jeremiah 18 years old when he delivers his Temple Sermon, which Holladay believes was his first public act. For a brief overview, see Holladay, *Spokesman out of Time*, 16–24, or *Fresh Reading*, 9–14.

Jehoiakim's royal coronation.[12] They were looking for some solace, some comfort, some hope in the wake of Josiah's death. Instead, Jeremiah mocked their false hope in the temple's inviolability. In his famous Temple Sermon, recorded in chapters 7 and 26, the prophet laid out his prosecution. "Do not trust in these deceptive words: 'This is the temple of the LORD, the temple of the LORD, the temple of the LORD.' For if you truly amend your ways and your doings, if you truly act justly one with another . . . and if you do not go after other gods to your own hurt, then I will dwell with you in this place, in the land that I gave of old to your ancestors forever and ever" (Jer 7:4–7). Jeremiah based his accusation on Deuteronomy's *if.* God promised to dwell in the land contingent upon faithfulness to the commandments. This theology put Jeremiah at odds with Jerusalem's favorite prophet, Isaiah, and made him sound like the false prophet, Micah. Standing at the temple, he told them that they treated the temple the way schoolchildren treat home base in a game of tag. "We're on the temple steps," they said with wagging fingers. "We're safe! And you can't touch us." These are deceptive words Jeremiah said. He mocked them, because their actions mocked God's covenant. God's presence was only assured if the people lived according to God's covenant. "Here you are, trusting in deceptive words to no avail. Will you steal, murder, commit adultery, swear falsely, make offerings to Baal, and go after other gods that you have not known, and then come and stand before me in this house, which is called by my name, and say, 'We are safe!'—only to go on doing [what you were doing]?" (7:8–10). They broke the Ten Commandments and then claimed God's protection on the temple steps. They turned God's temple into "a den of robbers" (7:11). If they didn't think God would allow the temple to be destroyed, Jeremiah told them to go look at the ruins of the old temple in Shiloh. If God destroyed one temple and moved the divine presence to another place, God could do it again.

The crowd was unmoved. They put Jeremiah on trial. They wanted Jeremiah put to death, but powerful connections spared his life, asserting that King Hezekiah had spared the prophet Micah. Tragically, they executed another prophet, Uriah, who spoke like Jeremiah (26:20–23). The divide was deep between the differing theological camps in 609 BC; life and death hung in the balance.

Fifteen years later Jeremiah had another famous confrontation (28). It was the year 594/3 BC. The Babylonians had already sacked Jerusalem, exiled

---

12. Holladay, *Jeremiah*, 2:27–28. The gathering was either for the king's coronation or for the annual Festival of the Booths. Holladay believes that Jeremiah's major readings took place every seventh year when the book of the law was read at the Festival of the Booths. If he gave his Temple Sermon at Jehoiakim's coronation, this would have been an exception—one year before the 608 BC reading.

the king and the aristocracy, and then placed the king's brother, Zedekiah, on the throne as a Babylonian puppet. Jeremiah was walking around Jerusalem with a donkey's yoke around his neck to symbolize that God had ordered Judah to serve King Nebuchadnezzar of Babylon. He could not have been popular. Imagine if he lived in the United States during post-9/11 days and carried a sign around his neck that said, "God says, 'Serve Bin Laden and Al-Qeada.'" What do you think Americans would have done to him? Babylon did far worse to Judah in 596 BC than terrorists did on 9/11.

One prophet who believed in the unconditional promises of the Davidic covenant challenged Jeremiah to a prophetic duel at the holy temple. A host of spectators gathered at the temple courtyard. Both prophets claimed to speak for God. Hananiah said the LORD was going to destroy Babylon and return the exiles within two years time. He used the same theological reasoning that Isaiah did while the Assyrians were besieging Jerusalem a hundred years earlier.[13] God would break Babylon and bring the exiles and the temple's treasures home.

"Bravo, bravo!" Jeremiah cheered. "May it be just as you say!" Then, he cautioned those quick to believe Hananiah, adding that only "when the word of [a] prophet comes true, then it will be known that the LORD has truly sent the prophet" (28:9). Jeremiah's words came straight from the book of the law: "If a prophet speaks in the name of the LORD but the thing does not take place or prove true, it is a word that the LORD has not spoken" (Deut 18:22).

At this point Hananiah walked over to Jeremiah, took off the yoke he had been wearing on his neck for months and broke it over his knee. Then, he held it up and yelled, "Thus says the LORD: This is how I will break the yoke of King Nebuchadnezzar of Babylon from the neck of all the nations within two years" (Jer 28:11). The patriotic crowd loved it. Overcome by theatrics and charisma, Jeremiah walked away in defeat. Round 1 went to Hananiah.[14] Sometime later, however, the LORD told Jeremiah to personally confront Hananiah, telling him that he had spoken falsely of the LORD and therefore the LORD would end his life. Hananiah soon died (28:17). Round 2 was a knockout by Jeremiah. These beliefs were a matter of life and death.

God gave Jeremiah a twofold message. "I have put my words in your mouth . . . to pluck up and to pull down . . . to build and to plant" (1:9–10).

13. Holladay, *Jeremiah*, 2:126.

14. Holladay comments, "Jeremiah's response was simply to 'go his way,' whether out of prudence, knowing that the optimistic word of Hananiah was popular with the crowd, or out of the conviction that he had already said and done all he could, or out of dread that perhaps Hananiah's action was at the instigation of Yahweh, one cannot say" (*Jeremiah*, 2:129).

He would declare a message of judgment upon Judah and a message of hope for the survivors. He accused Judah of breaking the Mosaic Covenant. They gathered wealth by unjust means, robbed, murdered, took bribes, and perverted justice. The rich didn't pay their workers' wages. They oppressed the poor and took advantage of the weak. They enslaved fellow Hebrews. They broke the Ten Commandments and worshiped other gods and idols. In Jeremiah's thinking the sins of idolatry led to the sins of injustice (19). Therefore, the LORD would bring "disaster upon them that they cannot escape; though they cry out to me, I will not listen to them" (11:10–11).

While Jeremiah believed God's judgment would bring destruction to Judah, some would be saved. He found hope in the idea of a righteous remnant, which we saw at the end of Micah (23:3–4). In his hopeful section, chapters 30–32, Jeremiah declared that God would forge a new covenant with the remnant.

> "Not like the covenant that I made with their ancestors," says the LORD, "when I took them by the hand to bring them out of Egypt—a covenant that they broke. . . . But this is the covenant that I will make with the house of Israel after those days, says the LORD: I will put my law within them, and I will write it on their hearts; and I will be their God, and they shall be my people. No longer shall they teach one another, or say to each other, 'Know the LORD,' for they shall all know me, from the least of them to the greatest, says the LORD; for I will forgive their iniquity, and remember their sin no more." (31:31–34)[15]

While destruction was coming, the time would come when houses and fields would again be bought and sold (32). Unfortunately, only a remnant would live to see it.

That was where Habakkuk had a problem with Jeremiah. He was a prophet caught between traditions. He was a contemporary of Jeremiah, but he followed in the footsteps of Isaiah.[16] When he wrote in chapter 2, "The earth will be filled with the knowledge of the glory of the LORD, as the waters cover the sea" (Hab 2:14), he quoted Isaiah 11:9. Twice he used the phrase "Holy One" to identify God, a term that was used extensively by Isaiah and rarely by other prophets. Of course, he didn't experience God's protection as Isaiah did. Habakkuk wrote at a time when he could say, "the LORD is in his

---

15. Holladay, *Jeremiah*, 2:35, 2:197. Holladay proposes that Jeremiah's new covenant passage was his last word preached in Jerusalem, at the Feast of the Booths in 587 BC, months after the city had been reduced to rubble. Shortly thereafter a group fleeing to Egypt took him with them.

16. Holladay, *Jeremiah*, 2:52; Hiebert, "Book of Habakkuk," 7:623.

holy temple" (2:20), because the temple was still there. Later he wrote after everything was destroyed, when the fields and vineyards produced no fruit and there were no herds in the stalls (3:17).

Habakkuk confronted this crisis by questioning God: "O LORD, how long shall I cry for help and you will not listen?" (1:2). He heard Jeremiah's message that the LORD was in the hand of the Babylonians, and God was using them to bring God's justice down upon Judah for her sins.[17] Yet, Habakkuk was not so easily persuaded. He complained to God that Jeremiah's prophecy made people "like the fish of the sea. . . . The enemy brings all of them up with a hook; he drags them out with his net" (1:14–15). Where was God's justice in that?

When he was finished with his questions, Habakkuk waited, "I will keep watch to see what [God] will say to me" (2:1). He does not tell us how long he stood watch. Months? Years? First, God told Habakkuk, "Write the vision; make it plain on tablets, so [clear] that a runner may read it" (2:2). God wanted this important message written in large, plain letters so that even those at a distance will be able to read it: "The righteous live by their faith," God told Habakkuk (2:4). Ponder that. We will come back to it later.

Ezekiel received a clearer vision from God than what Habakkuk saw. He was not sitting in the ruins of the holy city, either. The prophets Ezekiel, Jeremiah, and Habakkuk were peers. The Babylonians shipped off Ezekiel among the aristocrats in the first exile around 596 BC. Four years later in Babylon, he received his first vision from God. Ezekiel is another long text. Read chapters 1–3; 8–10; 16; 18; 33; 37; and 44 for an overview of Ezekiel's message.

Both Jeremiah and Ezekiel spoke of the first exile, the destruction of Jerusalem, and the second deportation. They did so from separate perspectives, geographical and theological. Jeremiah remained in Jerusalem, and wrote a letter to the exiles in Babylon. Ezekiel, exiled to Babylon, would have been among the Jews in Babylon that received Jeremiah's letter. Both were the sons of a priests. Ezekiel was a Zadokite, while Jeremiah came from the old Shiloh tradition of the northern Levites. Jeremiah preached as a Deuteronomistic prophet; Ezekiel wrote with a Priestly focus on the temple.[18]

17. In Habakkuk 3:3 the prophet states that God's wrath was coming from Mount Paran. This mountain was from the area of Mount Sinai. In Deuteronomy 33:2 the author used an older poem that spoke of how "the LORD came from Sinai" and "shone forth from Mount Paran." Mount Paran is portrayed like a rest stop on God's highway from Sinai to Jerusalem. Habakkuk pictures God's judgment tied to the Mosaic Covenant, which was given to Moses on Sinai. This viewpoint was a core Deuteronomistic belief.

18. Friedman claims, "Parallels between P and the book of Ezekiel are at least as noticeable and striking as those between D and Jeremiah" (*Bible*, 15–16). Von Rad,

Ezekiel saw an amazing vision. God's presence abandoned the temple that had been called by God's name. God's presence left his people and the land that God had given them. This vision was a judgment upon Israel. They were no longer fit for the presence of God.[19] More astonishing was that Ezekiel saw God's glory land in Babylon, by the River Chebar (Ezek 10). He preached to exiled Jews.

Ezekiel followed a classic prophetic theme that God was bringing judgment because Israel had broken God's covenant. Ezekiel described Israel as an abandoned child that God rescued. As with creation, so God created Israel with a word, "I said to you, 'Live!' and grow up like a plant in the field. You grew up. . . . I pledged myself to you and entered into a covenant with you, says the LORD God, and you became mine" (16:6–8). Though God lavished so much upon Israel, this devotion was betrayed, "But you trusted in your beauty, and played the whore because of your fame" (16:15).

Like Hosea, Ezekiel condemned his own people for worshiping other gods, for bowing down before idols. This spiritual adultery broke the marital covenant between God and Israel. Unlike Hosea, whose love for his adulterous wife caused him to believe that God's love never ends, Ezekiel approached Israel's unfaithfulness as Priests approached adultery, by purging the unholy. "I will judge you as women who commit adultery and shed blood are judged, and bring blood upon you in wrath and jealousy. I will deliver you into [the] hands [of your enemies] . . . they shall strip you of your clothes . . . and leave you naked and bare. They shall bring a mob against you, and they shall stone you" (16:38–40). God's judgment fell upon Israel because the nation had defiled God's name. The image Ezekiel painted was that Israel was unclean, like a woman during her menstruation period (36:17). God's holy name had been "profaned among the nations" (36:22). Ezekiel used the word *profane* more often (twenty-nine times) than the rest of the Old Testament combined (twenty-seven times). Israel's uncleanness contaminated God; therefore God rejected Israel.

Ezekiel condemned Israel using a measuring stick based on the holiness theology of the Priests.[20] When Ezekiel condemned Israel and Judah

---

Old Testament Theology, 2:220, states that "even a child" can see the distinct differences in how Jeremiah and Ezekiel understood and saw the terrible collapse of their nation.

19. Hanson adds, "The glorious presence of Yahweh in the temple, on which Israel depended for its existence, had been forced to leave, due to the total ritual depravity of the land" (*People Called*, 219).

20. He was the only prophet to condemn Israel for being in contact with women during their menstruation period. He was the only prophet who mentioned the sexual prohibitions of the Holiness Code as they pertained to familial relations. He was the only prophet to say that Israel "despised my holy things and profaned my Sabbaths" (22:8). The priests "made no distinction between the holy and the common, neither

for their sin, he continually returned to cultic and ritual activity. Most prophets had a low regard for religious ritual, specifying that such practices were only holy if they were substantiated by acts of justice or sincere devotion of steadfast love. Ezekiel, however, gave them first regard. Judah had "defiled the [temple] sanctuary (5:11), turned aside to other cults (8:7ff.), and taken idols into her heart (14:3ff.)—in other words, she 'had rendered herself unclean' in the sight of Yahweh."[21] Israel was unclean and unholy and therefore did sinful things. The sinful things did not make her unclean; they were a testimony of her uncleanness.

Ezekiel, like Jeremiah, believed that God was about to make a new covenant with the people Israel. Ezekiel's phrases and terms so closely followed Jeremiah 31 that he must have read Jeremiah's scroll, or both of them had to have been influenced by ideas being bantered about in Jerusalem before the first Babylonian invasion.[22] Several times Ezekiel declared that a new heart and spirit would be put within the people Israel and become part of a new covenant between God and Israel (11:19–20; 16:60–63; 18:31; 34:25; 36:25–28; 37:26). Here we see the Priestly belief that God's broken covenant could be restored. This new covenant would not be like the former broken covenant. It shall be everlasting, for God would change Israel's state of being.

Ezekiel believed this sinful and unholy nation broke God's covenant and deserved this punishment. Yet, this priestly prophet could not get those ruined divine promises out of his head. God would make a new everlasting covenant. God would set David on the throne forever. God would be present in the temple in the land of his people. If God had to raise dry bones to get it done, then that was what God would do (Ezek 37). Out of the punishment of exile, Ezekiel began to light a messianic hope.

Practicing Midrash

The seven prophets who spoke to Israel and Judah during days of crisis each claimed to be speaking the word of God. In each of the three periods we examined at least one pair of prophets, which created a binocular view of God's vision. Yet, sometimes the prophets' words were so different that a

---

have they taught the difference between the unclean and the clean, and they have disregarded my Sabbaths, so that I am profaned among them" (22:26).

21. Hanson, *People Called*, 219.

22. Hanson concludes, "There are striking parallels with Jer 31:31ff.; one feels that Ezekiel must somehow have had Jeremiah's prophecies in front of him (in particular, Jer 32:37ff.)" (Hanson, *People Called*, 235).

double-vision was created, instead. We know from Jeremiah's experience that prophets had duels in which a crowd judged the legitimacy of one message over another. Now, it is time for you to take your seat in the crowd to judge the true and false prophet.

(1) Free the Stories to Speak for Themselves

Unfortunately, the Bible does not help much when it comes to distinguishing a true prophet from a false one. Deuteronomy claimed that you could tell a true prophet from a false one by watching to see if what he or she said comes true (Deut 18:22). If it does not come true, then the prophet has spoken presumptuously. Jeremiah said as much to the cheering crowd when they liked Hananiah's message more than his own (Jer 28:9). This is all well and good when looking back historically. It is not very helpful in real time. Jeremiah also declared that a true prophet first stood in God's heavenly council before he or she proclaimed God's words (23:22). This makes for a great line in a sermon, but exactly how do you determine if someone has *stood* in God's council? There is simply no test for that. With no better guidance than this, it must be conceded that determining the difference between false and true prophets is an effort in spiritual alchemy. So, as we review the pairs of our prophets, try to lay aside assumptions you may have about these prophets and let their words speak for themselves, first and foremost for the times in which they lived, and secondarily as words for our day.

Amos, Micah and Jeremiah writing independently from each other spoke with similar convictions. When they looked at the military threats of the Assyrian and Babylonian armies, they saw God's judgment. God was behind this because the people had forsaken God's commandments. Jeremiah, whose theology was steeped in the thinking of Deuteronomy, believed that the Mosaic Covenant required God's punishment. The people had broken the covenant by injustice and therefore would have to be expelled from the land. All three acted as if God's relationship was conditional.

In reading Hosea, Isaiah, Habakkuk and Ezekiel, we heard critics of that message. Hosea was the first prophet to speak of a covenant between God and Israel. This relationship was likened to a marital covenant. In Hosea's mind this covenant had clearly been broken by Israel's practice of worshipping other gods along with worshipping the LORD. But Hosea did not take a Deuteronomistic point of view about Israel's unfaithfulness. Rather than casting Israel out with no appeal, God's voice through Hosea keeps making statements of faithfulness. "I will not execute my fierce anger; I will not again destroy Ephraim; for I am God and no mortal, the

Holy One in your midst, and I will not come in wrath" (Hos 11:9). The overriding message of Hosea's marriage to Gomer is that God keeps restoring a broken marriage with Israel. It is easy to forget what a radical message this was. When Ezekiel used the same image of Israel—an adulterous wife—he did not imagine God would buy her back from her pimp because of God's deep love. According to Ezekiel, Israel should be stripped and stoned to death (Ezek 16:38–40).

Hosea's hope had one insurmountable problem. The Assyrians destroyed Israel. "How can I hand you over, O Israel?" sounds a little hollow when the countryside is a wasteland. The possibility that God had nothing to do with Assyria's victory and Israel's defeat was never a consideration. What was certain was that the LORD did not save Israel. So, while Hosea had something to say about the steadfast love of God, it was his words of judgment that broadcast the loudest after 722 BC.

Micah, like Hosea, had a problem with accuracy, but for the opposite reason. Micah preached that Jerusalem would become a "heap of ruins" (Mic 3:12), but it did not occur. Isaiah, who kept telling King Hezekiah and the people to trust the LORD for God was going to save Jerusalem, was right. Sunrise one morning revealed a miracle. "The angel of the LORD set out and struck down one hundred eighty-five thousand in the camp of the Assyrians; when morning dawned, they were all dead bodies. Then King Sennacherib of Assyria left, went home, and lived at Ninevah" (Isa 37:36–37; 2 Kgs 19:35–36). The siege of Jerusalem in 701 BC was lifted and all of its inhabitants were saved. Micah's prophecy concerning God's judgment upon their sins of injustice simply did not happen. So why was Micah not considered a false prophet? It can only be because a century later Jerusalem did become a heap of ruins. But this adds more confusion to the identification of false and true prophets. If a prophet's words come true only after several decades and under different circumstances, then can there be any definition of true and false without debate?

EXCURSUS 4.2

Prophetic Messages of Destruction and Salvation: True or False?

	Destruction	**Salvation**
Israel 722 BC	*True*	*False*
	Amos: "I will punish you for all your iniquities" (3:2).	
	Hosea: "They shall not remain in the land of the LORD" (9:3).	Hosea: "I will not execute my fierce anger" (11:9).
Judah 701 BC	*False*	*True*
	Micah: "Jerusalem shall become a heap of ruins" (3:12).	Isaiah: "The Assyrians shall fall by a sword, not of mortals" (31:8).
Judah 594 BC	*True*	*False*
	Jeremiah: "I will do to the house that is called by my name . . . just what I did to Shiloh" (7:14).	Hananiah: "I will bring back to this place all the vessels of the LORD's house" (Jer 28:3).
	Ezekiel: "They shall know that I am the LORD, when I disperse them throughout the countries" (12:15).	
Judah 594 BC	*Why*	
	Habakkuk: "Why do you look on the treacherous, and are silent when the wicked swallow those more righteous than they?" (1:13).	

Habakkuk's concern went beyond which prophet was speaking truth. While Jeremiah's preaching convinced him of the coming of God's wrath, he had trouble accepting that God used the Babylonians. "Why do you look on the treacherous [Babylonians], and are silent when the wicked swallow those more righteous than they?" (Hab 1:13). Are the Babylonians going to keep on emptying their nets, "destroying nations without mercy?" (1:17). For Habakkuk, there had to be another answer than the justice of the Mosaic Covenant as Jeremiah understood it. He went in search for another answer.

While Ezekiel agreed with Jeremiah that God's judgment upon Judah was going to bring destruction and exile, he disagreed about the details.

Jeremiah had based God's judgment on issues of injustice. He rejected the Priestly Torah with its sacrifices and offerings. He concluded "the false pen of the scribes has made it into a lie" (Jer 8:8).[23] Ezekiel based God's judgment on issues of holiness and quoted the Priestly Torah to condemn his people. Ezekiel made justice a part of, but subordinate to, holiness theology.[24] He overwhelmingly dwelt on Israel's holiness sins—how they corrupted the worship of the LORD, profaned God's name, and became unclean.

Imagine two great prophets telling their people that God's judgment and punishment are coming unless they repent and change their ways. One prophet preaches that the people must repent and change their ways regarding an ABC list of sins, while the other prophet preaches that they must repent and change their ways regarding an XYZ list of sins. This difference between Jeremiah and Ezekiel continues today. There are a number of churches that call our society to repent from a number of economic and racial sins of injustice and yet do not consider many sexual issues to be sins. Then, on the other hand there are a number of churches that call our society to repent from a whole list of sexual sins and yet do not consider many economic and racial issues to be sinful. How do you decide which prophet is right and which problem to solve? This is the challenge of reconciling Jeremiah and Ezekiel's prophecies.

(2) Listen to the Stories as Contrasting Voices of God

The fact that at least a pair of prophets at each major crisis prophesied different messages from God suggests a pattern. Either God chose to speak with multiple voices to create a conversation around the crisis, or human beings in trying to conceive God's revelation consistently heard more than one message, or both of these affects were in play. Whatever beliefs you hold about biblical revelation, this pattern should be considered.

In the northern kingdom, both prophets indicated that there was a relationship with God that carried expectations. Hosea believed Israel had broken a marital covenant with God and deserved to be cast out of the land. However, Hosea imagined that God would keep rescuing Israel the way he kept rescuing his adulterous wife, Gomer. Amos believed that

23. Friedman, *Who Wrote the Bible*, 167–68, 209, points out places where Jeremiah criticizes the Priestly Writers.

24. Von Rad explains, "Where Ezekiel speaks of sin, he thinks in particular of offences against sacral orders. Complaints about transgressions of the social and moral commandments are very much less prominent" (*Old Testament Theology*, 2:224). Gammie says that Ezekiel 18 "should be ranked among those passages of the Old Testament that receive special attention in a course on biblical ethics" (*Holiness in Israel*, 50).

God's relationship with Israel was conditional. By the end of his book, God declared that Israel had lost her special status and had become like any other nation (Amos 9:7–8). Amos declared that Israel had broken God's commandments by their acts of injustice. Hosea hardly mentioned this at all. God was mad because the people loved other gods, too. It is noteworthy that Hosea speaks of love more than any other prophet, while Amos never used the word.

Amos and Hosea were at tension in two points. Was God's covenant conditional or unconditional? Would God's faithfulness override Israel's unfaithfulness? Despite his words of judgment, Hosea's last words centered on forgiveness and mercy. Then, however, the Assyrian army wiped everything out. Second, Amos thought the major area of sin was social injustice—oppressing the poor, the widow, and the outcast—while Hosea thought loving other gods was the major problem. Amos thought righteousness and sin were matters of action. Hosea thought they were matters of the heart.

At nearly the same time the two southern prophets believed a covenant was at work in Judah's relationship with God, but it was David's covenant not Moses' that was the primary concern. Despite Isaiah's awareness of idolatry and injustice in Israel, the prophet spends more time providing messages of God's deliverance than of God's judgment.[25] The LORD's protection of Jerusalem and Judah stemmed from the unconditional covenant with David. "There shall be endless peace for the throne of David and his kingdom" (Isa 9:7).

Micah thought this unquestioned confidence was deceitful. The prophets and priests said these words, "Surely the LORD is with us! No harm shall come upon us" (Mic 3:11), because people paid them. (Is that what Micah thought of Isaiah?) Such words did not come from the LORD. This deceitfulness, which caused the people to believe in a lie rather than to repent for their injustices, would cause Zion to be "plowed as a field," and Jerusalem to become a "heap of ruins" (3:12).

In Micah and Isaiah we see the same tension about God's covenants as we saw in Amos and Hosea. Would God's faithfulness override Judah's unfaithfulness? The miraculous salvation of Jerusalem when Assyria abandoned its siege of the holy city convinced everyone that Isaiah's message of God's faithfulness was true. This fueled Jeremiah's sermon nearly a hundred years later at the temple court, as he declared such a belief had led to disobedience of God's commands (Jer 7:4–11). The same argument that

25. Isaiah prophesied that God would protect Judah from the nation of Aram (Isa 7). God anointed King Hezekiah to be a wonderful counselor, who will rule in justice and righteousness (9). Finally, Isaiah declared God would protect Judah from the Assyrian Empire (10; 29–33).

existed between Micah and Isaiah a century earlier continued in the days leading up to the Babylonian conquest of Judah. However, the destruction of Jerusalem was so complete that no prophetic work proclaiming the unconditional covenant with David survived from this time period. There is no book of Hananiah in the Bible. Presumably, such a prophet could no longer get a hearing.

Ezekiel disagreed with Jeremiah in ways that went beyond the diagnosis of Judah's sinfulness, where Ezekiel focused on sins that defile holiness and Jeremiah emphasized sins of injustice. Ezekiel saw the pathway to righteousness in a vastly different manner. His most revolutionary vision—that God's presence had left the temple and the land given to the Israelites and traveled to Babylon—meant that God would not abandon the exiles, but instead would go with them into exile (Ezek 10). For those in exile, Ezekiel's words must have been great comfort. On the other hand, his vision, while offering a word of comfort and hope to the exiles, obviously rejected the inhabitants of Jerusalem still living under King Zedekiah's reign. God's glory had chosen to accompany the Jewish exiles at the expense of the Jews still living in Jerusalem. Given that the first Babylonian deportation consisted primarily of the aristocracy, including him, Ezekiel's vision could be accused of elitism.

Jeremiah, still receiving a word from the Lord in Jerusalem, certainly did not share his view. His letter to the exiles told the people to settle down, raise families, and seek the welfare of that city. Then, after seventy years the Lord's presence would visit them again (Jer 29:10). Ezekiel makes a substantial rebuttal of Jeremiah's letter through his vision, which declared the Lord's presence had already arrived! Even after the destruction of the city, the word of the Lord told Jeremiah to stay there (42:10–11). Ezekiel's vision directly contradicted with the word Jeremiah received while living among the survivors and vice versa. Was God with the exiles in Babylon or the survivors in Jerusalem? Ezekiel said one thing, Jeremiah the other.

There was one other significant criticism of Jeremiah's Deuteronomistic theology. When Habakkuk looked upon the ruins of Jerusalem and thought of the dead and departed exiles, he agreed that there was no question that God's judgment had fallen upon them. What else could explain this? But was this justice? What makes Habakkuk so interesting was that he was Jeremiah's contemporary. Habakkuk may have been in the temple courtyard and watched the prophetic duel between Hananiah and Jeremiah. He would have heard about Hananiah's death. Habakkuk was a person who was both persuaded and troubled by Jeremiah's message. He found a weak spot in Deuteronomistic theology. Was it God's justice to make the righteous die with the wicked? If Judah was guilty for not keeping the law, was it justice that her conquerors trampled the law? Was Judah worse than the Babylonians?

When he asked God for an answer, the word he received was: "The righteous live by their faith" (Hab 2:1–4). Live by faith is the answer you get when your questions go unanswered. Live by faith is what you do when your prayers do not receive a yes and you must find a way to live with your loss. Live by faith is what you think when your doubts will not be silenced but your hope will not die. For Habakkuk, "live by faith" was what happened to his belief in God when it got crossed by a theology in God's steadfast love and a theology of God's justice. Habakkuk did not get the clear answer he wanted from God. Instead he faced the unanswered questions, the hardships and the unknown mystery of God's ways with an undying faith in the LORD. He would live with his questions, and remain faithful to God. I imagine him ending his brief book while he sat in the ruins of Jerusalem and gazed over the scorched landscape.

> I wait quietly for the day of calamity
>
>> to come upon the people who attack us.
>
> Though the fig tree does not blossom,
>
>> and no fruit is on the vines;
>
> Though the produce of the olive fails,
>
>> and the fields yield no food;
>
> Though the flock is cut off from the fold,
>
>> and there is no herd in the stalls,
>
> Yet, I will rejoice in the LORD;
>
>> I will exult in the God of my salvation.
>
> God, the LORD, is my strength;
>
>> he makes my feet like the feet of a deer,
>
>> and makes me tread upon the heights. (3:16b–19)

(3) Find Where You Want to Join the Divine Conversation

The prophetic office brings with it a daunting challenge—to speak a word from the LORD to a people facing a particular challenge at a particular time. As we have seen prophetic messages are not necessarily transferable from one age to another, or from one place to another. Isaiah's message was fitting for one age; it was a hindrance in another age. It is particularly susceptible to hubris, empty rhetoric that comes from nothing more than ego. The diversity of the prophetic message is every bit as wide as what we have already seen in the Hebrew Bible.

One note needs to be mentioned before we work toward joining this conversation. The prophets, like virtually everyone in those days, assumed that God had a heavy hand in all matters—births, rainfall, growing crops, disasters, wars and any other major thing. So, when their nations faced military threats, they did not see it simply as a geopolitical problem. It was primarily a theological problem. They concluded that Israel or Judah's destruction or salvation was ultimately determined by God, rather than by military efforts, alone. This puts the prophets in a different mind-set from you and me. Few of us believe that God determines the outcomes of war. We may, as Lincoln revealed in his Second Inaugural Address, wonder if the folly of war comes back to haunt us, that God, in the way human nature is shaped, exacts a terrible price from even the victors of war. We may pray for the safety of our troops and for the safety of civilians in harm's way. But outside of a few peace churches, such as the Mennonites or Church of the Brethren, there is no major Christian voice calling for the slashing of the United States' military budget in order that we may put greater trust in God to protect our nation. Neither, do we argue about the reasons God has blessed or punished us by determining the outcomes of our wars in Vietnam or Iraq or Afghanistan. As a nation we believe guns and bombs, not God, wins war.

So, while the prophets were forced to reach for conclusions about God based on the outcomes of war in 722, 701, and 587 BC, we are not forced into those same conclusions. We can join this divine conversation from another vantage point. This will allow us to engage these disparate voices from a level playing field. Hosea's proclamation that God will keep returning for Israel no matter how many times it strays does not have to be silenced because Assyria overran the northern kingdom. Neither should Micah's rebuke of Judah's sins of injustice be invalidated because the Assyrians gave up the Jerusalem siege.

The prophets were all in agreement that the age and people to which they were speaking were in trouble. As we have seen, though, there was great disagreement about diagnosing those problems. Amos, Micah and Jeremiah believed that the sins of injustice had reached a point that God could no longer look away. Hosea, Jeremiah, Isaiah and Ezekiel all mentioned the worship of other gods as a major problem. Hosea spoke of this betrayal as adultery, that in loving the LORD and loving other gods, Israel had broken

God's heart. Alternatively, Ezekiel approached the problem of idolatry as a contamination of the holy. Isaiah thought Judah's reliance on military alliances was a breach of trust in God's faithfulness, which was most egregious of all the people's sins. The conversation between these prophets is a discussion about the nature of sin, a conversation that continues to be debated among Christians, today.

Amos, Hosea, Isaiah and Jeremiah all condemned the people's reliance upon cultic sacrifices and burnt offerings, while neglecting what was really important. Without justice, or faith in God, devotion from religious ritual "is like a morning cloud, like the dew that goes away early" (Hos 6:4). When Jeremiah dismissed male circumcision, an act of religious ritual, he told the people to circumcise their hearts (Jer 4:4; Deut 10:16; 30:6).[26] The prophet was trying to get to the faith that was behind the ritual, not eliminate the ritual altogether. While the prophets agreed that God was upset with their society, they did not agree about the biggest problems.

Where do you find a comfortable place joining this conversation? Think of how people of faith describe the problems of our society and nation, today. Some believe that the sources of our greatest problems are racial injustice or the systemic injustice of our economic system. Others believe sexual immorality and related issues have led to the destruction of the family. Some believe that multicultural diversity has ruined a unified America. Still others are convinced that until you change people's hearts, nothing will change. There is great debate about whether corporate sins—systematic racism, wealth inequality, economic injustice—are most destructive to our society, or whether it is personal piety and morality—honesty, sexual purity, charity—upon which our nation hinges. Numerous polls show that a majority of Americans think the country is heading in the wrong direction. Yet, people are divided as to the nature of the wrong direction. The division usually looks like the differences between Jeremiah and Ezekiel.

These modern debates about our own society were embedded in the prophetic arguments stemming from Israel and Judah's own national crises. Having reviewed the voices of God through these prophets, in what ways can this divine conversation inform our dialogue, today?

- In what ways can the injustices of economic systems and the oppression of the poor and outcast become destructive forces to a nation? Why might such things make God angry?

- In what ways do you think faith and morality is a matter of action?

26. Friedman, *Who Wrote the Bible*, 14.

- How might a lack of trust in God, or tangentially, a lack of trust in the founding values and documents of a nation, be detrimental to a country?

- In what ways can a shift in ultimate allegiances change the course of a society's history? How might such things break God's heart?

- In what ways do you think faith and morality is a matter of the heart?

- In what ways can matters of holiness—the shifting of cultural boundaries, the loss of rituals, the defilement of bodies through addiction or sexual exploitation—undermine the nature of a society? Why might such things upset God?

- In what ways do you think faith and morality is a matter of being?

The diversity of the prophets' messages reminds us that many of our contemporary arguments about ethics and morality originated out of Scripture. This reality should give us pause while debating such things and work at appreciating the faith at work in the persons who disagree with us. The word of God by speaking through several voices has created this divine conversation, from which people of faith may discern through dialogue wise and faithful responses to the challenges of their day. Such wisdom, however, only happens when we enter into conversation. Screaming Bible verses in accusation at one another to prove our point of view leaves us without one leg on which to stand.

Imagine the messages of the prophets as bands on a color wheel. Amos, Micah and Jeremiah are prophets of justice, while Hosea and Isaiah are prophets of grace, and Ezekiel a holiness prophet. The theological combinations of grace, justice, and holiness are unlimited, because like the primary colors of red, yellow and blue their combinations create the whole spectrum of the color wheel. The wisdom of God's word can be seen in the color wheel. Even if I personally reject one of the prophets' messages as being unfit for my faith relationship with God, it still informs and molds my faith through its absence.

Can you name ways in which your own faith and morality is a blend of these prophetic messages?

The messages of the prophets should also encourage humility among us. Jeremiah believed that Deuteronomy's blessing-and-curse theology had explained God's involvement in all that happened to Judah in 587 BC when Jerusalem and the holy temple were reduced to ruble. For the surviving remnant, however, it was not so clear what caused the effect. Months after the city's destruction, a band of Judeans carted Jeremiah off to Egypt, kidnapped him to be their talisman, a lucky charm, though they cared little for his preaching. When he rebuked them for worshiping other gods along with the LORD in their Egyptian refugee camp, they offered a chilling response.

> As for the word that you have spoken to us in the name of the LORD, we are not going to listen to you. Instead, we will do everything that we have vowed, make offerings to the queen of heaven and pour out libations to her, just as we and our ancestors, our kings and our officials, used to do in the towns of Judah and in the streets of Jerusalem. We used to have plenty of food, and prospered, and saw no misfortune. But from the time we stopped making offerings to the queen of heaven and pouring out libations to her, we have lacked everything and have perished by the sword and by famine. (Jer 44:16–19)

Jeremiah had declared that the people's injustices and idolatry had caused their fate. King Josiah's reforms had criminalized the worship of other gods, destroyed their shrines and temples, and reestablished the worship of the LORD according to Deuteronomy's book of the law. Still it had not been enough, which made others see things differently. They believed that King Josiah's reforms were the beginning of their bad times. Life had been good while they worshiped a deity called the *queen of heaven* along with the LORD. As soon as they stopped worshiping her and gave their total allegiance to the LORD, that's when bad things started happening. They reasoned that their tragedy had not been caused by the LORD's wrath, but by the queen of heaven's anger. It was such a convincing argument that all Jeremiah could do was to repeat his warnings and conclude, "All the remnant of Judah, who have come to the land of Egypt to settle, shall [one day] know whose words will stand, mine or theirs!" (44:28).

Surprisingly, that was Jeremiah's last word—wait and see! This is the difficulty of any religion that looks for a clear cause-and-effect relationship between faith and history. Your assurances are more apt to be frustrated than validated, which was part of the wisdom of President Lincoln's Second Inaugural Address.[27] Both read the same Bible, he said, and prayed to the same God—each to invoke divine aid against the other. "The prayers of both could not be answered; that of neither has been answered fully. The Almighty has his own purposes." The scourge of slavery, he stated, had become a judgment upon the whole nation, North and South, through "this terrible war." While he prayed for a speedy end to the war, he wondered if God would will it "until all the wealth piled by the bond-man's two hundred and fifty years of unrequited toil shall be sunk, and until every drop of blood drawn with the

---

27. Lincoln, "Second Inaugural Address," in *His Speeches and Writings*, 792–93.

lash, shall be paid by another drawn with the sword." Though the war ended, our nation is still paying the price of slavery and segregation.

"With malice toward none, with charity for all" may we continue this conversation with the humility to see that our "firmness in the right," should only be as "God gives us to see the right" through all the colors of the wheel.

CHAPTER 5

Which People Are Our People?

We must all learn to live together as brothers [and sisters].
Or we will perish together as fools. We are tied together in
the single garment of destiny . . . and whatever affects one
directly affects all indirectly. This is the way God's universe is
made; this is the way it is structured.[1]

—MARTIN LUTHER KING JR., PALM SUNDAY, 1968

ETHICS ARE NOT so hard to figure out. Nations around the globe have similar laws. Cultures throughout human history have focused on a handful of basic principles: do not murder or hurt others, do not take what does not belong to you, do not lie or cheat, take care of your own people, treat others as you would like to be treated. Whether you are talking about an ancient civilization, or an urban gang, religious commands, or federal laws, ethical boundaries have many parallels. However, there is one main difference—to whom are you ethical? How wide is the circle to which these rules apply? Do they apply to everyone the same way, or are there differences based on specific distinctions, such as between men and women, or insiders and outsiders, or different classes of people? An ancient tribe may have had very strict commands about behavior within the tribe, but could be barbaric to strangers from other tribes. Nations often have separate policies for how they treat citizens and noncitizens. Even criminals can treat their families and friends with high regard, while thinking nothing of stealing from or hurting people outside their circle.

This question has been at the heart of our nation's formation and reformation. Were slaves and Native Americans deserving of the same rights as all persons in the United States? Should undocumented immigrants have the same rights as citizens? How did our nation justify the internment of Japanese Americans during World War II, or the segregation of African Americans

1. King, "Remaining Awake through a Great Revolution," in *Testament of Hope*, 269.

89

for over one hundred years after the end of the Civil War? Should same-sex marriage be regarded as the same as traditional marriage, or should gay and lesbian citizens be treated by a different set of rules?

How big the circle should be drawn is one of the great arguments in the Bible. Who are the people of God? May Israelites marry people from other nations? How are aliens and strangers in the land to be treated? Which people are our people?

The postexilic stage in Israel's history offers a great place to study this question. When Persia conquered the Babylonian Empire in 539 BC, the new emperor permitted exiles to return to their homelands. Exiled Jews began returning to Judah and started to rebuild the holy city of Jerusalem. A new prophet sang of God's glorious restoration of Israel:

> Make straight in the desert a highway for our God.
>
> Every valley shall be lifted up,
>
> and every mountain and hill be made low;
>
> the uneven ground shall become level,
>
> and the rough places a plain.
>
> Then, the glory of the LORD shall be revealed,
>
> and all people shall see it together,
>
> for the mouth of the LORD has spoken. (Isa 40:3–5)

Unfortunately, it wasn't as glorious as Isaiah's poetry. There were plenty of rough places for the exiles when they returned. Jerusalem sat in ruins. They did not get along with the peasants scraping a living out of the land. When they laid the foundation of the Second Temple and celebrated with trumpets, music and loud cheers, "many of the priests and Levites and heads of families, old people who had seen the first house on its foundations, wept with a loud voice when they saw this house" (Ezra 3:12). The Second Temple built by an impoverished people would never match the glory of Solomon's temple. Poverty, and conflicts with local peoples, would delay construction for decades.

EXCURSUS 5.1

Who Should Comprise the Second Temple Community

In this chapter we will study how one set of books were written against policies recorded in another set of writings. Soon after Persia conquered the Babylonian Empire in 539 BC, King Cyrus permitted Babylonian exiles to return to their homelands. Within a few years Jewish exiles began returning to Jerusalem and Judah. This migration continued for decades. Ezra and Nehemiah cover events as early as 525 BC and as late as 400 BC.[2] Daniel supports the Priestly theology of Ezra and Nehemiah, and is briefly noted in this chapter.

Ezra and Nehemiah, originally written as one scroll in the fifth century BC, tell the story of how the returning exiles rebuild Jerusalem. The authors were returning exiles themselves and told the story from the Priestly tradition perspective. The descendants of Jews who survived the Babylonian conquest and remained in the land did not write a history of how Jerusalem was rebuilt. They are basically invisible in Ezra and Nehemiah, as if these returning exiles no longer recognized Jews who had not been exiles. One of the great challenges in the books of Ezra and Nehemiah is to renew God's covenant and rid the Second Temple community of foreigners. This policy to remove foreigners from the community—who may have just been the descendants of the Jews who survived the destruction of Jerusalem—generated the writings of resisters.

The scroll of Isaiah was expanded (chs. 40–66) to include the writings of a *second* Isaiah who spoke of Israel's return to the land. The first portion of Second Isaiah primarily talks about returning to Judah. Later chapters begin talking about how Israel should live in the land, including worship at the rebuilt temple. Chapters 56–66 add positions on justice for the poor and outcast that are absent in 40–55, leading many scholars to think a *third* Isaiah, or a guild of prophets completed the scroll.[3] These chapters speak more directly

2. The editing of these two books can make it difficult to follow the story. For instance, one section of a fifth-century BC event is inserted into the narrative of Ezra 4, which is happening in the sixth century BC. The text does not flow chronologically.

3. Conrad, *Reading Isaiah*, 3–20. He argues that while three or more authors have written Isaiah, it shows signs of being edited to be one piece. For this reason Conrad suggests that interpreters should not overly emphasize the differences of the three writers to the point of neglecting their common tradition and theology.

to Ezra and Nehemiah's policies that exclude outsiders. However, for our purposes, it does not really matter if Second Isaiah was the work of one or multiple authors. Therefore, I will speak of Second Isaiah as a single prophet.

Ruth and Jonah were independently written against the policies of Ezra and Nehemiah. Ruth's author took an older folktale and refitted it for this purpose during the Second Temple period.[4] Although Ezra and Nehemiah's policies are not denounced by name, these stories focus on characters that match the insiders and outsiders of the Ezra and Nehemiah community. In Ruth, an Israelite named Naomi returns to her homeland after living in a foreign land—just as the exiles had done. Her Moabite daughter-in-law, who proves to be more valuable than seven sons, provides for her. Ezra and Nehemiah's policies would have forced Ruth to leave Jerusalem, because she would have been a foreign wife—one of the peoples named in Nehemiah (Ezra 9:1–4; Neh 13:1–3, 23–27). In Ruth she is the hero.

Jonah is a prophet who is told by God to preach to Nineveh, the former capital city of the Assyrian Empire, the nation that destroyed the northern kingdom. Ezra defines the *people of the land* as descendants of Assyrian settlers. Jonah, who does not want to preach to these people and instead wants God to destroy them, takes on the persona of those for the policies of Ezra and Nehemiah. At the end of the story God forgives the people of Assyria and accepts their worship. If God would accept the worship of the Assyrian people, why would God not accept the mixed descendants of Assyrians and Israelites into the Second Temple community?[5]

Exiled Jews Are God's Holy People

In the exiles' minds they had been tossed from the land because they had broken God's covenant. Reestablishing the covenant was therefore paramount for their protection and prosperity. While in Babylon, Ezekiel had

4. Leuchter, "Sociolinguistic and Rhetorical Implications," 198n9. Leuchter dates Ruth to the mid-Persian period, though it possesses a compositional style comparable to sixth-century texts.

5. Trible, "Jonah," 7:466. She discusses the difficulty of dating Jonah, acknowledging a majority of opinions fall in the sixth, fifth, and fourth centuries BC, and concludes that it is best to let Jonah float between centuries.

visions of God making a new covenant with Israel. These included grand promises of what God would do for the people: banish wild animals from the land, send showers of rain, produce bountiful harvests, provide a baby for every crib, replant the garden of Eden, and be present with them forevermore (Ezek 34:25–29; 36:30–36; 37:26). The temple would be the conduit for this new covenant. Ezekiel spends eight of his forty-eight chapters describing God's vision for a new temple. Unfortunately, things did not happen as beautifully as Ezekiel imagined.

Problems with identifying the nation of God's people became an issue once construction began on the temple. The people of the land approached the leaders of the returned exiles and said, "Let us build with you, for we worship your God as you do, and we have been sacrificing to him ever since the days of King Esar-haddon of Assyria who brought us here" (Ezra 4:2). Instead of welcoming this offer the leaders of the exiles replied, "You shall have no part with us in building a house to our God; but we alone will build to the LORD, the God of Israel, as King Cyrus of Persia has commanded us. Then the people of the land discouraged the people of Judah, and made them afraid to build" (4:3–4). This confrontation occurred between the returned exiles and a group Ezra called the *people of the land*, who were the mixed descendants that claimed allegiance to the LORD. In time they would be called *Samaritans*.

Around 450 BC the Judean community renewed the covenant with God. Ezra made a long confessional prayer to God on behalf of the people in which he concluded, "Here we are, slaves to this day—slaves in the land that you gave to our ancestors to enjoy its fruit and its good gifts. Its rich yield goes to the kings whom you have set over us because of our sins; they have power also over our bodies and over our livestock at their pleasure, and we are in great distress" (Neh 9:36–37). This confession reveals that building the temple did not provide the blessing from God Haggai had promised in his short book. So, the returned exiles took another step to gain God's favor. They publicly renewed the covenant with God as a community. It was hoped God would then reward their faithfulness and free them from their oppression. While the people promised to observe all the commandments of the LORD, five items were specifically singled out. The people promised:

1. Not to intermarry with the people of the land,

2. To strictly observe the Sabbath, including interactions with the people of the land,

3. To regularly pay a tax for the work of the temple and to keep the altar fire burning,

4. To offer the first fruits of the harvest, the firstborn of sons and live-stock to the LORD,

5. And not to neglect the House of the LORD. (10:28–39)

The five emphases are all components of holiness theology of the Priests. There is no hint of Deuteronomy or Jeremiah's emphasis on justice for the poor and needy. The pledge to not marry people of the land became part of the answer to the question, "Which people are our people?"

Mixed marriages were banned in Ezra and Nehemiah and foreign wives were sent away. A proclamation was announced throughout Judah, that all should assemble at Jerusalem. This was so important that if any did not come within three days "all their property" would be seized and they would be banned from the "congregation of the exiles" (Ezra 10:6–8). "Ezra the priest stood up and said to them, 'You have trespassed and married foreign women, and so increased the guilt of Israel. Now make a confession to the LORD the God of your ancestors, and do his will; separate yourselves from the people of the land and from the foreign wives.' Then all the assembly answered with a loud voice, 'It is so; we must do as you have said'" (10:10–12). This meant that men, who had been exiles, now were forced to exile their own wives and children. Their destination is not recorded. A list of 113 offenders concludes the book of Ezra. The offenders included even priests and Levites. The writer announced this ban on three separate occasions—in Ezra 10 and twice in Nehemiah 13—leading to the impression that enforcement was less than perfect. Perhaps, *Romeo and Juliet* love flourished in postexilic Judah.

This desire to separate as a people was emphasized in the exilic stories of Daniel as well. The heroes in the book of Daniel honor God by remaining holy and separate while living among the Babylonian people. Its stories address the question, "How does one remain a faithful Jew when there is no Jewish state?" In three of the stories Daniel and his friends resolve "not to defile themselves with the royal rations of food and wine," they refuse to worship a golden statue, and he refuses to cease praying to the LORD (Dan 1; 3; 6). In each story they prove themselves superior in faith, intellect and character. Daniel becomes a trusted adviser to the emperor.

The second half of Daniel was written much later than the first half and had a distinct end-of-times theme to it. This apocalyptic Daniel (7–12) concluded his book with a chapter on the resurrection of the dead. By the judgment of God, those who were holy and righteous would be raised from the dead to "everlasting life," while those who are unrighteous would be raised to "everlasting contempt" (12:2). The desire to separate the holy from the impure, the righteous from the unrighteous, found an eternal and permanent solution. The hunger to believe that living a righteous life for God did have dividends, which was not self-evident living for centuries under occupying military powers, found its fulfillment in the afterlife. This was the apocalyptic answer to the unfairness of life and the unfulfilled promises of God—in heaven everything would be as it should be. Like the stories of Daniel and his three friends, the people of God should continue to live holy lives and wait upon the LORD. The righteous would find their reward in heaven and the wicked would be punished in the judgment to come.

All Who Seek the LORD Are God's People

The second prophet in the book of Isaiah (chs. 40–66) would have agreed with Ezra and Nehemiah that the returning exiles must not make the mistake of their grandparents. Just what that mistake was, however, would be a point of contention. Ezekiel had rejected God's promise to Abraham as having any lasting significance. Yet, some fifty years later Second Isaiah returned to that promise. Defying Ezekiel, he spoke of how Abraham's promise was the cornerstone to the hope of Israel's restoration.[6] Ezra and Nehemiah, however, focus exclusively on the Mosaic covenant without ever mentioning God's covenants with Abraham or David.

Among the prophets only Hosea mentioned love more often than Second Isaiah. God's steadfast love for Israel was more permanent than the mountains (Isa 54:10). "For a brief moment I abandoned you, but with great compassion I will gather you . . . with everlasting love I will have compassion on you" (54:8). Though Judah had been exiled, Second Isaiah knew that God had not forgotten them and would now bring them home (46:3–4).

Despite the fact that foreigners had destroyed Israel and Judah, Second Isaiah believed there was room for all nations in God's kingdom. He daringly declared that King Cyrus of Persia, a non-Jewish person, was God's anointed, a word that has Davidic and Messianic overtones. He said foreigners, who loved the LORD, would be welcomed into the temple. "Do not let the foreigner joined to the LORD say, 'The LORD will surely separate me from his people.' . . . The foreigners who join themselves to the LORD . . . who keep the Sabbath . . . and hold fast my covenant . . . will be accepted [at] my altar; for my house shall be called a house of prayer for all peoples" (56:3–7). Second Isaiah proclaimed that the LORD is the God of all the earth and therefore the God of all peoples, not just for Israel (45:22–23).

---

6. Sanders, *Canon and Community*, 67n10. Sanders reveals the polar opposite positions Ezekiel and Second Isaiah take on Abraham's promise (Ezek 33; Isa 51).

In addition to Second Isaiah, Ruth and Jonah also resist Ezra and Nehemiah's narrow definition of God's holy people. The book of Ruth is a love story that dramatically makes a theological statement to counterbalance the Priestly tradition's xenophobia during the reconstruction period.[7] The main hero, Ruth, stands out because she is a woman operating in the patriarchal world of ancient Israel. Phyllis Trible introduces Ruth this way: "The book of Ruth presents the aged Naomi and the youthful Ruth as they struggle for survival in a patriarchal environment. These women bear their own burdens. They know hardship, danger, insecurity and death. No God promises them blessing; no man rushes to their rescue. They themselves risk bold decisions and shocking acts to work out their own salvation."[8] Ruth's character reveals her righteousness. Boaz took notice of her not because of her beauty but for her loyal deeds. "Seven sons" could not have been more valuable to Naomi (Ruth 4:15).

Even more surprising than this hero's gender was her ethnic heritage— Ruth came from Moab. The story began soon after both became widows. Ruth declares her loyalty to her mother-in-law saying, "Your people shall be my people, and your God my God" (1:16). The people of God, according to Ruth, cannot be defined by bloodlines. Like Moses' father-in-law, Jethro, she was a righteous foreigner devoted to the LORD. Ruth became a part of God's people by her acts of faithfulness. Her status as a foreigner becomes poignant at the end of the story when it declares that she became King David's great-grandmother. Despite the fact that Ezra and Nehemiah banished Moabites from the Second Temple community (Neh 13:1), the book of Ruth reveals that King David was one-eighth Moabite. Would Ezra and Nehemiah banish Ruth? Would they banish King David?

Whereas Ruth used a love story to speak of God's all-embracing reach, Jonah used an adventure story to proclaim the same message. Sometime after the Babylonian exile and the return to an occupied Judah, the book of Jonah was written.[9] This parable shows that God opened salvation to all who were devoted to the LORD. Paul Hanson describes Jonah "as a protest against the

---

7. Hanson, *People Called*, 314–16. Hanson dates Ruth to the fourth century BC and calls Ruth an alternative vision to the Priestly claims that foreigners should be excluded from the reconstructed Jerusalem.

8. Trible, *Rhetoric of Sexuality*, 166.

9. Hanson also describes Jonah as an alternative vision to the Priestly claims that God is only for the Jewish people. Jonah's author uses a "classic expression of early Yahwistic faith in God's compassion" (*People Called*, 318). He dates Jonah to the late fifth to early fourth century BC. A late date is almost a certainty since the Assyrian Empire is not even mentioned in the book, with the people known only as citizens of the city. For Hanson's brief discussion of Jonah, see *People Called*, 316–21.

exclusivism and isolationism of the Ezra and Nehemiah reform movement."[10] The books of Jonah and Ruth along with Second Isaiah's prophecy reveal that theology focused on God's steadfast love survived the exile and worked as a counterbalance to the holiness theology of the Priests.

The story began with the flawed hero Jonah, who is the only prophet to walk out on God. He refuses the job God gave him to do and took passage on the first Mediterranean cargo ship heading to the far end of the world.[11] He nearly drowns in the sea till God sends a very large fish to swallow him to save him. After three days in the fish's belly Jonah begrudgingly agrees to do God's bidding, which was to preach to one of Israel's most hated enemies. Jonah personally hoped that God would rain down fire from heaven upon the citizens of Nineveh. After his assignment of preaching hellfire and damnation, he found a little knoll outside the city in hopes of watching divine fireworks.

To his disappointment he did not get to watch fire rain down on Nineveh. Surprisingly, the people believed God and repented. They cried to God and put away their violent ways. "When God saw what they did, how they turned from their evil ways, God changed his mind about the calamity that he had said he would bring upon them; and he did not do it" (Jonah 3:10). That God's mind might change was part of Jonah's issue.[12] He could hardly contain his anger, "O Lord! Is not this what I said while I was still in my own country? That is why I fled . . . for I knew that you are a gracious God and merciful, slow to anger, and abounding in steadfast love, and ready to relent from punishing" (4:2). Jonah's indictment of God was based on the preamble to the Ten Commandments found in Exodus 34. Phyllis Trible explains his dilemma, "Since Jonah himself willed the destruction of Nineveh, the merciful God was for him not redemption but wrath. Reciting words of love, Jonah convicted God."[13] The mercy of God had been stretched and expanded, which made Jonah furious. God was merciful and abounding in steadfast love not only for Israel, but also for Israel's enemies.

10. Hanson, *People Called*, 321.

11. Trible notes, "Nineveh is east; Tarshish is west. Nineveh specifies Yhwh's direction; Tarshish signifies 'from-the-presence-of Yhwh' (*millipnê*)" (*Rhetorical Criticism*, 128).

12. Trible suggests that Jonah's anticipation of God's mercy was the cause of his flight from God, "Through acts of penance and repentance Nineveh overturns, as Jonah predicted but not as he intended. Paradoxically his prophecy is both true and false" (*Rhetorical Criticism*, 190).

13. Trible, *Rhetoric of Sexuality*, 3.

Practicing Midrash

Ezra and Nehemiah describe the challenge the exiles faced upon returning to Jerusalem. They aimed to create a holy nation by renewing God's covenant, building the temple and excluding foreigners from God's holy people. Daniel took this a step further when his vision imagined a judgment day when the righteous and the unrighteous would be separated for eternity. The prophecy of Second Isaiah and the books of Ruth and Jonah rejected this narrow definition of God's people and declared that God's love and forgiveness was available for all who seek the Lord. They resisted Ezra and Nehemiah's rulings and advocated for a more inclusive Second Temple community.

(1) Free the Stories to Speak for Themselves

In defining the true people of God, who were to rebuild Israel, the contrast between the writings of Ezra and Nehemiah and those of Second Isaiah, Ruth, and Jonah could not be greater. The Priestly tradition of Ezra and Nehemiah believed God called Israel to be holy as God is holy. This command separated Israel from other nations and peoples. The covenant with God required circumcision of all males, dietary and purity commands from Leviticus and Deuteronomy, Sabbath regulations, and adherence to the religious rituals of the temple. This, they concluded, meant the exclusion of foreign peoples who would pollute and defile the holiness of God's temple and people.

It may be hard for us to read Ezra and Nehemiah's definition of God's people from our twenty-first-century perch, for we might see only legalism and xenophobia. To read about forced divorces with wives and children sent away in exile sounds like bigotry. In order to let these passages speak for themselves, it is important to lay aside our enlightened biases and try to imagine their world. Without a strong homogenous drive the exiles would not have survived Babylon as an identifiable Jewish people. Babylon wanted to strip away the exiles' Jewish identity. They gave Daniel a Babylonian name, Belteshazzar, as well as his friends whom we remember by their Babylonian names, Shadrach, Meshach, and Abednego. They wore Babylonian clothes, ate Babylonian food, and learned Babylonian ways, so that they would forget how to be Jewish. Empires have done this to countless refugees and captured exiles throughout history, leading to the extinction of cultures and civilizations. The exiles' exclusivity at this crucial time retained their religious and cultural heritage. When they returned to Judah they brought those hard lessons with them. The Priestly writings of the Torah, as well as Chronicles, Ezra and Nehemiah were all completed at a time when the Jewish people did not control their circumstances. There was no king on the throne. Powers foreign and distant controlled the land. One of the few things they could control was their circle of people and who would be allowed to worship God in the temple. Perhaps the context of persecution bends faith toward a desire to be holy. If society separates you as different and inferior, you flip the separation into a mark of purity, of holiness, and of being superior in the eyes of God. Can you picture religious groups today that use this type of thinking?

We know almost nothing about the second prophet in Isaiah. He does not share any biographical information, and no other book spoke of him.[14] He would have been a descendent of Israel's aristocracy, because that is whom the Babylonians took into exile. Anonymously, he wrote some of the most beautiful poetry in the Hebrew Bible.[15] The Babylonians took away his identity, but not his hope. The very first words of Second Isaiah announce God's compassion and salvation, "Comfort, O comfort my people, says your God" (Isa 40:1). The exiles would return on a highway where "every valley shall be lifted up, and every mountain and hill be made low" (40:4).[16] The Davidic covenant anchored Second Isaiah's theology. God has great plans for Israel, to make it a "light to the nations" so that God's salvation may reach the "end of the earth" (42:6; 49:6). God's steadfast love not only offers forgiveness and mercy to Israel, but to all who seek the LORD.

Likewise the books of Ruth and Jonah reveal the power of love and faithfulness to overcome great obstacles. Just as the exiles returned to their homeland with great challenges, so did Naomi as she returned to her home-land a widow with no living sons. Fortunately, Naomi returned with her Moabite daughter-in-law Ruth, who was better to her than seven sons. As the LORD blessed Naomi by partnering her with a foreigner, so the LORD would bless the returning exiles should they welcome foreigners who would say to the Israelites, "Your people shall be my people, and your God my God"

14. There is one verse, Isa 49:1, in one of the Servant Songs, which is written in the first person and describes being called in the womb. This may be the only autobio-graphical information in Second Isaiah.

15. Holladay notes, "Chapter 40 opens a sequence of 16 chapters of the most sus-tained, lyrical expression of hope and renewal to be found within the Old Testament" (Scroll of a Prophetic Heritage, 117).

16. Holladay explains that a highway presumes travelers, "The prophet proclaims that a road is to be prepared in much the same way for the triumphal march of God himself, the heavenly king. But if God is to lead a procession across the desert, then there is a procession to be led, another hint . . . that people are going to go home and that God will lead the procession of homecomers" (Scroll of a Prophetic Heritage, 125–26).

(Ruth 1:16). Jonah's amazing story of how the LORD forgave the people of Assyria for their many sins—including the destruction the northern kingdom—showed the returning exiles that they should forgive the people of the land and welcome them into the Second Temple community.

The writers of Ezra, Nehemiah, Daniel, Second Isaiah, Ruth and Jonah all experienced life as an exile or as a returned exile living under military occupation, but they approached these circumstances from very different perspectives. Ezra, Nehemiah, Daniel believed God would have them hunker down, circle their wagons, live as a holy and separate people until God restores everything as it should be. Second Isaiah, Ruth, and Jonah believed that God would have them welcome the foreigner, and live as transformed people so that they may be a "light to the nations." To allow both viewpoints to speak is to acknowledge that while people may experience the same crisis they can respond to it in very different ways. Neither the ancients nor we are determined by our circumstances.

(2) Listen to the Stories as Contrasting Voices of God

The contrast in these two theological arguments may be most easily seen in their end-time conclusions. Daniel described a future judgment day where God would raise the righteous for "everlasting life" and the unrighteous for "everlasting contempt," and the two groups would be separated forever (Dan 12:2). Meanwhile, Second Isaiah imagined that God would create "new heavens and a new earth" where "the wolf and the lamb shall feed together, the lion shall eat straw like the ox" (Isa 65:25). Rather than be separated for eternity, Second Isaiah pictures a harmonious new earth where former enemies live as one.

These are two basic theological concepts arguing with each other in these writers. The Priestly tradition, which included Ezekiel, Ezra, Nehemiah, Haggai, Zechariah, and Daniel, placed a priority on God's holiness and believed that Israel must be holy as God is holy. The priority was to make the people acceptable to God by the ways they separate themselves from common peoples. What began as piety to keep persons in a right relationship with God became a xenophobic struggle. The Priestly texts repeatedly prohibit Israelites from marrying foreigners. (Remember the Priestly version of Jacob's story and how Esau broke his parents' hearts by marrying Canaanite women.) Ezra and Nehemiah's forced exile of foreign wives and children plays out a continuing theme. Just who were foreigners is a bit of a mystery. They used terms for peoples—Moabites, Ammonites, Canaanites, Hittites, and Jebusites—of nations that no longer existed (Ezra 9:1; Neh 13:1). All of these tribal nations had been wiped out along with the northern kingdom of Israel and the southern kingdom of Judah by either the Assyrian or Babylonian empires. First, the Persians, then Greeks and Romans would rule all the territory for centuries. This polemic condemns all the people of the land as other, even their own cousins who survived the wars. It seems that in the postexilic community foreigners were everyone who was not a member of the "congregation of the exiles."[17]

The writers of Second Isaiah, Ruth and Jonah spoke with an inclusive vision for God's people. Informed by the Davidic tradition, Second Isaiah believed God would transform the way things had been, "See, the former things have come to pass, and new things I now declare" (Isa 42:9). Of all the prophets, only Hosea spoke of love more than Second Isaiah. These writers had a different vision for a reconstructed Jerusalem, and resisted Ezra and Nehemiah's rulings. They believed that any one who joins themselves to the LORD would be welcome at God's altar in the temple. Maybe the banished wives and children kept returning to the Second Temple community because they had heard the words of Isaiah, "Do not let the foreigner joined to the LORD say, 'The LORD will surely separate me from his people'" (56:3). They chose to listen to God as Isaiah heard the LORD, and to disobey the rulings of Ezra and Nehemiah. God's love would not be denied.

Ruth's story made a good partner piece to Second Isaiah's prophecy. Naomi stands in the place of the returning exiles as she, too, returns to her homeland to rebuild a life that had lost everything. The extravagant love of her Moabite daughter-in-law saves her. Naomi's son had married a foreigner, one of the nations named by Ezra, and she comes to Naomi's rescue when none of her Israelite kin cared for her. Ruth's connection to King David changed the dynamics of this story from a faith folktale into a theological and political treatise. Yet, Ruth's own story, as a righteous foreigner, speaks to the value for Israel to include people like Ruth in the Second Temple community. Could Ruth have been written by a returning exile whose life had been blessed by a righteous foreigner?

The book of Jonah was a direct challenge to the exclusive rulings in Ezra and Nehemiah. Ezra had identified the "people of the land" as descendants from Assyria, which even though they worshipped the LORD,

---

17. Klein, "Books of Ezra & Nehemiah," 3:667, discusses the division between returning Jewish exiles and those Jews who never left the land after the Babylonian conquest. There are a lot of unknowns of what happened between these two groups. One possibility is that Jews who remained in Palestine were grouped in with all the other "people of the land." They, of course, had not been schooled in the Priestly-dominated Judaism that evolved over the roughly hundred years of exile. Klein states, "In any case, the books of Ezra and Nehemiah thoroughly back those who had returned from exile (the Golah) and virtually ignore those who had remained in the land."

disqualified them from building and entering the temple or having any part of the Second Temple community. The book of Jonah rejects this bigotry. It shows God forgiving the people of Nineveh, the capital of Assyria, the country that had destroyed the northern kingdom of Israel. The LORD does this because God is gracious, merciful, abounding in steadfast love, and "ready to relent from punishing" (Jonah 3:2). The story's moral was that the LORD's love for Israel was available to the whole world, even to Israel's enemies and to their descendants. If Ezra and Nehemiah, like the prophet Jonah, brooded about God's graciousness, then they misunderstood the gift of God's steadfast love.

The Priests spoke little of God's love. In the long Priestly collection in the Torah it was never stated that God loved Israel. Ezra and Nehemiah, which was written after the Torah was collected, did incorporate phrases about the LORD's steadfast love. Each of the half dozen times God's love (*hesed*) was mentioned, however, it came in the form of official speech—congregational singing, a letter, or as a salutatory greeting to God in prayer. To use parental metaphors, when Ezra and Nehemiah spoke of God's steadfast love, you got the feeling they were not picturing a warm, motherly hug, but more like a cordial letter from dad while you're away at boarding school, signed, "Love, Father."

(3) Find Where You Want to Join the Divine Conversation

The questions "Who are God's people?" and "Which people are our people?" remain debated topics in Christian circles and our nation, today. This chapter has focused on the period of reconstruction—the Second Temple community—because the returned exiles had to start from scratch. In the arduous task of rebuilding Jerusalem they were given the chance to intentionally remake their community and culture, to build a new society. Like the Exodus community before them, or the colonial settlers of North America, they had to decide whether to incorporate the indigenous people and how to relate to them as insiders or outsiders. It is not surprising that opinions were not unanimous. Nor is it surprising that people heard God's voice in different ways.

Ezra and Nehemiah's reforms eventually became the law of the land. When the Priests collected scrolls of sacred writings and passed them down for generations, however, they included the words of Second Isaiah, Ruth and Jonah even though those authors spoke against Ezra and Nehemiah's reforms. After the Romans destroyed Jerusalem in AD 70 and either killed or drove Jewish persons from their homeland, the Jewish diaspora retained their identity as a people because they lived as an ex-clusive community with strict dietary, Sabbath, and religious laws. Had they been more inclusive of others and had they been willing to assimilate into the cultures where they settled, it is questionable if there would be a recognizable Jewish identity today.

"Who are God's people?" is theological question about identity. Chris-tians may also see it as a question about salvation, but here in the discussions between Ezra and Nehemiah and Second Isaiah, Ruth and Jonah identity is the focus. Who do you have to be to become God's people? How does a person outside the circle become a part of the community? Are there ways that a person inside the community may be excluded and removed from the circle? These are questions that Christian groups have considered over the centuries—the Amish, colonial Congregational Churches with the adoption of the Half-Way Covenant, Christian congregations in lands where Christi-anity is a minority religion, and Southern churches during the Civil Rights movement—each with decisions that fit their context and theology.

This argument between Ezra and Nehemiah and their resisters—Sec-ond Isaiah, Ruth, and Jonah—can be read in a nationalistic way, and affect issues regarding immigration, multiculturalism, and citizenship. People of faith living in the United States can look at this argument from sacred and secular angles.

Where do you care to join this divine conversation?

- How do you feel about the desire to be God's holy people—to be a people separate from others in order to be for God and God's ways?

- Can you name some positive traits of understanding *our* people in this way?

- Can you name some inherent liabilities of creating an exclusive, holy group?

- Do you see parallels in Ezra and Nehemiah's understanding of God's people to the way some want to create a USA for Americans? Describe them.

- How do you feel about a sense of call for God's people to be an inclu-sive "light to the nations"? (Isa 49:6)

- Can you name some positive traits of understanding *our* people in this way?

- Can you name some inherent liabilities of creating an inclusive group that welcomes all sorts of people on the basis of God's love?

- Do you see parallels here in Ruth, Jonah, and Second Isaiah's under-standing of God's people to those who want to welcome all the tired, the poor, and the "huddled masses yearning to breath free" as citizens of the United States? Describe them.

Nearly all Christian churches would affirm God's holiness and God's love. So, why is it hard when defining identity to create meaningful standards that set the faithful apart, and yet at the same time emphasize that all are welcome at God's table? One difficulty is setting boundaries that work for individuals as well as for large groups. Welcoming Ruth into Naomi's Israelite community is one thing. Her words, "your people shall be my people, and your God my God," were proved by her devotion to her mother-in-law. In telling the story of Ruth the author portrays a Moabite so sympathetic and honorable that only the hardest of hearts could not welcome her with open arms into the Israelite community. The claim that she was King David's great-grandmother was a final blow to convince the unmoved. But should welcoming Ruth have meant that Israel should have welcomed all Moabites as a thirteenth tribe of Israel? What if the Moabites repeated Ruth's promise—your people shall be my people, your God my God—except that the men refused to be circumcised, or did not observe the Sabbath, or also kept some traditions with their Moabite god?

The book of Jonah does depict a whole city repenting to the LORD as one. However, in the story God relents from destroying Nineveh, but God does not welcome them as part of Israel. Even when Second Isaiah speaks of the foreigner being welcomed into God's holy temple, it was a foreigner who had been joined to the LORD (whatever that meant), who had kept the Sabbath and held fast to God's covenant with Israel. What may be allowable, even compassionate and encouraged on an individual basis, could still be a problem on a wider scale. There are no identifiable Moabite people today. They have all vanished into the sands of history. Would that have happened to the Jewish people if they would have welcomed other peoples into their society and merged their religious and cultural distinctions?

Noah's ark is a good way to picture Ezra and Nehemiah's way of thinking about God's people. The world is going to hell in a hand basket, but there is this holy ship sailing through the midst of all this chaos. The best thing the church can do is to be the best Noah's ark it can be, preserving God's holy people until Christ comes again.

Luke's telling of Jesus' Parable of the Wedding Feast (Luke 14:15–24) is a good way to picture Second Isaiah, Ruth and Jonah's way of thinking about God's people. The world is a mess, but there is always room at the table for more at God's feast. If we share bread together, it just might change the world. There is truth in both of these images, even if they are held in tension.

If God put the pen in your hand, how wide would you draw the circle? Would you make the circle wide enough to include everyone, thereby diluting the commitment of the true believers? Or would you draw the circle narrow enough to keep those who do not deserve it out, while making the commitment of the true believers mean something? Or can you imagine another way of drawing the circle of God's people?

CHAPTER 6

Countertestimonies

The fundamental cause of the trouble is that in the modern world the stupid are cocksure while the intelligent are full of doubt.[1]

—BERTRAND RUSSELL

DANIEL'S ENDING WHERE ALL the righteous people receive eternal life and the wicked are condemned to everlasting punishment did not bring a smile to everyone's face. But no one had an answer that did. Neither the Priests of Judah, the Levites who crafted Deuteronomy, the Storyteller who celebrated God's steadfast love, nor any of the prophets and psalmists could completely make sense of the calamities that fell upon God's chosen people, at least not in a way that satisfied everyone. Within one hundred fifty years the two ancient kingdoms of Israel had been wiped out by empires, and except for two groups of exiles sent to Babylon in 596 and 587 BC, their people were largely lost to history. The exiles kept their Judean identity, but lost every material possession and the right to live in their homeland for generations. None of the core teachings of Israel's faith had satisfactory answers for such devastation. None of them had an answer for the future except to wait for God to fulfill unmet promises.

The three ideas about God—God is love, God is just, God is holy—had strengths and weaknesses. That is in part why they existed. The weakness in one became a strength in another. The idea that the LORD was a God of steadfast love, forgiving iniquity and sin for a thousand generations, who mercifully protected Israel from all enemies, had sustained the faithful through many troubling times. And after all, who does not want to believe that God unconditionally loves you. The idea that the LORD was a God of justice, who lifted up the poor and lowly and brought down the rich and powerful, who punished the wicked and rewarded the righteous, had

1. Russell, *Mortals and Others*, 28.

formed Israel's ideas of ethics and justice. And after all, who does not want to believe that God works out things in fairness, that everyone gets what they deserve. The idea that God was holy, not like humans who were mortal and fallible, gave Israel a hope beyond their limited existence. And after all, who does not want to believe in a God greater and more powerful than ourselves. But these noble ideas about God and the promises God made to Abraham, Moses and David did not stop the Assyrians and the Babylonians. That was why many people stopped believing in the old way:

> But now you have spurned and rejected [David];
>
> you are full of wrath against your anointed.
>
> You have renounced the covenant with your servant;
>
> you have defiled his crown in the dust. . . .
>
> How long, O LORD? Will you hide yourself forever?
>
> How long will your wrath burn like fire? . . .
>
> LORD, where is your steadfast love of old,
>
> which by your faithfulness you swore to David? (Ps 89:38–49)

Israel had to find a theology to help them conceptualize God in their current circumstances. The Deuteronomy and Priestly traditions, which blamed the people for their own destruction, were not without their critics, as we saw in the writings of Habakkuk. He questioned the justice of condemning a nation when unknown thousands of righteous and faithful people would be swept up in the tragedy along with the wicked. This issue of justice became a centerpiece for two of the most astonishing books in the Bible. They took Habakkuk's questions and pushed them to their logical conclusions. Walter Brueggemann called them countertestimonies to Israel's witness about God. They accuse God of abandonment and held up the pain of real life experience to confront the theological concepts of Israel's faith. They condemned all the old traditions for inadequately speaking of God in the face of human suffering and for constructing a meaning for human life.

EXCURSUS 6.1

Countertestimonies to Israel's Core Teachings

There are two books in the Old Testament that argue with the rest of the Hebrew Scriptures. They did not debate one aspect of God's actions as we saw in the first two chapters of Genesis, nor is it the case of one writer going back and changing an earlier text. The books of Job and Ecclesiastes argue against the core teachings of Israel's faith. Walter Brueggemann calls them "countertestimonies" and includes with them lament psalms, Lamentations, and a small number of assorted texts.[2]

Job was written during or after the Babylonian exile, capturing the loss and despair that came from the exile. It demands to know where God was when the Babylonians were destroying a whole civilization. It rejects any theology that lays blame upon the people for the disaster they endured. The author uses an old folklore to create a righteous man blessed with an overwhelming bounty of prosperity, who then loses everything. The author of Job borrowed the ancient myth, probably taking some poetic liberties and then composed the major middle section of the book.[3] Three so-called friends—who represent Israel's traditional teachings— visit Job and most of the book is their discussion. Near the end, though, God shows up to have a word with Job.

2. Brueggemann, *Theology of the Old Testament*, 317–403. He proposes a wider circle of counter-testimonial texts, including lament psalms, certain proverbs, portions of Second Isaiah and other texts than is being described in this study. However, Brueggemann's comments about countertestimony are applicable for our more narrow examination. Hanson concludes Job resists his friends who tried to "defend the traditional notion of community based on the doctrine of retribution and belief in a rational, moral universe" (*People Called*, 212).

3. Newsom, "Book of Job," 4:322–29. She dates Job to the early postexilic times, roughly the sixth or fifth centuries BC. There are divergent theories about whether Job originally existed as an older myth, with poetry inserted, or was written by a single author (with the exception of the later Elihu dialogue). Newsom claims to be an agnostic regarding its composition, and is more interested in its canonical form. The character of Job didn't need the Jewish exile to be invented; human suffering is universal. One piece of evidence that stands out is the passage in Ezekiel 14 where the prophet mentions three persons of faith—Noah, Danel and Job. Noah was a pre-Israelite person. Danel was a legendary Canaanite king. Job's pairing with these two would suggest that he, too, was a legendary non-Israelite character of some past day. See also Crenshaw, *Old Testament Wisdom*, 100. He believes that the narrative and the poetry are two separate works, with the poetry being inserted into the older folklore.

Ecclesiastes was written well after the exile at a time when foreign empires had occupied Israel for generations.[4] A philosopher (the Teacher) wrote Ecclesiastes, and he wonders if God interacts with human beings at all. He questions whether religious teachings have any value, if anything has lasting value, or if all of life is simply vanity.

This chapter also includes an exploration of the Song of Songs. This poetic love story is not a countertestimony in the same way as Job or Ecclesiastes. However, as erotic poetry spoken from the mouth of a young woman and her lover it rejects the gender boundaries upon women and the prohibitions regarding sexuality that are found throughout the Hebrew Scriptures. Modern readers may find some of the metaphors in this love poetry unusual and far from erotic. Other metaphors still communicate over two thousand years later and will surprise the reader for its immodesty. The Song of Songs, also called the Song of Solomon, was written during the postexilic period as well. Its inclusion into the canon of the Hebrew Bible created an argument with the Deuteronomy and Priestly texts that regulated boundaries upon women and sexuality.

These three books have the audacity to cross-examine the core teachings of Israel's faith. They force us to consider the value of asking questions.

When Being Good Is Not Enough

The story of Job was an ancient tale concerning a rich man with a large family, who lost everything in a series of calamitous events. Robbers looted his land and business, and murdered his employees. A terrible storm killed all of his children. He lost his health, and suffered in pain. Only his wife survived with him, and she nagged him to "curse God and die" (Job 2:9). Such was the tragedy that befell Job.

At this point a poet inserted what became the bulk of the book. Once the scene had been set, a dialogue ensued between Job and three friends, who visited him in an attempt to console and comfort him. The struggle to understand why these terrible things happened to him, and to anyone who

4. See Hanson, *People Called*, 213, for a fourth-century BC dating of Ecclesiastes. See also Towner, "Book of Ecclesiastes," 5:271. He thinks the fourth century is plausible, but assumes the work was generated in the third century BC. Horne concurs with a third-century dating (*Proverbs-Ecclesiastes*, 374).

identified with him, began. Job was a surrogate for the exiles; his suffering matched their suffering. Job's friends represented the insufficient theologies of Israel's faith. The poetic author used Job's ancient folktale to challenge the conventional views of the day.

The book of Job wants to know where God is when tragedy strikes. Why does God not save humans in times of their greatest need? Job's friends do not believe that God is at fault when tragedy occurs. They believe humans bring suffering upon themselves. Job's plight had to have been due to some sin that he had committed. If Job would confess his sin, repent from his actions, God would restore him. "If you return to the Almighty," Eliphaz tells him, "you will be restored, if you remove unrighteousness from your tents . . . you will pray to him and he will hear you, and you will pay your vows . . . and light will shine on your ways" (22:23–28). This type of thinking was at the heart of Priestly theology. When you sin, you could be restored by making sacrificial offerings and by religious rituals with the priest. Without being cleansed, the unrighteous—Job—would continue to suffer God's punishment.

Job's friends represented a theology of blessing and curses, or rewards and retributions.[5] They believed that God rewarded the righteous with good things and punished the unrighteous with suffering. The genesis of this type of thinking was first seen in Deuteronomy. James Crenshaw notes that the friends are more concerned with themselves than with Job: "The friends' consolation was at least partially self-serving. . . . After all, their religious convictions depend on the reliability of their claim to moral excellence, for they are healthy and prosperous. Their faith requires them to prove that Job has committed some awful crime, for his calamity called for precisely this conclusion. That is why their tolerance gradually fades, and open accusation replaces subtle hints."[6] If Job's suffering had an arbitrary cause, then Job's friends were in danger as well. As long as Job's suffering could be explained in rational, cause-and-effect terms, then it could be avoided. A rational, logical explanation for Job's suffering comforted *them*, even as it angered the unrepentant Job. One scholar noted, "The friends turn their backs on Job as they defend their deeply held beliefs."[7]

After first suffering agony and grief and then accusations by his self-serving, so-called friends, Job challenged Deuteronomy's theology of

---

5. Crenshaw claims that Job's friends appeal to "at least *eight different kinds of authority* in their vain attempt to justify God's ways" (*Old Testament Wisdom*, 113). The idea of reward and retribution was not as simple as we might imagine and was influenced by cultural as well as religious forces.

6. Crenshaw, *Whirlpool*, 70.

7. Humphreys, *Tragic Vision*, 103.

blessing and curse. Job maintained his innocence, or at least his proportional innocence. Job would admit he was not perfect, but he certainly did not do anything deserving the great tragedy that befell him (13:26–28).[8] Notice in the following passages Job carefully declared that he had fulfilled his obligations of justice and devotion. He had followed God's commandments, worshiped only God, cared for the poor, the widow, the orphan and the stranger.

> My foot has held fast to [God's] steps;
>
> > I have kept his way and have not turned aside.
>
> I have not departed from the commandment of his lips;
>
> > I have treasured in my bosom the words of his mouth. (23:11–12)
>
> When I went out to the gate of the city,
>
> > when I took my seat in the square,
>
> the young men saw me and withdrew,
>
> > and the aged rose up and stood . . .
>
> because I delivered the poor who cried,
>
> > and the orphan who had no helper.
>
> The blessing of the wretched came upon me,
>
> > and I caused the widow's heart to sing for joy.
>
> I put on righteousness, and it clothed me;
>
> > my justice was like a robe and a turban.
>
> I was eyes to the blind, and feet to the lame.
>
> > I was a father to the needy,
>
> > > and I championed the cause of the stranger. (29:7–16)

Job defended his life before God: "Here is my signature! Let the Almighty answer me!" (31:35). He told God to make a case against him. If he had broken the commandments, done any of the things God had prohibited, then openly bring charges. Job's poet created an indisputably righteous man, who

---

8. Crenshaw writes, "Job realizes that he committed the usual youthful peccadilloes, but he does not think those innocent mistakes should be held against him now" (*Whirlpool*, 65).

nonetheless suffered greatly, in order to put God on trial.[9] If the righteous suffer, then the idea of divine rewards and retributions based on human behavior is meaningless.

Not only did Job show that the righteous suffer, but to truly add insult to injury, he furiously declared that the wicked prosper (24). The so-called justice of Deuteronomy was a farce! Righteous persons like Job suffered greatly and yet the truly wicked prospered and were granted long life. Job wanted to be put on trial so he could accuse God! The poet who wrote Job discredited the whole theological structure championed by Israel's core teachings. Life had proved how absurd their positions were. Then, he dared them to "prove me a liar" (24:25).

Job was not without criticism for those who advocated a God abounding in steadfast love. God had become an oppressive presence to Job. In a brief parody of Psalm 8, Job wrote:

> What are human beings, that you make so much of them,
>
> > that you set your mind on them, visit them every morning,
>
> > test them every moment?
>
> Will you not look away from me for a while,
>
> > let me alone until I swallow my spittle?
>
> If I sin, what do I do to you,
>
> > you watcher of humanity? (Job 7:17–20)

Far from being a God of love, Job described God as malicious. God did not forgive Job's sins. Instead, God tortured him with nightmares that caused him to desire death over life. Why would his sin even matter to God? Job appealed for mercy, but he did not believe God would respond (9:17–18). There was no future but death. "For there is hope for a tree, if it is cut down, that it will sprout again, and that its shoots will not cease. . . . But mortals die, and are laid low; humans expire, and where are they? . . . They will not awake or be roused out of their sleep" (14:7–14). In rejecting an afterlife, Job would take no solace from apocalyptic Daniel's hope that everything would be worked out in heaven.

While Job effectively tore down the scaffolding of Israel's core teaching, he was not so successful at constructing an alternative. Crenshaw said that this was in part because "Job has no case at all against God apart from

9. Humphreys, *Tragic Vision*, 106–11. He explains the poet's use of a trial metaphor as a context for meaning.

an operative principle of reward and retribution, for in a world devoid of such a principle good people have no basis for complaining that the creator has abandoned the helm and thus allows the ship to wander aimlessly amid submerged rocks."[10] Without the presupposition of a holy, just, or loving God who directs matters, Job was left with a God of mere power. Beginning in chapter 38, God answered Job with an extended monologue, in which God sounded like the Wizard of Oz when Dorothy, Tin Man, Scarecrow, the Cowardly Lion, and Toto first entered his receiving room.

> Who is this that darkens counsel by words without knowledge?
>
> Gird up your loins like a man, I will question you,
>
> And you shall declare to me.
>
> Where were you when I laid the foundation of the earth?
>
> Tell me, if you have understanding. (38:2–4)

Thus begins three chapters of poetry that declares how powerful God is and comparatively how small Job is. God looks like a bully, distant, and overbearing.[11] God's power is undeniable in the monologue, but this was never in question. Job had already attested to God's power in his earlier venting. The question is the compassion of God's justice, or the justice of God's compassion, in the face of human suffering, which God's deep-voiced monologue never addresses.[12] Crenshaw believes that God's silence toward Job's questions is a way for the poet to brush aside the idea that the universe operates on a principle of rationality—as if our ideas of justice, of holiness, of blessing and curse, do not begin to comprehend how the universe works.[13]

Since there was no curtain for Toto to pull back, Job was left to humbly repent in the face of God's overwhelming presence.[14] His confession,

10. Crenshaw, *Whirlpool*, 63.

11. See Ham, "Gentle Voice," 527–41. He offers a more compassionate view of God's response to Job.

12. Humphreys writes that the divine speeches are "non sequiturs." God's questions for Job "take no cognizance of Job's oath and demand, nor of the debate and the issues set out in it. Even the suffering of Job is ignored. It now becomes clearer that the whole book is built of questions, questions upon questions" (*Tragic Vision*, 112).

13. Crenshaw, *Old Testament Wisdom*, 125.

14. Humphreys believes the error Job makes is the typical "hubris of the tragic hero. . . . If not setting himself up as equal to his god, he claims to be at least equal to the task of defining the context into which his god must fit" (*Tragic Vision*, 109). He says the text points to this as well at the beginning of chapter 32, "So these three men ceased to answer Job, because he was righteous in his own eyes" (Job 32:1). This changed after his encounter with God.

however, threw one more jab at the Deuteronomistic and Priestly Writers. "I had heard of you by the hearing of the ear, but now my eye sees you" (42:5). Not only had Job seen God (something that just wasn't done in the D and P collections, because if people saw God they died), but Job shook his fist and dared God to stand up to him. Yet, he saw God and lived to tell about it. God stated that Job had spoken "what is right," while rebuking Job's friends for defending their traditional blessing-and-curse religion. Maybe Job saw God because of, not in spite of, his honest, though irreverent, questioning.

Of course, if that were true, what would be the point of all those religious rituals and behavior scorecards? Exactly. What *would* the point be?

When Having Everything You Want Is Not Enough

Ecclesiastes in many ways is like Job's criticism. However, whereas Job asks the questions of someone who has suffered unjustly, Ecclesiastes is the musing of someone who had every reason to be thankful in life, but instead asks, "Is this all?"[15] As with Job, this Teacher did not speak of Israel's covenant with God, or of God's salvation history for Israel. In Ecclesiastes, God is silent. Brueggemann observes, "There is only silence on Yahweh's part, perhaps to match the resignation and the cold concession of the witness."[16] At best we might learn how God operates through nature and by observing life. Unfortunately, even this proved unsatisfactory. Milton Horne notes that this sage "finds that the once reliable order of the universe, which guaranteed goodness and assured justice, is not in fact reliable in an unqualified sense."[17]

Ecclesiastes declared that God's justice is not evident in life. "In the place of justice, wickedness was there, and in the place of righteousness, wickedness was there as well" (Eccl 3:16). Daily toil, the deeds of humankind, the accumulation of wealth, these are all vanities. After a life of work, we then die like the dogs at our feet. "The same fate comes to all, to the righteous and the wicked, to the good and the evil, to the clean and the unclean, to those who sacrifice and those who do not sacrifice. . . . The living know that they will die, but the dead know nothing; they have no more reward, and even the memory of them is lost" (9:2–6). Where is the justice in that? The teacher had

15. Michael V. Fox writes, "Qoheleth possessed wealth, pleasure and wisdom, but his satisfaction in his achievement is marred by a sense of injustice" ("Wisdom in Qoheleth," 126–27).

16. Brueggemann, *Theology of the Old Testament*, 398.

17. Horne, *Proverbs-Ecclesiastes*, 376. Horne notes that Ecclesiastes begins and ends his book with poems reflecting upon creation and that creation acts as "a theological foundation" for Ecclesiastes, hence, the similarity to the contemporary thought called "natural theology."

hoped in his heart that God would judge the righteous and the wicked, but his observations of life led him to conclude that God is indifferent to the ways of humans, whether righteous or wicked (2:15–17).

The Teacher's questioning broached the absurdity of life. There is no greater cause-and-effect operating in life. One can imagine the Teacher pushing Sisyphus's rock up the hill, only to watch it roll down and start the process all over again until finally the cycle is broken with his death. The Teacher's response is similar to Albert Camus's writings on life's absurdity.[18] "This is what I have seen to be good: it is fitting to eat and drink and find enjoyment in all the toil with which one toils under the sun the few days of the life God gives us" (5:18). Life's mortality adds to the urgency to enjoy the here-and-now. "Go, eat your bread with enjoyment, and drink your wine with a merry heart; for God has long ago approved what you do. . . . Enjoy life with the wife whom you love. . . . Whatever your hand finds to do, do with your might; for there is no work or thought or knowledge or wisdom in Sheol, to which you are going" (9:7–10).

Ecclesiastes tore down the theological framework of Israel's faith. To those who proclaimed God's steadfast love, the teacher concludes God is indifferent to human beings. To the Deuteronomists, who proclaimed God's justice, he asks them to look at people's lives and honestly defend that the righteous are rewarded and the wicked are punished. To the Priests, who proclaimed God's holiness, the teacher remarks that holy or unholy, righteous or unrighteous, all would get the same bed of death in the end.

His criticisms came after generations of unfulfilled promises in the postexilic age. Rebuilt Jerusalem did not look like the prophets' dreams. Persians, then Greeks, ruled the holy city and Jews lived as aliens in their own land. His cynicism evolved generationally. Hopes that God would restore Israel by a righteous remnant had grown stale after centuries of occupation.

18. Albert Camus popularized absurdism in the mid-twentieth century, even though he regretted being attached to that school of thought. His novel *The Stranger* and nonfiction *The Myth of Sisyphus* confronted the idea that life is absurd, but he saw himself separate from the absurdism philosophers. "Si rien n'avait de sens," he wrote in *Second Letter to a German Friend*, "vous seriez dans le vrai. Mais il y a quelque chose qui garde du sens" ("Deuxième letter," *Lettres À Un Ami Allemand*, 42). ("If nothing had meaning, you would be correct. But there is something that still holds meaning.") Despite the belief that death ends our lives and transports us into nonexistence, Camus believed that we could and should enjoy life while we have it.

Love Conquers All

A third countertestimony of the Old Testament is very different from Job and Ecclesiastes. The Song of Songs did not attack the leading theological ideas of Israel's faith. It did not address God's justice, or the meaning of life, though it could be seen as a positive companion to Ecclesiastes.[19] The Song of Songs is a love poem. "The Song is affirming, even boldly so, of human sexuality," says Carey Walsh. "Given the taciturn nature of other biblical materials on sex, the Song is startling, refreshing, even flamboyant. . . . Sexuality and desire are not viewed as problems to repress or punish; nor are they sources of shame."[20]

> He brought me to the banqueting house,
>
> > and his intention toward me was love.
>
> Sustain me with raisins, refresh me with apples;
>
> > for I am faint with love.
>
> O that his left hand were under my head,
>
> > and that his right hand embraced me! (Song 2:5–7)
>
> Upon my bed at night I sought him whom my soul loves . . .
>
> > when I found him whom my soul loves.
>
> I held him, and would not let him go
>
> > until I brought him into my mother's house
>
> > and into the chamber of her that conceived me. (3:1–4)

In speaking of young love, unmarried love, from the voice of lovers—the only place in the Bible spoken from a woman's voice—the Song rejects the Priestly and Deuteronomistic boundaries for women and about sexuality. It directly challenged the misogynistic way Proverbs spoke of female sexuality. It was such a troublesome book to the church that for most of Christianity's history the book was interpreted as an allegory.[21] The young lovers were

19. Weems suggests, "One might argue that the protagonist in Song of Songs accepts the author of Ecclesiastes' invitation and revels in the joys of nature, work, and play when one is in love" ("Song of Songs," 5:364).

20. Walsh, *Exquisite Desire*, 136.

21. See Kingsmill, *Song of Songs*. While an interpretive shift of the Song to a plain reading as love poetry is nearly half a century old, the idea that it could be read allegorically is not completely dead. This recent analysis of the Song attempts to salvage allegorical interpretations along with a plain reading of the poetry.

not portrayed as real people, but as a metaphor for Christ and the church, or God and Israel. (Apparently the poetry was real enough to celibate medieval monks, who made it one of the most frequently read books in monasteries!)[22] Even today, the Song of Songs is rarely studied in Sunday School curriculum. Only one passage (2:8–13) is included in the Common Lectionary. Rarely do pastors preach from its text.[23] And it certainly is not cited for Vacation Bible School!

Phyllis Trible suggests that the Song of Songs reclaims the tragic love story from the garden of Eden.[24] Paradise Lost, as Milton called it, is found in the coupling of these two young lovers. The partnership Adam and Eve lost in the aftermath of the forbidden fruit is recovered in the equality created by shared love. Trible writes, "In the Song, male power vanishes. His desire becomes her delight."[25] Whereas Eve had been shackled by a desire for her husband (Gen 3:16), the young woman in the Song is liberated by mutual desire.

> How fair and pleasant you are, O loved one, delectable maiden!
>
> You are stately as a palm tree, and your breasts are like its clusters. . . .
>
> O may your breasts be like the clusters of the vine,
>
> And the scent of your breath like apples,
>
> And your kisses like the best wine. . . .
>
> I am my beloved's and his desire is for me.
>
> Come my beloved, let us go forth into the fields,
>
> And lodge in the villages. . . .
>
> There I will give you my love. (Song 7:6–13)

This book more than any other in the Bible speaks to the mutuality of lovers and partners. While Eve and Adam had been banished from the garden

22. Murphy, *Word according to Eve*, 113.

23. Judaism does make space for the Song of Songs. It is read on the Passover Sabbath, where Jews are reminded that God saved Israel because God loved Israel. While Judaism makes the Song a part of its annual rituals, it is heard as an allegorical reading of God's love and not as the affections between two young lovers.

24. Trible, *Rhetoric of Sexuality*, 144–65. See also Landy, *Paradoxes of Paradise*. She lays out a thorough thesis that the Song of Songs was written as a response to the Genesis 2–3 story.

25. Trible, *Rhetoric of Sexuality*, 160.

of Eden, the garden of sexual intercourse and partnership was available to
these lovers any time they escaped the restrictions of their family, community, or conventional values and fell into each other's arms.

The Song of Songs calls into question the values of the community,
which restricted a young woman from following the love of her heart and
denied her sexual expression of that love. Her family does not approve of
her actions (1:6; 8:8–9); neither do the night watchmen of her community.
When they find her in the evening at a time no maiden should be out, they
beat her as they would a prostitute for attacking the integrity of the community. Does her torn garment suggest they raped her as well (5:7)?[26] She
refrains from showing public affection of her lover, saving them both from
the wrath of others (8:1). Although, the Song does not quote any of the
prohibitions of the Priests or Deuteronomy, the disapproval of the woman's
family and the community stand as protectors of the accepted boundaries
of sexuality and family. Yet, she will not be bound by them. She will keep
her "own vineyard" (1:6). She risks her family honor, her reputation, and
her health to love the man of her choosing. Renita Weems notes that the
young woman is sexually vivacious, while nearly all other biblical women
are sexually constrained. This poet "speaks openly and immodestly about
her erotic desires, while the latter are portrayed as the archetypal other
whose sexuality must be regulated and guarded against."[27] When the rabbis
added the Song among the Hebrew Scriptures, it became a countertestimony to the sexual prohibitions and the familial boundaries placed upon
women throughout the Bible.

The poetry of the Song proclaims the equality of the two young lovers.[28] The woman asserts herself and initiates her sexual liaisons. Her lover's
desire for her is as strong as her desire for him. The garden of their love casts
aside any secondary role of biblical women. These unmarried lovers elevate
the scandal of the Song's countertestimony. The young maiden does not belong to her lover, nor do her brothers or father control her. She is her own
person, unbounded by convention or patriarchy. As with Ecclesiastes, God's
voice is absent in the Song of Songs. She is liberated not by God's steadfast

26. Weems, "Song of Songs," 5:412.

27. Weems, "Song of Songs," 5:368.

28. Trible notes the level of mutuality in the poetry, "Throughout the Song [the
woman] is independent, fully the equal of the man. Although at times he approaches
her, more often she initiates their meetings. Her movements are bold and open: at night
in the streets and squares of the city she seeks the one whom her [soul] loves (3:1–4). . . .
Never is this woman called a wife, nor is she required to bear children. In fact, to the
issues of marriage and procreation the Song does not speak. Love for the sake of love is
its message" (*Rhetoric of Sexuality*, 161–62).

love, but by the union of her own erotic love with her lover. God has not placed her in a garden's paradise. She has discovered the garden's paradise by her own sexual self-expression. Truly, love is the greatest of powers.

> For love is strong as death, passion fierce as the grave.
>
> Its flashes are flashes of fire a raging flame.
>
> Many waters cannot quench love, neither can floods drown it.
>
> If one offered for love all the wealth of one's house,
>
> it would be utterly scorned. (8:6–7)

Practicing Midrash

These three countertestimonies argue in a different way from our previous explorations. The authors cross-examine the core teachings of Israel's faith in God. In short they reject all the theologies of the Hebrew Bible as being either insufficient to explain suffering, to find meaning in life, or to find the liberation of love. They will not allow the Priests of Judah, the Levites who wrote Deuteronomy, or the collection of writers who spoke of God's steadfast love to go unquestioned. They compare the core teachings of faith with their life experiences and conclude that they are wrong. Both their cynical and suggestive responses invite us into a larger conversation about faith in God.

(1) Free the Stories to Speak for Themselves

The clearest way to hear the critique of these countertestimonies is to accept them as arguments with the dominant voices of the Hebrew Bible. When Job is arguing with his so-called friends, he is arguing with Scripture, or at least Scripture as understood by Job's poet. He declares in the face of tragedy, the inequality of prosperity, or the persistence of wickedness that righteousness in any of its forms is unreliable. In the face of abandonment, he questions God's justice, holiness, and love.

When Ecclesiastes says all is vanity, he is arguing with Scripture. He declares that religious ritual has no enduring meaning, that neither righteousness nor wickedness have any effect upon God, nor does God care for human beings in any tangible way. The best we can do is to enjoy the life that we have—love your family, delight in your work, and find pleasure when you can—for we are all heading toward the meaninglessness of death. At least Job speaks to God and more importantly hears God speak to him. The Teacher does not believe God cares enough about humans to interact with them. The stories of God making covenants with Abraham, Moses, and David have no meaning to the Teacher. He never mentions them. The stories of God interacting with Eve, Sarah, and Miriam were nothing more than vanity to him.

When the Song's poet proclaims the pleasures of the erotic love of an unmarried young woman, she is arguing with Scripture. She rejects the boundaries placed upon women by religious patriarchy, codified at the end of the second creation story in Genesis and numerous commands in Exodus, Leviticus, and Deuteronomy. When her family forbids her love, she escapes to meet her lover. When the night watchmen catch and beat her as a prostitute, she remains undaunted and will not be dissuaded from pursuing her lover. In praising the pleasures of forbidden love, she declares good what had been defined as unholy.

To listen to these countertestimonies is to value the act of questioning. It is to believe that theological truth must not be accepted without question. It is to create a safe space for doubt, for inquiry, and for mystery whenever there is a gap between theological concepts and life experience. To let Job, the Teacher, and the Poet speak for themselves means to resist the temptation to defend the positions of Job's friends, the Teacher's critics, or the young lover's brothers. Instead, it is to try to empathize with these critics, to try to imagine what it would be like to be in their position.

(2) Listen to the Stories as Contrasting Voices of God

It is amazing that the books of Job, Ecclesiastes, and the Song of Songs were included in the canon of the Hebrew Bible. Job and Ecclesiastes's criticisms call into question basic teachings of Israel's faith. The Song provoked religious and cultural values with her suggestive poetry. Those who collected and compiled the revelation of God's word included the voice of these critics and conferred upon them the same status. It is not a level playing field, of course—dozens of stories, commandments, and covenants on one side and three solitary voices on the other. Still, it is remarkable, and it is a missing attribute in the New Testament.

These three voices in God's word provide of a bit of humility. For every prophet sure of his cause, for every ritual that indisputably confers God's salvation, for every command to keep women and sex within boundaries, these voices create doubt and dismiss certainty. The book of Hebrews declared, "Faith is the assurance of things hoped for, the conviction of things not seen" (Heb 11:1). Whatever faith is, it is not certainty.

These countertestimonies remind us of that. They offer the hope of being heard and understood for those searching when religious teachings and life experience deviate rather than synchronize. When the faith in which you have believed no longer provides answers that make sense, these critics give you a divine voice once again. At such times Anne Lamott finds comfort in Wendell Berry's lines, "It may be that when we no longer know what to do, we have come to our real work, and that when we no longer know which way to go, we have begun our real journey. The mind that is not baffled is not employed. The impeded stream is the one that sings."[29] These critics get our faith unstuck with a jolt of doubt, permission to break the rules, or with an angry fist shaking at God. They call us back into the mystery of God, where we may once again enjoy the song of the impeded stream.

These three countertestimonies offer the reader a fresh way to hear the core teachings of Israel. The rocks and branches that clog the river of God's word create the babbling in the brook. We will not read Deuteronomy's justice theology the same way after reading Job. We will read the ending of the Second Creation story differently having read the Song of Songs. We will balance the prophets' hope of God's salvation with the Teacher's cynical conclusion about God's indifference in our minds and reach our own conclusions. The countertestimonies demand that we reread the faith testimonies of Israel with them in mind as we enter the divine dialogue.

(3) Find Where You Want to Join the Divine Conversation

Walter Brueggemann suggested that "tension between the core testimony and the countertestimony is acute and ongoing . . . that this tension between the two belongs to the very character and substance of Old Testament faith, a tension that precludes and resists resolution."[30] The idea that this tension resists resolution is a core thesis of this entire study. One aspect of entering into the divine conversations of any of the Bible's arguments is learning to let go of the need to resolve the Bible's disagreements. We do not need to fix Job as his companions tried to do. We just need to hear him. Neither do we need to fix Deuteronomy or any of the justice prophets—Amos, Micah, or Jeremiah—who spoke of God directly interceding on behalf of the poor and needy. We do need to hear that testimony alongside Job's critique in order to figure out what we believe—individually and in community.

---

29. Wendell Berry, "Poetry and Marriage: The Use of Old Forms," in *Standing by Words* (New York: North Point, 1983); as quoted in Lamott, *Small Victories*, 6.

30. Brueggemann, *Theology of the Old Testament*, 400.

Harold Kushner's *When Bad Things Happen to Good People* brought Job's critique into the households and congregations of thousands of Jews and Christians during the late twentieth century. Rabbi Kushner reflected upon the illness and death of his teenage son through the voice of Job. To make sense of his faith in a loving and just God through the intersection of the tragic death of his son, he concluded that "God can't do everything, but He can do some important things."[31] Kushner refused to believe that God wished ill upon his son, or his grieving family. He gave up on the idea of an all-powerful God in order to cling to an all-loving God.

> I believe in God. But I do not believe the same things about Him that I did years ago, when I was growing up or when I was a theological student. I recognize His limitations. He is limited in what He can do by laws of nature and by the evolution of human nature and human moral freedom. I no longer hold God responsible for illnesses, accidents, and natural disasters, because I realize that I gain little and I lose much when I blame God for those things. . . . The God I believe in does not send us the problem; He gives us the strength to cope with the problem. . . . I believe that God gives us strength and patience and hope, renewing our spiritual resources when they run dry.[32]

Job's critique gave Kushner a way to continue to believe in the love and justice of the God of Abraham, Isaac and Jacob as well as to find comfort in the strength God gave him in the days of his son's illness and following his death. He did not believe in God the same way, but he continued to be a person of deep faith. Kushner's experience was his spiritual journey. The circumstances of where your life experience begins diverging from your theological concepts will be your journey. But his story encourages us to use the countertestimonies to cross-examine the theological ideas of our faith as a way to start that journey.

Job and Ecclesiastes were brutally honest and critically attacked the weaknesses of Israel's great theological ideas. But they offered little in the way of constructive counsel. The best Ecclesiastes advised was to party until you died, which while being fun for a while, may lack the substance most of us are seeking. Job's poet still believed in a powerful God, though a capricious one—killing off the rich man's children, then offering a new

---

31. Kushner, *When Bad Things Happen*, 113–31. "God can't do everything, but He can do some important things" is the title of the second to last chapter in Kushner's book, in which the rabbi works at constructing what faith could look like for a person who had been through Job-like tragedy.

32. Kushner, *When Bad Things Happen*, 134; 127–28.

set to make amends. The countertestimonies serve as a useful check upon biblical certainty, but their skepticism does not offer a positive alternative. That's what Kushner did for himself. At least of the three, the Song's poet offers the freedom and ecstasy of mutual love as a positive alternative to the holiness boundaries meant to protect purity and family. Unfortunately, she is silent about God.

The countertestimonies do not offer a positive alternative in part because they do not want to replace the core teachings of Israel's faith. They simply want to challenge them to be more true to the human experience of loss and longing. The Teacher explained that he was searching for answers till he had exhausted all possibilities he could imagine. Yet, should another way open up it is certain that this seeker would be off on the chase once again. He longed to find satisfaction in Israel's faith. Job begs God for a response, though unfortunately he gets one that does not answer his questions. While he is finally comforted and offered sympathy by those who knew him (Job 42:11), it is hard to imagine that he ever stopped searching. The Song's poet expressed her desire to be allowed to publicly share affection with her lover, to break down the walls, and be out in the open with her love—a longing shared by many who have had to closet their love.

The work of listening to the countertestimonies is to allow them to temper the certainty of the core teachings of Israel's faith while still hearing the confessions of the psalms, prophets, the storytellers, the Priests and the Levites. They remind readers that though those confessions stated God's love, justice and holiness, they also spoke of God's absence (where was the LORD when the serpent began talking to Eve and Adam), unreliability (God's blessing of Joseph seemed to be on and off again), and God's breaking of promises (lament psalms accuse God of not honoring the covenants). The countertestimonies serve as witnesses—through the voice of God's word—that the faithful endure injustice, tragedy, and mortal limits that fall short of a soul's eternal gaze. They force the core teachings to acknowledge human angst.

Finding a place to join this divine conversation may depend on your life situation. If you have been waiting for a liberating voice for women in God's word, the Song of Songs may be a welcome sign. If you have struggled through hardship and doubted God's presence at such times, Job could be an invitation for you to share your questions. Or maybe life has treated you well, but you cannot help but notice in our information age how millions of people experience hardship at no fault of their own. Ecclesiastes gives you permission to ask about meaning in life.

While much of twenty-first-century Christianity has embraced the Song's poet in her advocacy for mutual relationships, an affirmation of sexuality, and freedom for women from cultural and religious restrictions, the longing she and her lover express is very much still a desire to be fulfilled. It was one of the most powerful ways the poetry was read allegorically throughout the church's history. Maybe that is the best way to enter into this divine conversation between Job, Ecclesiastes, the Song of Songs and the core teachings of the Hebrew Bible.

- Where is your heart longing? What questions do you have for God that are not being answered by beliefs you have held?

- Could seeking God through questions take you into a deeper spirituality than one that gives answers? If so, how would you know what that looks like?

- Where does mystery—the gap between your experiences and the beliefs you have held—invite you into a journey, maybe a lifelong journey, of exploration and discovery and further exploration?

- Imagine your faith as a mystery to be explored—like the ancient Polynesians who somehow discovered Hawaii, or Christopher Columbus who sailed the ocean blue in 1492, or Lewis and Clark searching for a northwest passage—in what way would you gather information, interpret the new things you were seeing, and determine your location?

It is also here in longing that the core teachings of Israel and the countertestimonies meet. The messianic hopes of the major theologies of the Old Testament expressed longings every bit as much as the Song's poetry, Ecclesiastes's philosophy, and Job's questioning. Some present Christianity as the fulfillment of those longings, but while Jesus fulfilled many messianic hopes, his arrival did not make everything right in the world, or bring the consummation of history. The last words of the New Testament join the last words of the poet's longing in the Song:

Come, Lord Jesus! (Rev 22:20)

Make haste, my beloved, and be like a gazelle

or a young stag upon the mountain of spices! (Song 8:14)

As we move from one testament to another, we would be wise to hear the countertestimonies not only as a cross-examination of Israel's faith as it had been, but also as a cross-examination of Christianity's faith to come.

CHAPTER 7

Following Jesus

To [the Hebrew] way of thinking, the face of a man is not a front for him to live his life behind but a frontier, the outermost, visible edge of his life in all its richness and multiplicity, and hence they spoke not of the face of a man or of God but of his faces.[1]

—FREDERICK BUECHNER

FOR DECADES MY GRANDFATHER, a bi-vocational pastor (during the week he worked at a manufacturing plant), used *Harmony of the Gospels*, by A.T. Robertson, to prepare sermons for rural congregations in West Virginia and Ohio. Robertson's father-in-law, John Broadus, wrote a harmony in 1893, which was innovative because it gave priority to Mark's gospel. Robertson updated it in 1922 to include "the light of modern synoptic criticism and research into every phase of the life of Christ."[2] Today, that copy holds a special place in my library, and with it my continuing struggle to understand the four messages about Jesus' life and ministry.

As early as the second century, Christians tried to work out the problems created by having multiple accounts of Jesus' life and ministry. Tatian, a Syrian Christian, compiled a composite gospel, called a Diatessaron, in which he weaved the four gospels, and possibly a fifth, together into one narrative. The Lutheran reformer Andreas Osiander first coined the term harmony in 1537 when he arranged the gospels in four parallel columns, comparing them to the pleasant sound of soprano, alto, tenor and bass in four-part harmony.[3] The idea of harmonizing the gospels to solve their divergent voices is almost as old as the Christian church. It

1. Buechner, *Faces of Jesus*, 10.

2. Robertson, *Harmony of the Gospels*, vii.

3. Grobel, "Harmony of the Gospels," 2:525. See also Ehrman, *Jesus Before the Gospels*, 119.

emphasizes the similarities of the gospels, and over time has made us "blind to the differences of these Gospels."[4] There is no doubt that the four separate gospels have plenty of similarities. They all proclaim that Jesus is the Messiah and the Son of God, though they may differ on what those titles mean. Each gospel depicts his humanity and ministry, his death and resurrection. Each speak of God's salvation made possible through Jesus, though they explain that differently.

The harmonies of the gospels, meant to demonstrate the unity of the narratives, also uncover the dissonance in the gospels. The Bible reader that actually compares the gospels one with the other will be confronted with both similarities and differences. Bart Ehrman notes the paradox that the different recollections of Jesus' story create:

> For some readers of the New Testament the different memories of Jesus found throughout its pages are more striking than the similarities. For others, it is the similarities that are both more profound and significant. That is a debate we will never resolve. People simply see things differently. Those who are more analytical tend to see difference; those who are more synthetic tend to see similarity. . . . People [who] read [the Bible] as a single book—especially people who think that rather than having a number of different authors, it has one author, God . . . see unity everywhere and very little diversity. On the other hand, people who focus on the fact that the New Testament has a number of different authors tend to read the book—or rather, the books—differently.[5]

I am certain that when my grandfather used Robertson's *Harmony* he used it to show the unity of God's message in Jesus Christ. My curiosity has been drawn to the disharmony in the gospels, which provides another setting for arguments in the Bible. Therefore, in this chapter and the next we will explore the discord in the gospels, not to sow doubt about the good news, but to fully hear each gospel voice.

4. Colwell, *New or Old*, 55.

5. Ehrman, *Jesus Before the Gospels*, 281–82.

EXCURSUS 7.1

The Six Gospels of Jesus Christ

Even a first-time reader of the New Testament quickly recognizes that the gospels repeat stories about Jesus. The reason is fairly simple. They copied one another. Luke admits doing so in his opening verses.

The most accepted theory is that Mark's gospel was the first of the four to be written. Most scholars place it around AD 70, though some are willing to push that date into the sixties.[6] Mark focused on what Jesus did. He presents a very human Jesus, which led to some disconcerting details that Matthew, Luke, and John later leave out.

Matthew and Luke used Mark's gospel in composing their own. Nearly all of Mark's gospel (94 percent) is in Matthew. Over half of Matthew's text is Mark's gospel, which he copied and altered as he desired. Luke heavily relied on Mark as well, using nearly 80 percent of Mark's text in his own. Also embedded inside Matthew and Luke, but not in Mark, is a shared common source that comprised about a quarter of each of those gospels. Scholars call it Q, which is short for *quelle*, the German word for source. Think of this collection of Jesus' teachings as a hidden gospel inside Matthew and Luke. It may have been written as early as Mark.[7] Though this sayings gospel has never been found, it explains the shared material within Matthew and Luke's gospels.[8] A second, but less accepted, theory is that Matthew was written second, then Luke copied from both Mark and Matthew, and Q never existed.[9] For the purposes of this study, it does not really matter whether Q existed or not. The arguments between the texts remain; only the names of the authors would change. With that in mind, I will work under the theory that Q was a second source for Matthew and Luke.

---

6. Garland, *Theology of Mark's Gospel*, 81–82; Brown, *Introduction*, 127; Perkins, "Gospel of Mark," 8:517–18; Griffith-Jones, *Four Witnesses*, 61–67.

7. Brown, *Introduction*, 122. He makes the point that since Matthew and Luke both use Mark and Q, "it is not unreasonable to assume Q is as old as Mark," but it cannot be proved that one is older than the other.

8. Tuckett, "Jesus and the Gospels," 8:75–76; Brown, *Introduction*, 116–22; Ehrman, *Apocalyptic Prophet*, 80–82.

9. Mosbo, *Luke the Composer*, 11–14, 120–21. The Farrer Hypothesis was proposed by Austin Farrer in the 1950s. It has been more recently been championed by Goodacre, *Case against Q*, 2002.

Matthew and Luke also brought unique material to their gospels. About 20 percent of Matthew is unique, while over a third is in Luke. How Matthew and Luke changed Mark and Q along with their unique passages suggest clues about their theology. Luke also wrote a second volume, the book of Acts, which gives us significantly more material to analyze Luke's perspective. The general consensus is that Matthew and Luke were both written around AD 80.[10]

John's gospel developed an original framework. Though he did not copy any other gospel word for word, it is reasonable to suspect he had a copy of Mark and/or Luke, given many of their shared details, particularly during the events of Holy Week.[11] Another theory about John is that he shared pre-gospel texts with Mark and Luke, instead of actually having copies of Mark and Luke.[12] When using other material John felt much freer to change the story than Matthew and Luke had been. Scholars date his gospel as early as AD 80 and as late as AD 120.

Thomas is a sixth gospel worth noting. Though not included in the New Testament it contains many sayings from Q that are in Matthew and Luke, which gives us another way to see how Christian communities repeated these stories.[13] Thomas collected Jesus' teachings; its existence as a book of sayings models how Q might have looked.[14] Elaine Pagels suggested that John was written, in part, to refute the *Gospel of Thomas*.[15]

10. Ehrman, *Apocalyptic Prophet*, 82; Brown, *Introduction*, 172, 226.

11. Bruce, *Gospel of John*, 5; Tuckett, "Jesus and the Gospels," 8:76–77.

12. Dodd, *Historical Tradition*, 423–32. Dodd uses a substantial analysis to conclude John did not have copies of the Synoptics, though possibly shared earlier sources. "The evidence of the few passages which suggest *prima facie* literary dependence of the Fourth Gospel upon the others in the Passion narrative is not sufficient to prove such dependence" (*Historical Tradition*, 150). See also Brown, *Introduction*, 365; O'Day, "Gospel of John," 9:502.

13. Miller, *Complete Gospels*, 315; Borg, *Lost Gospel Q*, 102–3; and Crossan, *Sayings Parallels*, 152.

14. Goodacre, *Case against Q*, 170–84. While noting that Thomas's discovery in the mid-twentieth century bolstered Q theory, Goodacre thinks that a close study of Thomas supports the Farrar theory that Luke copied Matthew and no Q existed. "[Q's] similarity to Thomas is the relatively superficial one that it is largely constituted by sayings material; it is its difference from Thomas that provides us with the clue about Q's true nature, that what we have here is no more and no less than the material extrapolated from comparison between the non-Markan elements common to Matthew and Luke" (*Case against Q*, 184).

15. Pagels, *Beyond Belief*, 30–73.

While theories on the gospels continue to redevelop, all of them point to a multilayered direct or indirect interaction between the gospels, including Thomas. This interaction presents a platform from which we can see their disagreements and similarities.

The fact that the New Testament begins with four competing gospels, four versions of Jesus' life and ministry, should be a clue that there will be disagreements about understanding and following Jesus. Luke begins his gospel by saying as much: "Since many have undertaken to set down an orderly account of the events that have been fulfilled among us . . . I too decided after investigating everything carefully from the very first, to write an orderly account for you, most excellent Theophilus, so that you may know the truth concerning the things about which you have been instructed" (Luke 1:1–4). Luke did not want to write another account; he wanted to write the truth about Jesus, an improved account. If he had been satisfied with Mark's version he would have sent Theophilus a copy of Mark's Gospel and been done with it.[16] Instead, he wanted his viewpoint to be the glue that pasted his collection of accounts together. Luke was not alone. Indeed, the gospels found in the last century indicate Luke was right. The gospels of Thomas and Judas are among the two dozen that have drawn a great interest.[17] Within the New Testament Luke and Matthew, Paul and James, John and Mark each wrote their "accounts of the events that have been fulfilled." As we read their accounts we will begin to see some of the same arguments that we saw in the Old Testament. Here, as there, writers act to counterbalance one another. If Buechner's reflection on how the Old Testament used a plural form of the word face is helpful, hearing the different voices about Jesus may open us to the full "richness and multiplicity" behind what was once a solitary face.

Following Jesus

Jesus is a busy man in Mark's gospel. He heals, cures, commands wind and sea, teaches, debates, travels and finally dies and lives again. *Immediately* was one of Mark's favorite words. He used it more than twenty-five times, fully one-fourth of all the times it is used in the Bible. Immediately described Jesus' urgency as he moves from one event to the next. What Jesus

16. Ehrman, *Apocalyptic Prophet*, 46–47. He notes that Luke's statement is rather bold considering he used Mark. When he says he is writing so others will "know the truth," he is implying that Mark did not tell the whole truth.

17. See Miller, *Complete Gospels*, for a reading and overview of the noncanonical gospels.

does dominates the narrative. Jesus does more than he talks in Mark. The memorable parables he told are absent in Mark. There is no Prodigal Son, or Good Samaritan. There is no Sermon on the Mount. This is an action-packed gospel. It focuses on God's actions through Jesus.

"The kingdom of God is near," were Jesus' first words (Mark 1:15). When he does talk in Mark the kingdom is on his mind. Perhaps the coming kingdom made him urgent. "There are some standing here who will not taste death until they see that the kingdom of God has come with power" (9:1; cf. 13:30). The clock is ticking. Jesus calls his disciples by saying, "Follow me," with no instructions, no persuasive sales pitches, no teachings. "Immediately," Mark says, they left everything and followed him (1:16–20; 2:14). In Mark the emphasis in discipleship is always on Jesus, not on the disciple, or the disciple-reader.[18]

The Markan Jesus imparts few ethical standards for disciples to keep. He dismisses or diminishes the Sabbath and dietary rules of the Mosaic law. While there are no specific requirements, discipleship in Mark means to dedicate your life to following Jesus. "If any want to become my followers, let them deny themselves and take up their cross and follow me. For those who want to save their life will lose it, and those who lose their life for my sake, and for the sake of the gospel, will save it" (8:34–35). "Whoever wants to be first must be last of all and servant of all" (9:35). The high cost of following Jesus is addressed in the story of the rich man (10:17–31) who asks Jesus, "What must I do to inherit eternal life?" When he professes to have kept the law all his life, Jesus tells him to sell his possessions and come follow him. The man, who was rich, walks away. Then, Jesus tells his disciples it will be hard for the wealthy to enter the kingdom of God. Surprised, they ask, "Then who can be saved?" To which Jesus says, "For mortals it is impossible, but not for God; for God all things are possible."

Discipleship in Mark is a paradox. Disciples give their whole lives to follow Jesus, though nothing they do can earn God's salvation. Correspondingly, God, for whom all things are possible, can grant it to anyone. Faith is the centerpiece of discipleship. It makes miracles possible. When Jesus visits his hometown, he can only do a few miracles because of their lack of faith—predictably Matthew changes that verse to say that Jesus *chose not* to do any miracles (Mark 6:5; Matt 13:58). Furthermore, Mark shows that faith can be given by God and provided to those who lack it. When the disciples cannot heal a boy with seizures the father turns to Jesus, "If you are able to do anything . . . help us." Indignant, Jesus responds, "If you are able!" Then, puts the burden back on the father, "All things can be done for the one who believes."

18. Garland, *Theology of Mark's Gospel*, 263–65.

It is the father's lack of faith, not Jesus' ability, which prohibits his son's health. To which the father immediately responds, "I believe; help my unbelief!" The boy is healed (Mark 9:14–29). If you lack faith, it can be provided. If you have faith without doubt you can move mountains (11:22–24).

Matthew emphasizes faith almost as much as Mark does, but he does not believe faith alone is enough. Matthew as well as Luke includes a collection of Jesus' teachings from a source scholars call Q. In these teachings disciples have a code of conduct to follow. What they do validates their faith in Jesus. "Not everyone who says to me 'Lord, Lord,' will enter the kingdom of heaven, but only the one who does the will of my Father in heaven" (Matt 7:21).

Early in Mark's gospel Jesus says, "No one puts new wine into old wineskins; otherwise, the wine will burst the skins, and the wine is lost, and so are the skins; but one puts new wine into fresh wineskins" (Mark 2:22). Luke counterbalances Mark's emphasis on the new, "And no one after drinking old wine desires new wine, but says, 'The old is good'" (Luke 5:39). In Matthew Jesus treasures both old and new, "Every scribe who has been trained for the kingdom of heaven is like the master of a household who brings out of his treasure what is new and what is old" (Matt 13:52). Matthew and Luke wanted to preserve the old Mosaic law by embracing Jesus' new way of interpreting it. Jesus did not "come to abolish the law or the prophets" but to "fulfill" them (5:17). The Sermon on the Mount is set up to establish Jesus as the new Moses. He uses a formulaic phrase, "You have heard that it was said . . . but I say to you" six times, and in each case he takes a statement from the law and reinterprets it. Raymond Brown observes, "The Matthean Jesus presents God's demand not by dispensing with the Law but by asking for a deeper observance."[19] Each time the Markan Jesus dismisses or diminishes the cultic rituals of the Mosaic law, Matthew alters the text. "The Law must be upheld," notes Robin Griffith-Jones. "Matthew's Jesus relaxes no command that was issued with the authority of Moses."[20]

Discipleship in Matthew involves much more than faith. In Mark Jesus is a busy man; in Matthew disciples are busy. To follow Jesus means keeping the law as well. "For truly I tell you, until heaven and earth pass away, not one letter, not one stroke of a letter, will pass from the law until all is accomplished" (Matt 5:18). Only those who forgive and are merciful can receive God's acts of mercy and forgiveness. Disciples who hear Jesus' teachings and act on them will be like the person who built a house on solid rock,

19. Brown, *Introduction*, 179.
20. Griffith-Jones, *Four Witnesses*, 162.

while those who hear Jesus' teachings but do not act on them will be like the person who built a house on shifting sands (7:24–27).

EXCURSUS 7.2

Exchanging One Parable for Another

Both Mark and Matthew record Jesus telling three parables about seeds within a single chapter. Jesus told the Parable of the Sower first, and the Parable of the Mustard Seed last. Between those came two different, but similar parables. Mark records the Parable of the Growing Seed (Mark 4:26–29). Matthew either replaces it with another parable, or changes it into another parable—the Parable of the Weeds (Matt 13:24–30).

Mark 4:26–29	Matthew 13:24–30
"The kingdom of God is as if someone would scatter seed on the ground."	"The kingdom of heaven may be compared to someone who sowed *good* seed in his field."
The farmer sleeps.	The farmer and workers sleep.
	An enemy sows weeds among the wheat.
The seed sprouts.	The plants bear and grain; then the weeds appear.
The farmer does not know how it grows.	The farmer knows "an enemy has done this."
The earth produces. The plants bear grain.	The farmer lets the wheat and weeds grow.
When the grain is ripe, the farmer harvests the wheat.	The weeds are collected and burned; the wheat is harvested.

While Matthew does not directly follow Mark the details in the two parables are very similar. Seed is planted. There is sleep. Seed grows. Grain appears. Harvest is reaped. The only difference is that weeds are inserted into the story. This addition changes Mark's parable. The farmer, who does not know how the seed grows while she sleeps, is full of knowledge in Matthew's parable. She knows an enemy has planted weeds, but that pulling the weeds would inadvertently "uproot the wheat along with them." Whereas the earth produces the plant in Mark, which is a sign of grace, in Matthew an enemy produces the weeds, which means judgment must follow.

Since Matthew needs a contrast to the enemy that sows weeds, his
farmer sows good seed, whereas in Mark there is no adjective that
describes the seed.

The way Matthew rewrites the Parable of the Growing Seed from
Mark's gospel, turning it into the Parable of the Weeds, exhibits this main
difference between the two. Both parables begin the same way with seed
being sown and a night's rest coming to the farmers. The farmer's sleep in
Matthew, however, becomes an opportunity for an enemy to plant weeds
among his wheat. Later in Matthew's chapter Jesus explains the parable and
identifies the good seed from the weeds. The good seed are "the children
of the kingdom," while the weeds are evildoers and sinners who are ille-
gitimately mixed in with the kingdom's children (Matt 13:38). They will be
thrown in the "furnace of fire, where there will be weeping and gnashing of
teeth" (13:42). Mark's parable suggests that all seeds will sprout and grow
and be harvested. Matthew turns a parable of grace into a parable of judgment. It serves as a warning to people in the church who are not meeting the
standards of discipleship.

John's gospel had a clear message. Those who believed in Jesus Christ by
name shall have eternal life. John is adamant that it is *in Jesus' name* whereby
one receives salvation. John explains that his stories were "written so that
you may come to believe that Jesus is the Messiah, the Son of God, and that
through believing you may have life in his name" (John 20:31). Believing in
Jesus' name means to believe the correct things about him.

John's gospel is unique among the four. His style of writing was more
reflective than the Synoptics. Rudolf Bultmann said that while speeches in
the Synoptics "are mostly sayings strung on a string, in John they are coher-
ent discussions on a definite theme."[21] Whereas Luke and Matthew usually
copy Mark and Q closely, John freely uses a few selected stories from Mark
and Luke to suit his purposes. Richard Hays notes that John cited the Old
Testament far less than the Synoptics, but this is partly due to fewer and longer episodes.[22] John leaves out a lot of events and details from the Synoptic
Gospels. Jesus is not baptized in John, nor does he face temptation in the
wilderness. There are no parables in John, and there is only one commandment. No longer does Jesus preach about the coming kingdom of God. It
is mentioned only twice, both during Jesus' conversation with Nicodemus

21. Bultmann, *Theology of the New Testament*, 4.

22. Hays, *Scripture in the Gospels*, 284. He tabulates gospels references to the Old
Testament as follows: "Matthew, 124; Mark, 70; Luke, 109; and John 27."

(3:3, 5), whereas in the Synoptic Gospels it is mentioned 121 times. Curiously, the following are also missing in John: poor people, widows, children, women travelers with Jesus, prostitutes, and the wicked rich.[23]

Whereas Mark emphasizes faith with little specificity, John wants to define correct belief in Jesus. Having faith is not enough in John. In fact the word faith is never used in John, which is surprising since it was central to understanding how to follow Jesus in Mark and essential in Matthew and Luke as well.[24] Followers must believe in Jesus' name. John mentions *believing in Jesus* twenty times in his gospel, and the verb *to believe* is used ninety-five times. Knowing and believing in Jesus is the most important thing to him.[25] Salvation comes by believing that Jesus is the Son of God, fully human and fully divine, the Jewish Messiah who is one with the Father.

The four gospels present three different ways in which persons may follow Jesus and become his disciples. In the Gospel of Mark, disciples put their faith in God and follow Jesus with their whole lives. Matthew, as well as Luke, affirms this trust and faith in Jesus, but adds that disciples must also adhere to the law as reinterpreted by Jesus. Disciples who listen to Jesus' words but do not do them will not be received into the kingdom. John takes another path, focusing specifically on words. Disciples believe in Jesus' name, meaning they believe certain things about Jesus. John's gospel is the beginning of orthodoxy—believing the right things about God brings eternal life. Salvation in John is knowledge, or belief. In Matthew and Luke, it is action. While in Mark salvation is faith.

Practicing Midrash

It is difficult to hear each of the four unique gospel voices. The tendency is to conflate the gospel stories into a composite picture when thinking of Jesus. That was the point when the early church created the Diatessaron—a narrative that merged the gospels into one story—which remained popular into the Middle Ages. The later harmonies of the gospels placed the texts parallel to each other in order to help readers and scholars create a complete portrait of Jesus. When Mel Gibson produced *The Passion of Christ*, he merged the gospels together to create one storyline. This study, however, asks us to view the gospels on a split screen, to watch Jesus' story unfold

23. Colwell, *New or Old*, 65.

24. Colwell, *New or Old*, 59, 64–65, 78.

25. Colwell, *New or Old*, 72. Colwell states that John used the verb "to believe" 95 times and the verb "to know" 133 times in his gospel. Yet, the noun "faith" (*pistis*) is never used.

separately from different perspectives at the same time. As we did with passages from the Hebrew Bible let us allow the gospels to practice midrash by arguing with one another.

(1) Free the Stories to Speak for Themselves

One of the consistent changes Matthew and Luke make in Mark's gospel when they recopied it was to remove negative statements about the disciples or Jesus. When Jesus tells the disciples the Parable of the Sower, they do not understand it and Jesus wonders if they will understand other parables (Mark 4:13). In the story of Jesus walking on water, the disciples were "utterly astounded" and did not understand what Jesus was trying to teach them because their "hearts were hardened" (6:51–52). Misunderstanding Jesus' messianic purpose, James and John ask to be his second in command when he becomes king, leading to an argument when the other disciples find out that James and John were trying to grab power for themselves (10:35–45). Matthew and Luke cut out these criticisms in their gospels. Matthew even points the finger at James and John's mother, who comes out of nowhere to take the blame for her sons' lust for power (Matt 20:20). There are at least seventeen instances in which Matthew and/or Luke either remove or mitigate the disciples' lack of faith, fear, or misunderstanding of Jesus as recorded in Mark. (There are another fourteen instances where Matthew and/or Luke alter disconcerting statements about Jesus in Mark.) Mark consistently shows the disciples to be flawed. They follow Jesus imperfectly.

We saw a similar storytelling style in how Samuel portrayed King David and how the Storyteller wrote tales about Abraham, Jacob, and Joseph. In those cases God's steadfast love embraces the flawed hero. A similar dynamic is at play in Mark's gospel. God makes salvation possible for mortals, which is impossible for them alone (Mark 10:27). Those who are not actively against Jesus are for Jesus (9:40). And when you find your faith lacking, cry out, "I believe; help my unbelief" (9:24). When people considering Jesus read Mark's gospel, they find that Jesus' disciples are just as flawed and full of doubt as they are. Nonetheless Jesus invites them to follow him completely—to carry their cross and be servants to all. Absent are ethical or moral commandments. When a scribe of the Mosaic law states that loving God with your whole being and loving your neighbor as yourself "is much more important than all the whole burnt offerings and sacrifices," Jesus tells him that he is "not far from the kingdom of God" (12:33–34).

Matthew, Luke, and John will try to correct what they thought was lacking or wrong in Mark. When reading their additions to Mark's gospel it is natural to start developing a composite view of Jesus in our minds. To do so, however, violates Mark's message. It erases his emphasis that following Jesus is found in this mysterious idea of faith—a concept that is beyond a mere affirmation of belief and embodied by the way we live our lives, yet which will not be bound by any ethical, ritual, or moral scorecard.

Let Mark's Jesus speak to you absent the noise of the other gospels. Simultaneously, listen to the differences in the way Jesus speaks in the other gospels. Watch the way, for instance, that Matthew changes Mark's story of when the rich man meets Jesus. Both Matthew (19:16–30) and Luke (18:18–30) follow Mark (10:17–31) closely in retelling this encounter. Luke's minor changes do not alter its meaning, so he will sit this argument out.

A rich man approaches Jesus, asking, "What must I do to inherit eternal life?" In Mark Jesus says, "You know the commandments," and then repeats five of the Ten Commandments as well as adding a command not to defraud, which is not in the Decalogue.[26] Matthew changes Jesus' statement to read, "If you wish to enter into [eternal] life, keep the commandments." He also removed the incorrect addition about fraud. The young man pushes Jesus to be explicit, "Which ones?" This heightens the importance of Jesus' answer in Matthew. According to the Matthean Jesus, if you want to enter eternal life keep the Ten Commandments. In Mark, Jesus' reference to the Decalogue begins his conversation with the young man, whereas in Matthew it becomes a final answer to his question. Therefore, while the young man's response is the same in both gospels, "I have kept all these," his answer takes the conversation in divergent directions in the two gospels.

Mark tells us that Jesus looked at him and loved him. He is the only person Jesus loved in the Synoptic Gospels. Does Jesus love him because he is sincere and faithful? Does Jesus love him because he is naïve and blind to his own flaws, believing he has faithfully kept the commandments when Jesus knows his lack of generosity has defrauded both the poor and God? Whatever the case Jesus invites him to join his disciples. Like them, he will have to leave everything to follow him. They dropped their fishing nets and a tax collection booth; he must leave behind his possessions and give his wealth to the poor.

26. Hicks, "Markan Discipleship," 179–99. The reference to defraud could be a citation to Malachi 3, in which there is both a proclamation of a messenger who will prepare the way for the messiah and also a rebuke of those who defraud. Mark cited Malachi's verse about God's messenger in ch. 1, v. 2, but incorrectly attributed it to Isaiah. Now, he takes a reference about fraud and acts as if it is part of the Ten Commandments. This makes two inaccurate references from the same chapter in Malachi, a curious coincidence. When Mark's Jesus includes this additional commandment he may be indicating that the young man's riches are ill-gotten gains, or even if legally gained have defrauded both the poor and God by his lack of generosity.

Matthew cuts out the comment about Jesus loving the young man as he usually does when Jesus shows emotion in Mark. It is the young man, not Jesus, who questions what he still lacks, as if he does not believe that keeping the Ten Commandments is enough. The Matthean Jesus says, "If you wish to be perfect," and then tells him to sell his possessions and follow. The shift is subtle and significant. In Mark, the young man's allegiance to his wealth was a barrier to following Jesus and consequently entering eternal life. In Matthew, Jesus tells the young man eternal life can be achieved by keeping the Mosaic law, as he had already done. He, therefore, did not lack anything. His wealth was a barrier to perfecting the law. Following Jesus included the task of following Moses, for Jesus came not to abolish the law, but to fulfill it.

Jesus' teachings in Matthew's Sermon on the Mount portray Jesus as a new Moses, who redefines the law. "Unless your righteousness exceeds that of the scribes and the Pharisees," who diligently but incorrectly observed the law according to Matthew, "you will never enter the kingdom of heaven" (Matt 5:20). His retelling of the rich man's encounter with Jesus conformed to the emphasis he placed on the continued observance of the law for the Christian church.

John's problem with Mark had nothing to do with keeping the Mosaic law. John wanted to define Mark's generic focus on faith. John wanted to make sure the faithful believed specific things about Jesus. Jesus talks a lot in John. However, Jesus' sayings in John were mostly about himself.[27] Where Matthew, Luke, Q, and to a lesser degree Mark recorded numerous commandments from Jesus, John is nearly devoid of them because he did not believe that faithful actions, or good deeds, were important to salvation. John does not define sin as bad morals in which forgiveness and good deeds are the antidote. Sin is the refusal to believe in Jesus. Gail O'Day explains, "Sin is defined not by what one does, but almost exclusively by one's relationship to Jesus, and more specifically, by whether one believes that God is present in Jesus."[28] Therefore, only believing in Jesus' name brings salvation. This is why Jesus spends most of his time in John's gospel explaining what disciples are to believe about him, not how they should live. John introduced a handful of

27. Ehrman notes, "In these earlier Gospels, Jesus constantly proclaims the Kingdom of God and urges people to live in ways that are appropriate to it. Not in John. Jesus does not talk about the coming kingdom here. He talks about himself, who he is" (*Jesus Before the Gospels*, 262).

28. O'Day further suggests, "This flies in the face of views that want to define sin in relation to right actions and thereby establish the norms for judgment." ("Gospel of John," 9:664). See also Kruse, who stated, "In John the fundamental sin is unbelief" ("Paul and John," 207).

new images and titles for Jesus—living water, bread of life, good shepherd, resurrection and the life, the way, the truth, and the life—as if the old titles and old expectations could not tell the whole truth about him.[29]

The emphasis on beliefs about Jesus created a couple of ironies in John. The gospel kept repeating that Jesus spoke the words of God. However, he never recounted "a message delivered to him by God."[30] In a similar manner disciples were told to obey Jesus' commandments, but with one exception Jesus never taught them any commandments. In John the words of God were less important than the belief that Jesus was the Word of God (John 1:1).

(2) Listen to the Stories as Contrasting Voices of God

The evidence that the gospels describe three different ways to follow Jesus goes beyond the gospels themselves. The early church struggled to define just what Christian salvation, discipleship, and following Jesus meant. There are echoes of the gospel arguments elsewhere in the New Testament.[31]

Mark did not think the whole Mosaic law was essential to following Jesus—loving God with your whole being and your neighbor as yourself "is much more important than all the whole burnt offerings and sacrifices" (Mark 12:33). This emphasis on faith, coupled with a disregard of the law, created a gospel that reinforced Pauline theology. Paul came to believe that Judaism as he knew it had become a religion based on doing good deeds and keeping certain rituals, what he called "works of the law."[32] While Paul preached a gospel proclaiming Christian salvation by grace through faith alone, Mark told the story of that gospel. Arguing that Mark portrayed Jesus preaching a gospel of salvation by faith is no different from recognizing that Paul proclaimed the same. While Mark wrote the first gospel his words

29. Griffin-Jones, *Four Witnesses*, 351. Griffin-Jones says that the old titles did not provide the answers for people asking, "Who is this Jesus?" What matters is not just the new titles found in John, but the importance that each one has in revealing Jesus' true nature and thereby revealing God's true nature.

30. Thompson, *God of the Gospel of John*, 237.

31. Kruse explains, "Within the New Testament there is evidence for three major streams of early Christianity. It is widely recognized that expressions of Christianity in the Jerusalem church differed significantly from its expression in the churches founded by Paul. . . . There is evidence for a third stream of early Christianity, one represented in the NT by the Gospel and letters of John (and some would add Revelation)" ("Paul and John," 197–98).

32. Crossan and Reed, *In Search of Paul*, 220–21. They argue that Paul did not give his fellow Jewish devotees a fair hearing, and has suggested Paul called for "faith-works" as opposed to "law-works."

remain as a witness debating Matthew, Luke, and John as surely as Paul argued with his opponents.

The argument that Matthew started when he altered Mark's gospel and added numerous passages from Q, making Jesus into a new Moses, matches the argument that James took up against Paul. Both thought the idea of faith alone to be insufficient as a practice of discipleship. They had a similar understanding of Jesus' teachings. James makes nineteen references to Jesus' sayings in his short book; they are all found in Matthew.[33] Matthew's Jesus states that only those who do the will of God, who are doers of Jesus' words and not hearers only, will enter the kingdom of heaven. Matthew was not against faith; he just thought that faith required obedience to God's commandments. One place we can see this is how Matthew changes the Parable of the Banquet (Matt 22:1–14; Luke 14:15–24) from its original version in Q. The *Gospel of Thomas* also tells the story, which allows us to compare three versions; Matthew, Luke, and Thomas. There are two reasons to conclude Matthew significantly rewrites the parable: (1) Thomas's version is a close parallel to Luke's, making it more likely that they closely followed the original in Q, and (2) Matthew's middle section of the parable disrupts the flow of the narrative to the extent that it hardly makes sense, making it unlikely this was the original version.

A rich man plans a feast and invites a number of guests. On the day of the banquet servants scatter across town to tell the guests that the feast will be beginning shortly. Surprisingly, the guests each offer lame excuses and inform the servants that they will not be attending. The rich man furious at being snubbed tells his servants to go out into the streets and bring in the poor and outcast. His food will not go to waste and those who dishonored him will not enjoy the party. At this point in Thomas the story ends. Luke adds another dose of grace and sends his servants back out into the streets with instructions to "compel people to come in, so that my house may be filled" (Luke 14:23).

In Matthew's version the rich man becomes a king, who sends his troops back to the invited, but ungracious, guests to destroy them and burn down their city—all while the feast is cooking in the oven. Despite these substantial changes, Matthew also reaches a point in the story where the servants "went out into the streets and gathered all whom they found, both

---

33. Donelson, *Hebrews to Revelation*, 41–42; Brown, *Introduction*, 734–35. My sum of nineteen references is a conflation of their charts, which agree on most verses. The fact that James talks about the poor instead of the "poor in spirit" as Matthew does may indicate that James' source for Jesus sayings came before Matthew altered Q's version of the Beatitudes. Brown suggests that his source was an early "Jesus tradition of the type that Matthew knew, similar to Q" (*Introduction*, 736).

good and bad; so the wedding hall was filled with guests" (Matt 22:10). Luke's version ended here. Matthew adds a new ending that changes the whole meaning of Jesus' parable. The host walks through the banquet hall, notices a man not wearing the proper attire, and asks, "Friend, how did you get in here without a wedding robe?" Given that the poor and outcast filled the house, it is an odd expectation that they would be well dressed, but Matthew's version has already pushed details beyond reason. Then the host tells his attendants to bind him and throw him into the "outer darkness, where there will be weeping and gnashing of teeth" (22:11–13).

What was first a parable of grace, where the kingdom of God is opened to outcasts, Matthew turns into a parable of judgment in which a former outcast, feasting at the banquet, is thrown to a worse fate. Those who come to the church through faith in Jesus must also put on proper clothing. This new ending repeats the conclusion Matthew created when he changed the former Parable of the Growing Seed into the Parable of the Weeds.

So, what is a disciple supposed to wear at the kingdom's banquet? Well, the Sermon on the Mount is a good place to start. The book of James would say that faith without works is dead. Matthew did not use those words, but apparently faith without action makes for a bad wardrobe, which will get you kicked out of the kingdom's banquet.

The Johannine Letters support the Gospel of John's emphasis on believing correctly about Jesus. To believe in Jesus' name meant that you believed in orthodox beliefs about Jesus. (The Greek word *orthodox* means *right praise*, but is usually translated as *right belief*.) These beliefs included that Jesus is the Son of God, and one with the Father; that Jesus is fully divine and fully human; and is the Jewish Messiah. You must believe all these things about Jesus or your belief in Jesus is not valid.

John significantly altered the way Mark and Luke recorded the events from Palm Sunday to Easter. The brief story of Jesus before Pilate is worth our review (Mark 15:1–5; John 18:28–38). Once betrayed by Judas, Jesus was first taken to the high priest and the Jewish Council, who found him guilty of blasphemy. The next morning, Friday, they take him to Pilate, the Roman governor of Jerusalem and surrounding Judea.

In both Mark and John, Pilate asks him, "Are you the King of the Jews?" The Markan Jesus replies, "You say so."[34] Then the chief priests, who were in the room with Pilate, accuse him of many things. Pilate cuts them

34. Schwiebert, "Jesus's Question to Pilate," 937–47. He makes the case that Jesus responds to Pilate's question with a question, "Do you say so?" This is consistent with Jesus elsewhere in Mark. It makes his response more ambiguous as well as throwing the decision back on Pilate. "Who do you say that I am?" is a question Jesus poses to his disciples at the turning point in Mark's gospel. Now at a key moment in fate he tosses a similar question to Pilate. And the reader is forced to ask the question for himself/herself.

off and asks Jesus, "Have you no answer? See how many charges they bring against you." Mark concludes the episode by saying, "But Jesus made no further reply, so that Pilate was amazed."

When Pilate asks the Johannine Jesus, "Are you the King of the Jews?" Jesus is not silent. He tells Pilate, "My kingdom is not from this world. If my kingdom were from this world, my followers would be fighting to keep me from being handed over to the Jews. But as it is, my kingdom is not from here."

"So you are a king?" Pilate responds. To which Jesus says, "You say that I am a king," echoing his brief response in Mark, and then continues, "For this I was born, and for this I came into the world, to testify to the truth. Everyone who belongs to the truth listens to my voice." And Pilate asks, "What is truth?" Only then does the Johannine Jesus go silent.

By this point in Mark Jesus is in the midst of becoming a victim, swept up by events that he is now powerless to stop if he wished. His silence before Pilate recalls a prophecy in Isaiah regarding the Suffering Servant, who "like a lamb that is led to the slaughter . . . so he did not open his mouth . . . because he poured out himself to death, and was numbered with the transgressors; yet he bore the sin of many and made intercession for the transgressors" (Isa 53:7, 12). The Markan Jesus chooses the cross and its suffering. He chooses defeat in order that he may be one with the defeated—the poor, the outcast, the sinners—and to somehow be their intercession to God. This is a defeated Jesus, even if his defeat was chosen and had a purpose.

John's Jesus is not silent, nor defeated. He makes sure Pilate knows that his kingdom is not of this world, and tells him that he came into the world to testify to the truth. Truth is an important word in John, who uses it twenty-six times as opposed to the Synoptic Gospels, which only use it uniquely four times. The truth to which Jesus testifies is the truth about him. Jesus is God's only Son; he and the Father are one, and whoever believes in him will have eternal life. This truth will set you free (John 8:32). John's Jesus is victorious heading to the cross. He is the one lecturing Pilate, not the other way around. O'Day comments, "On one level, Jesus is on trial for his life, but on . . . the most important level, the world is on trial for its life. The world thinks it is judging Jesus, but in reality, Jesus is judging it."[35] His suffering must be endured, though like labor pains will ultimately give birth to eternal life.

Considering the different perspectives of the four New Testament gospels and the other gospels not included, Gregory Riley wrote: "All were produced by one early Christian community or another generally with knowledge of and in contrast to the views of neighboring Christian communities. Again, sometimes those differences were friendly, and a new Gospel was meant to be

35. O'Day, "Gospel of John," 9:826.

complementary, merely drawing out some additional aspects of Jesus' person or teaching particularly important to one community. But often the intent was polemical; the aim was contrast and correction."[36] For John's letters confessing correct beliefs about Jesus became a test of one's salvation. You could imitate Jesus, carry your cross, and worship regularly, but if you believed the wrong things about Jesus you were a deceiver and the antichrist. There was no room for a diversity of beliefs in Christianity. There was only one way to God and eternal life, through belief in Jesus Christ, the Son of God, who came in the flesh as God's messiah. "I am the way, and the truth, and the life. No one comes to the Father except through me" (14:6).

(3) Find Where You Want to Join the Divine Conversation

Imagine for a moment that we meet face-to-face at a social gathering and when the topic of religion comes up in our conversation you tell me that you are a Christian. Then I ask you, "What makes you a Christian? What distinguishes you as a Christian from a person of another religion or of no religious affiliation?"

How would you answer those questions?

Your answer probably says a great deal with how you enter the divine conversation of this chapter's study. Most people reading this book will either be practicing Christians or persons interested in faith though not members of a worshiping community. Therefore, the argument in the gospels about how to become a disciple may trigger personal feelings for readers.

Every Sunday in churches around the world worshipers stand and repeat the Apostles' Creed in unison. Together they state what they believe about God, Jesus, the Holy Spirit, and the church. Belief becomes a defining marker. In *The Book of Common Prayer* the service of holy baptism includes a Baptismal Covenant in which the congregation joins the candidates for baptism in stating their promises to God.[37] The *Lutheran Book of Worship* and the Presbyterian *Book of Common Worship* follow similar formats.[38] Moreover, non-creedal denominations, such as Baptists, often have statements of faith that are non-creedal in name only, and they baptize candidates after asking do they believe or accept Jesus Christ as LORD and Savior.

It is not surprising that beliefs dictate the process of how persons become Christian in Protestant churches. Martin Luther attempted to reform Christianity because he thought it had become a religion based on good

---

36. Riley, *One Jesus Many Christs*, 5.

37. *Book of Common Prayer*, 304–5.

38. *Lutheran Book of Worship*, 122–23; *Book of Common Worship*, 406–10.

works. Though he promoted salvation by grace through faith, it did not take long for faith to be exchanged by belief and new Protestant factions argued about which beliefs were orthodox and essential. The Protestant Reformation became a movement divided by beliefs—papal and scriptural authority, the meaning of the Lord's Supper, baptism, and other sacraments. The first two reform communities, Lutheran and Swiss, were unable to unite after Martin Luther and Huldrich Zwingli could not agree on their beliefs about communion.[39] Over the following century thousands died while the church let military battles determine their beliefs. What you believed became a matter of life and death.

Harvey Cox in *The Future of Faith* contends that for centuries Christianity has been in an Age of Belief. Events of the twentieth century began to undercut beliefs of the church from scientific advances, such as Darwin's evolutionary theory and Einstein's theory of relativity, to human terror, such as the Holocaust and the atomic bomb. The old belief system had insufficient answers for these things, so that in the twenty-first century, "a religion based on subscribing to mandatory beliefs is no longer viable."[40] Cox is among a chorus of scholars and pastoral leaders who think Christianity is shifting into a new age—an Age of the Spirit.[41] "If the Age of Faith was a time of 'faith in Jesus' and the Age of Belief a period of 'belief about Christ,' the Age of the Spirit is best understood as . . . an 'experience of Jesus.'"[42]

This transitional phase in Christianity means that each of the gospel's arguments about following Jesus still have a case to be made. John's emphasis on orthodoxy will continue to be an essential focus in some Christian denominations. Increasingly many will find it intellectually impossible to continue to believe in parts of the Apostles' Creed, or other church doctrines. Meanwhile, in other faith communities belief will become a secondary matter, where persons will meaningfully commit to following Jesus as a way of life, while being agnostic about God's existence. For some this will include Matthean Jesus' emphasis on an ethical and moral life, while others will be drawn to the Lukan Jesus' attention to justice for the poor and outcast. Then, others will eschew any categorical definition of faith and highlight the Markan Jesus' call to carry their crosses and become servants to all—however they interpret that in everyday life.

The conversation between Mark, Matthew/Luke, and John about what it means to follow Jesus is going to be passionately debated in congregations, seminary classrooms, emergent faith communities, and small group studies

39. Hillerbrand, *Reformation*, 108, 154–63.

40. Cox, *Future of Faith*, 221.

41. In addition to Cox's *Future of Faith*, see Butler Bass, *Christianity After Religion*; Tickle, *Great Emergence*; and McLaren, *New Kind of Christianity*.

42. Butler Bass, *Christianity After Religion*, 109.

during the next generation. Where you, the reader, joins this conversation will be one voice among a cacophony of expressions.

- How important do you think beliefs are to being a Christian? If you attend church, how important were the beliefs of that particular congregation or denomination in your decision to become a part of that fellowship?

- Is a person that is fully committed to following Jesus by the way she lives her life, but who doubts many of the church's beliefs and teachings as much a Christian as someone who affirms all the orthodox beliefs of the church? What about someone fully committed in faith to Jesus, but who doubts the existence of God?

- If you were going to be baptized as an adult today, would you prefer the pastor or priest to ask, "Do you accept Jesus Christ as Lord and Savior?" or "Do you commit yourself to follow the way of Jesus Christ?" Would you prefer to read and affirm the Apostles' Creed, or share a brief testimony of the faith experience that motivated you to seek baptism? Why would you choose one or the other?

- How persuasive do you find the following criticism from James about salvation by faith alone? "If a brother or sister is naked and lacks daily food, and one of you says to them, 'Go in peace; keep warm and eat your fill,' and yet you do not supply their bodily needs, what is the good of that? So faith by itself, if it has no works, is dead. . . . Show me your faith apart from your works, and I by my works will show you my faith" (Jas 2:15–18).

- How would you guide a teenager exploring a decision to follow Jesus and become a Christian—with an emphasis on beliefs, on faith, on faithful actions, or with some combination? Why?

- If questions like these are not being discussed in your congregation or faith community, what do you imagine would happen if you began asking them?

Recognizing how Jesus speaks differently in Matthew, Mark, Luke, and John about following him will create conversations that will help the church be relevant and vibrant for the next generation of disciples.

CHAPTER 8

Who Is My Neighbor?

And they'll know we are Christians, by our love, by our love,
Yes, they'll know we are Christians by our love[1]

—PETER SCHOLTES

As A TEENAGER THERE were many summer nights I sat around a campfire with friends from my church or at camp singing songs from the silly to the serious. Guitar-playing college students told stories and jokes that had been passed down to them, which my peers and I would pass down to those younger than us. When the fire died down and the mood became a little more reflective songs about love and service were sung in more reverent tones—*They will know we are Christians by our love* and *The gospel in a word is love*. It was not until years later that I began to wonder what we meant by singing those songs. What love were we singing about? It is easy to say, "Love is the answer." The Beatles sang, "All we need is love," and multitudes have been singing it for half a century. But the world continues to have a shortage of love. Even when people practice love in a healthy manner, whom they love becomes an all-important question—how wide is their circle of love?

Most people love those who love them. Love is commonly shared between family and friends. The wider the circle becomes, the more difficult it is to love others. This is true for the church as well. It has been an argument for Christianity since the four evangelists wrote the gospels. If the gospel writers could have sat with me at summer camp, they would have all enthusiastically sang, "Yes, they'll know we are Christians by our love." But what they would have meant by those words would have been drastically different things.

John argues with the Synoptic Gospels, Matthew, Mark, and Luke, about whom Christians should love. The argument continues in the Christian church, today. What is the best way a church shows its love, by how it

---

1. Scholtes, *They'll Know We Are Christians.*

loves its own people, or by how it loves outsiders? What should a church's ministry emphasis be: taking care of its members, or serving its community?

EXCURSUS 8.1

Reading John's Gospel through John's Letters

Although it is doubtful that the author of the fourth gospel and the author of John's letters were the same person, there are too many common phrases and ideas for them to be completely independent of one another. Both use the term little children for believers, refer to love more than other New Testament books, see the world as hostile to believers, and speak of abiding in Christ/God. There are also enough differences that lead most scholars to reject the idea of a single author. For instance the gospel is christocentric, while the epistles are more theocentric.[2] The gospel has long sections about the Spirit, which is absent in the letters. The letters also have a different understanding of sin and atonement compared to the gospel. The context of the writings is also different. The gospel is in conflict with Judaism, while the letters have conflicts within their Christian community.[3] The authors were likely a part of a community that connected them in a Johannine tradition.[4]

This leads to a more curious and strategic question—which came first and subsequently who reacted to the ideas of whom. Though this is less clear, I am persuaded by those who think the gospel was first, or at least an early version of it was known to the author of the letters.[5] John's letters give us an insight to interpreting the gospel, because the letters are written through the eyes of people who knew and loved the gospel. Of course, they should not be the only lens used for seeing the gospel. Gail O'Day cautions, "Much of the conflict to which 1 John is addressed seems to be generated by disagreement over the interpretation of the theology contained in the gospel."[6] If part of the conflict in the Johannine

---

2. Jones, *1, 2 & 3 John*, 6.

3. O'Day, "Gospel of John," 9:499; Brown, *Introduction*, 381.

4. Black, "First, Second, and Third Letters of John," 12:366–68.

5. Brown concludes, "1 John makes most sense if understood as written in a period following the appearance of the Gospel, when the struggle with the synagogue and 'the Jews' was no longer a major issue" (*Introduction*, 383).

6. O'Day, "Gospel of John," 9:499.

community was interpreting the gospel, then in reading the letters we are only getting half the story when using them to help us read the gospel. Be cautious seeking insights to the gospel through the letters. Perhaps if Diotrephes had authored an epistle we would be getting a fuller picture (3 John 9–10).

From Love One Another to Love Your Enemy

In the Gospel of John Jesus gives only one commandment. This is quite surprising when you compare it to the teachings of Jesus in Matthew and Luke, where Jesus instructs the crowds with numerous commandments. Jesus offers over twenty-five commandments in the Sermon on the Mount alone. John's gospel mentions commandments; Jesus tells his disciples that if they love him they will keep his commandments (John 14:15, 21; 15:10). However, the Johannine Jesus never mentions any of them save one, "I give you a new commandment, that you love one another. Just as I have loved you, you also should love one another" (13:34).

The phrase "love one another" is used five times in John's gospel as well as seven additional times in John's letters. It is only used sixteen times in the New Testament, meaning that 75 percent of those references are in John's gospel and letters—the others are twice in Romans, once in 1 Thessalonians, and once in 1 Peter. Curiously, the Synoptic Gospels never use the phrase. John talked about Christian love in a different way from the other gospels. Less clear is what he meant by "love one another." The way Paul used the phrase in 1 Thessalonians indicates it was known in the early church. Yet, the first gospels never use it. Instead, in Q Jesus is critical of such an idea, as seen in Matthew and Luke.

The fact that Jesus calls this a new commandment is odd. New compared to what? To whom was this commandment new? Did John, who wrote the last of the four gospels, think that the others had left something out? Furthermore, Jesus shares this commandment only with his disciples. He did not teach it to the crowds. The audience affects the commandment's message. He tells the disciples to love one another. The crowds, who were full of Jesus' adversaries as much as his followers, do not hear the commandment. If Jesus had taught this commandment to the general public its meaning would have been broader. As it is the audience reinforces the commandment's language, which implies sectarian love.

John's gospel and letters mention the English word love, through four different Greek terms, 117 times, more than in anywhere else in the New

Testament.[7] Unfortunately, they rarely define it, so readers have to imagine what love means in the Johannine books. The best illustration occurs when Jesus washes the disciples' feet as they arrive for a meal on the night he was betrayed (13:1–20).[8] After Jesus plays the role of a servant by washing their feet, he tells them to be servants to one another. Later that same evening Jesus gives them the commandment to love one another. Being a servant illustrates how to love one another. As with the command, Jesus gives this example only to his disciples.

Jesus scoffed at such love in Q. "If you love those who love you, what credit is that to you? For even sinners love those who love them. If you do good to those who do good to you, what credit is that to you? For even sinners do the same" (Luke 6:32–33). In Q it was already assumed that Christians would love other Christians in the church. That would be expected. The mark of a true disciple was one who was able to love those who hated and persecuted her. "Love your enemies," Jesus says (6:35; Matt 5:44). "Be merciful, just as your Father is merciful . . . for he is kind to the ungrateful and the wicked" (Luke 6:35–36).

The Lukan (and Matthean) Jesus argues with the Johannine Jesus. While John emphasized the importance of the Christian community to love one another, Luke thought that the only love worth measuring in the Christian community was to love one's enemies—including the ungrateful and the wicked. We also see this in how Luke interprets a third common phrase about love in the gospels.

The command to "love your neighbor" was first taught by Moses, according to the Priestly tradition (Lev 19:18). It became central to Christian teaching. The Synoptic Gospels state that loving your neighbor is the second half of what Jesus called the greatest commandment and tethered it to the command to love God with your whole being. In Mark, a Jewish scribe says that all of the law and the prophets are based on this tandem teaching of loving God with your whole being and loving your neighbor as yourself. Jesus replies by telling him that he was very near to the kingdom of God (Mark 12:34).

Luke takes Jesus' command to love your neighbor and pushes the interpretation further. A scribe of the law asks Jesus what must he do to inherit eternal life. Jesus tosses the question back to him, what did he think? The scribe replies with both parts of the greatest commandment and receives Jesus' commendation. Then, the scribe asks him, "And who is my

---

7. Skinner, "Virtue in the New Testament," 307.

8. Skinner, "Virtue in the New Testament," 308–9.

neighbor?" (Luke 10:29). This becomes the setting for the Parable of the Good Samaritan (10:30–37).

The key to understanding the Good Samaritan is the character development in the story. Because parables are so short characters act according to type in order to quickly tell the story. If a character acts out of type it is always part of the plot twist in the story. The parable begins with a Jewish man being robbed, beaten and left for dead by the side of a road from Jerusalem to Jericho. One by one three travelers see the injured man. The first two, a priest and a Levite, were officers of the Jerusalem temple. Touching a corpse would have made them ritually unclean and temporarily prohibited them from temple duties. Some have suggested that this was the reason the two avoided the man and that Jesus used this part of the story to criticize the practice of putting the rituals of the law ahead of human compassion. Shrewdly, Jesus picked characters that should have been especially governed by the command to love your neighbor. The book of Leviticus, a central text for the Priestly tradition, originally recorded the command from Moses. Instead of helping the man, or at least checking to see if he was alive, the priest and the Levite separately avoid him and continue traveling.

EXCURSUS 8.2

A Good Samaritan?

Samaritans were the descendants of the former northern kingdom of Israel, taking their name from Samaria, the capital city of the kingdom. When Assyria destroyed it in 722 BC they assimilated the survivors into the empire. They intermarried with other nationalities, but continued to worship the LORD, the god of Israel.

When Babylon conquered Judah in 587 BC they exiled the best and brightest and left the remaining survivors in rubble. A century later Jewish exiles began returning in large numbers and dedicated themselves to rebuilding Jerusalem and the temple. As we examined in chapter 5, the exiles believed they were the true people of God and excluded Samaritans and other people of the land from the rebuilt temple. Animosity grew with time. Samaritans eventually built a rival temple to the LORD on Mount Gerizim, near Shechem the site of the first Israelite temple. During the Jewish independent state, the Maccabean army demolished the

Samaritan temple in 112/111 BC, which has generally been viewed as the final breach between the two peoples.[9]

Jews believed Samaritans had tarnished the Israelite faith by marrying foreigners and integrating practices from other religions into the worship of the LORD. Samaritans believed they represented the ancient Israelite religion and that Judaism had been corrupted by Babylonian influences. Jewish and Samaritan hostility can be briefly seen in all four gospels. When Jesus told his parable Jewish persons in the audience would not have imagined a *good* Samaritan, because the two cousin peoples had bred an ethnic hatred for one another for centuries.

To gain a new appreciation for the parable replace the hero and the audience with contemporary groups or persons hostile to one another. Imagine the parable of the good lesbian along the road to an evangelical Christian conference, or the parable of the good Klansman near the parking lot of an NAACP meeting.

The third traveler was a Samaritan. In Jesus' day Jews and Samaritans were enemies. Jesus selected an enemy of the Jewish people to be the hero of the story. The Samaritan acting out of character type—at least in the mindset of Jewish persons in the first century—creates the plot twist in the story. After two men who should have been upholding the command to love your neighbor leave the injured man to die, a hated Samaritan obeys the command to the fullest extent. First, he risks his own life—the robbers could have been still lurking—to save a Jewish stranger. Next, he provides first aid and transports the man back to the city. Finally, he takes him to an inn, pays the innkeeper to nurse him back to health, and promises that if his expenses exceed the amount paid he would reimburse him the next time he traveled through town. In Luke's gospel the phrase love your neighbor becomes love your enemy. The answer to the scribe's original question, "What must I do to inherit eternal life," was completed when Jesus said, "Go and do likewise," at the end of the parable. Consequently, the Good Samaritan becomes part of Luke's argument with the Gospel of John.

9. Van Beek, "Samaria," 4:182–88; Gaster, "Samaritans," 4:190–97. For another view on the temple's destruction, see Bourgel, "Destruction of the Samaritan Temple," 505–23.

Practicing Midrash

This argument between the Lukan Jesus and the Johannine Jesus is similar to the one we studied in chapter 5, when the returning exiles to Jerusalem were debating who constituted the nation of Israel. In this version of the argument the early church is debating the obligations to love neighbor. Do such obligations extend to all persons—even enemies—or are they limited to those among the faith community?

As we have done with previous chapters, make sure to listen to John's Jesus give the commandment to love one another as well as to Luke's Jesus criticize that idea and make the case that Christian love must move beyond love for one another and extend to enemies.

(1) Free the Stories to Speak for Themselves

When John wrote down the only commandment that Jesus would say in his gospel, did he mean for it to be interpreted as a sectarian rule? Or did he think this phrase was synonymous with love your neighbor?

The setting in John's gospel tells us much about the way he understood the commandment. It is the day before Jesus' crucifixion, the disciples have gathered with Jesus for a meal, which will become the last supper. (John portrayed Jesus as the Passover lamb, so he changed the synoptic timeline and made the last supper the day before the Passover.) A series of episodes from the evening run from John chapter 13 through half of chapter 18—a quarter of the whole gospel. It begins with Jesus washing his disciples' feet and follows with the last supper. John makes the narrative about the meal short, skipping over details found in the Synoptic Gospels, which leaves scroll space for Jesus to have an extended talk with his disciples. Jesus directs the conversation to the disciples and to future readers, who will become disciples. A few times the narrative notes that these words are not for outsiders.

We see this acted out when Judas leaves while being identified as the one who will betray Jesus. Remove him from the inner circle and it becomes more exclusive. The betrayer is not included. When the disciples are told to love one another, Judas has already been removed from the club. They do not have to love him, but only those who remain faithful. Twice Jesus explains that when he is talking to the disciples, he is not including Judas (John 13:11, 18). Later in the evening, at the moment when the soldiers arrive to take Jesus away, he claims that he did not lose any of disciples (18:9). Losing Judas to betrayal does not count because Judas was never really one of them anyway; he was "destined to be lost" (17:12).

Judas's outsider status among the disciples represents a dynamic in Jesus' long soliloquies in chapters 13–17. He serves as a contrast to the true disciples. These speeches emphasize Jesus' close bonds with them. They are his branches; he is the true vine. Jesus abides in them and they in him. The Spirit will guide them in all truth. If they ask anything in the Father's name, it will be given. They belong to Jesus and he protects them, so that they may be one. And while they are in the world, they do not belong to the world.

In contrast, the world cannot receive the Spirit, "because it neither sees him or knows him" (14:17). While Jesus reveals the Spirit to the disciples, the Spirit is not revealed to the world.[10] Likewise, Jesus prays for the disciples, but not for the world. Ultimately, the world does not know God. Whoever does not abide in Jesus is thrown into the fire and burned (15:6).

Jesus gives the disciples the command to love one another as a part of a long discourse, which contrasts the favored status of Jesus' disciples, including future followers, with everyone else. It is unlikely, then, that when the Johannine Jesus gave the commandment to love one another, he was thinking of anything more than his followers loving each other.

The letters of John reinforce such a reading. They interpreted Jesus' commandment in a sectarian way. First John repeatedly instructs brothers and sisters in the faith to love one another. "Those who say, 'I love God' and hate their brothers or sisters are liars; for those who do not love a brother or sister whom they have seen cannot love God whom they have not seen" (1 John 4:20). Yet, while brothers and sisters in the faith should pray for those committing sin so that God would "give life to such a one" (5:16), they should not pray for those committing mortal sin (whatever that is). No life would be given to them. "If you see a brother or sister committing a 'mortal sin,' you must not pray for such a person" (5:17). It is hard to imagine how *not* praying for someone is showing God's love to them.[11] Once they lost their status in the community, the mandate to love them no longer applied.[12]

In 2 John as soon as the writer repeats the commandment to love one another, he then begins talking about deceivers in the church, who must be excluded. "Do not receive into the house or welcome anyone who

10. Brown, *Introduction*, 353, notes that the Spirit's "hostile relationship to the world" is "characteristic" in John.

11. Brown writes, "Some find almost a contradiction in 1 John's insistence on love . . . and the refusal to pray for those who commit a deadly sin. . . . Christians should be careful about deciding that such people are radically evil in themselves and cannot be prayed for" (*Introduction*, 393).

12. Brown, *Introduction*, 377, raises the point that John's shift seems narrow and sectarian.

comes to you and does not bring [correct] teaching; for to welcome is to participate in the evil deeds of such a person" (2 John 10–11). Those who will not abide in the "teaching of Christ" must be excluded from the church (9). The letters of John reinforce a sectarian intent of the Johannine Jesus' command to love one another.

The Jesus in Luke and Matthew criticizes such love. "If you love those who love you, what credit is that to you? For even sinners love those who love them" (Luke 6:32). Instead, this Jesus tells his followers, "Love your enemies, do good to those who hate you, bless those who curse you, pray for those who abuse you. . . . Do to others as you would have them do to you" (6:27–31). In John's gospel and letters love strengthens the bond of the community, unifies it with God, and protects it from outsiders. In Luke and Matthew the love of the Christian community is supposed to have a transformative effect on outsiders, even upon its enemies.

Mark, Matthew, Luke, Paul, and James all record the command to love your neighbor. As we have already seen, Luke pushes the interpretation of love your neighbor toward a command to love your enemies by the way Jesus tells the Parable of the Good Samaritan. He is not alone in doing this. Matthew also connects the command to love your enemies with love your neighbor. "You have heard that it was said, 'You shall love your neighbor and hate your enemy.' But I say to you, Love your enemies and pray for those who persecute you" (Matt 5:43–44). There is no need for a scribe in Matthew to ask, "Who is my neighbor?" Matthew's Jesus plainly says that loving neighbor and enemy are the same.

The Apostle Paul expands the circle of Christian love in the same way. In Romans Paul uses the phrases love one another and love your neighbor interchangeably—the only place this happens in the New Testament (Rom 13:8–10). He characterizes Christian love with phrases that sound like gospel teachings from Q. "Bless those who persecute you. . . . Live in harmony with one another. . . . Associate with the lowly. . . . Never avenge yourselves. . . . 'If your enemies are hungry, feed them; if they are thirsty, give them something to drink.' . . . Do not be overcome by evil, but overcome evil with good" (12:14–21).

The phrases *love your neighbor* and *love your enemies* occur a dozen times in the New Testament, but not once do John's gospel or letters repeat them. Likewise, Matthew, Mark, or Luke never use John's phrase *love one another*. Consequently, when Luke's Jesus says, "Love your neighbor," and John's Jesus says, "Love one another," they mean two different things.

(2) Listen to the Stories as Contrasting Voices of God

We saw in chapter 7 that the Markan tradition, which Matthew and Luke inherited when they used the gospel as a core for their own retelling of the story, placed a premium on faith, or a total trust in following Jesus. Disciples carry their crosses daily, become servants to all, and lose their lives for Christ's sake. To this Matthew and Luke add the sayings of Jesus from the Q collection, in which Jesus reinterprets the Mosaic law by placing higher demands upon his followers. Disciples give without reward, forgive unendingly, do not judge others, treat others as they would want to be treated, bless those who persecute them and love their enemies.

In combining Mark's gospel and Jesus' sayings in Q along with their own unique material Matthew and Luke envision a Christianity that transforms communities. The coming kingdom of God would alter human history—either as an ending of the world as we know it, or as an ushering in of a new era. That the future did not come as these writers in the New Testament imagined—the world is still around two thousand years later—should not diminish the transformative motives of their gospels.

Earlier we saw where the act of Jesus washing his disciples' feet in John illustrated how they were to love one another. Although the Synoptic Gospels do not tell that story, they do include two other stories when Jesus commands his disciples to be servants. They contrast John's story on servanthood. Both originally came from Mark with noticeable changes in Matthew and Luke. Both begin with disputes between the disciples, and in both Jesus equates greatness with becoming a servant to all. In one Jesus holds a child in his arms as an illustration, indicating that those who would be great must serve the least among them (Mark 9:33–37). In the other James and John asked Jesus to place them in positions of power, which starts an argument among the twelve (10:35–45). Like the previous story, Jesus says that to become the greatest of all, they must become a servant to all. The command is given to the disciples, as was Jesus' example of washing his disciples' feet in John. In the Synoptic Gospels, however, all people become the beneficiaries of the command. Jesus compares the disciples' leadership as servants with the rulers of the Roman Empire. Whereas in John the disciples are to be servants to one another, in the Synoptic Gospels Jesus offers a principle for being leaders in the world. Their servant leadership should be the opposite of Roman rulers who "lord it over them" (10:42).

Jesus' command to love your neighbor in the Synoptic Gospels and its extension to love your enemies in Luke and Matthew create an ethic that foreshadows the coming kingdom of God. It imagines the transformation of society.

Jesus never preaches about the kingdom of God in John. The phrase only appears in his private conversation with Nicodemus (John 3:3–5). He never asks his disciples to bless those who persecute them, or to turn the other cheek, or to walk a second mile. John does not picture the transformation of society. In fact *the world*, to use John's term, does not know Jesus and will be hostile to his disciples. "You do not belong to the world, but I have chosen you out of the world—therefore the world hates you" (15:19).

After the last supper Jesus prays before the soldiers arrest him. In John the prayer does not take place at the Garden of Gethsemane and Jesus does not ask God to "remove this cup from me" (Mark 14:36). Instead, Jesus prays for his disciples. He asks God to protect both current and future disciples from the world, which hates them (John 17:12–15). Second, he prays that his disciples would be unified (17:20–23). The prayer indicates John's vision for believers. The church is supposed to be a sanctuary, a refuge from the world. Jesus sends them into the world to be witnesses of truth, but they are not of the world. From this perspective Jesus says to his disciples, "I give you a new commandment, that you love one another" (13:34).

Compared to the vision of the Synoptic Gospels a focus on loving one another in the Christian community was a new commandment. It was a different perspective. Jesus' followers must love one another because the world hates them. Rather than transform society by being part of the coming kingdom of God and its new ethic, disciples should create a sanctuary from the world. The church does have a ministry to the world. It testifies to the truth of Jesus Christ, so that those in the world might come to believe in Jesus and become a part of the sanctuary from the world. The command to love one another was a new vision for the church, an alternative vision of the church.

John's focus on orthodoxy—correct beliefs—made this new command a double-edged sword. Sectarian beliefs could make loving one another a selective command that creates division rather than unity, as seen in 3 John. "I have written something to the church; but Diotrephes, who likes to put himself first, does not acknowledge our authority. . . . He refuses to welcome the friends, and even prevents those who want to do so and expels them from the church" (3 John 9–10). The Christian community that produced the letters of John had a split over doctrine, possibly on how to interpret John's gospel, which then led to a breakdown in relationships. Jesus' command to love one another, frequently mentioned in John's letters, exacerbated this split rather than to become a bridge to reconciliation.

The law scribe in Luke's gospel got to the heart of the argument when he asked Jesus, "Who is my neighbor?" Are my neighbors just the people in my group? Or do they include outsiders, even enemies? John's and Luke's gospels answered that question differently based on how they saw the purpose of the church.

(3) Find Where You Want to Join the Divine Conversation

I must confess that it is difficult for me to appreciate John's emphasis to love one another. We live in global, multicultural world, where the sins of racism continue to bring heartache to church and society. John's argument has been used in ways he may not have intended. Nevertheless, it has been so used and forces me to ask—Why would God inspire a gospel telling Christians to love each other and exclude those who do not believe correctly, or who commit certain sins? Unfortunately, the church has given us plenty of terrible examples when it excluded people—the Spanish Inquisition, segregated American churches, and the way the Reformation broke out into war because factions could not agree on doctrine. In minutes you could make a list a page long. The church continues to struggle with being inclusive. John's argument that the church should focus its love upon those in its fellowship could be blamed for some of the church's darkest days. Perhaps naming the way John's argument has been used will allow us to find a healthier place to join this conversation.

The commandment to love one another argues about engaging society, a society that may have been hostile to Christians in John's part of the Roman Empire. The author of the book of Revelation felt the oppression of Rome; it is the dominant theme of the book. Did John's community of faith face similar persecution? If so, it is easier to understand his focus on strengthening love within the community. A persecuted community survives by its bond of love.

Luke was not arguing that Jesus' followers should not love one another. When Matthew's Jesus said, "You have heard it said to love your neighbor and hate your enemy," he did not flip the saying into, "Love your enemy and hate your neighbor." Loving one another, loving friends and family was assumed. This Jesus wanted his disciples to go beyond tribal love, to break down the walls of hate between different peoples.

John, who was writing after Luke and Matthew's gospels, may have been trying to restore an emphasis he felt was missing in the early church. Loving one another was important as well. Loving one another was needed to create a strong and sustainable faith community.

On a practical level every church has to wrestle with the argument between the Lukan Jesus and the Johannine Jesus. Every congregation has to decide its priorities for ministry. Should it have an inward focus, taking care of members, or an outward focus, serving the surrounding community? Will it spend most of its resources—money, time, and energy—on strengthening the fellowship of its membership? Or will it spend most of its resources on serving the needs in its city or town? Or will it try to do both equally, as well as possible?

If you are part of a worshiping community, does your congregation see its mission to be an agent of God's peace and justice in your city or town? Or does it see its mission to be a safe place in the world, where a body of believers loves one another? Does it spend the bulk of its dollars on ministry for the poor, hungry, and outcast, and its energy on enlisting church folks to actively do ministry in the area where you live? Or does it spend the bulk of its dollars creating programs for church members and its energy on inviting friends and neighbors to join them for these programs?

If you think your congregation tries to balance both of these foci, would you be willing to get a copy of the church budget and church calendar and track what your congregation does with its time and money? What do you think you would find? If you asked your pastor(s) what she spends most of her time doing, do you think more of it would be spent on ministering to people in the congregation, or on serving people in the surrounding community as a ministry of the congregation?

The argument about whether Christians should love one another or love their enemies is an argument about the mission and purpose of the church. Luke's Jesus claims that the church should engage the world, even when it persecutes the church. Loving your enemies transforms disciples regardless of what it does to enemies. Some—like Gandhi and Martin Luther King—thought it could also transform enemies. Luke's charge to love enemies points the church in the direction of changing the world by making enemies friends.

John's Jesus thought the church should disengage from the world, and serve as an oasis, or a sanctuary, for those who wanted to escape it. John's charge to love one another directs the church to be such an accepting, loving community that enemies want to become friends. The command to love one another can be as inclusive as the command to love your enemies as long as the invitation to join the community does not discriminate. It could be argued that both the Lukan Jesus and the Johannine Jesus have the same goal in mind, but offer different strategies to make it happen.

With the American church in decline this argument—how to engage society—is more important than ever. Beginning forty years ago with Dean Kelly's book *Why Conservative Churches Are Growing*, many argued that liberal theology, accused of rejecting orthodox beliefs, caused the decline in mainline Protestant denominations.[13] The emphasis on orthodoxy in John's gospel and letters could support that point. It often painted mainline Protestant efforts at social justice, including a more inclusive church, as part of the problem. Now that decline has been hitting evangelical Protestant denominations over the past decade the church's exclusivity is seen as part of the problem. The Barna Group, an evangelical organization that has been researching American religion for over thirty years, has repeatedly reported that one of the reasons young people are leaving or staying away from the church is because they view it as being judgmental in general and homophobic in particular.[14] So, both sides have ammunition to make their arguments about what is wrong with the church. What makes this conversation between love your enemy and love one another a part of God's living word, however, is the discussion about what should the church's emphasis be now and for the near future. How should a congregation engage the society in which it meets?

Which strategy tugs at your heart?

- If you are in a faith community, should your congregation act like Noah's ark in the world, a sanctuary safely floating midst a flooding chaos? What would that look like? What would you do?

- Or should it be a part of the transformative reign of God in society? What would that look like? What would you do?

- If you closed your eyes and started singing, "Yes, they'll know we are Christians by our love," how would you visualize that love?

13. Kelley, *Why Conservative Churches Are Growing*, 174–79.

14. See Barna Group, "New Generation Expresses Its Skepticism"; "Six Reasons Young Christians Leave Church"; "Spiritual but Not Religious." For further reading, see Kinnaman, *You Lost Me*, and *UnChristian*.

CHAPTER 9

Saints and Sinners

Sin is not the adult bookstore on the corner. It is the hard heart, the lack of generosity, and all the isms, racism and sexism and so forth.[1]

—ANNE LAMOTT

GUILT AND SHAME ARE two of the blemishes of twentieth-century American Christianity. In an attempt to talk about the biblical notion of sin, churches instead merely made people feel bad about themselves. Catholic and Protestant—Evangelical and Mainline—carry on a faith passed on to them, and for better or worse, Western Christianity has been formed by obsessed sinners.

Paul, the church's first theologian, said that he was the least of the apostles because he had persecuted the church, which according to Acts included his involvement in Stephen's murder (Acts 6). Later, he confessed, "I do not do what I want, but I do the very thing I hate. . . . It is no longer I that do it, but sin that dwells within me" (Rom 7:15–17). Augustine, the fourth-century theologian that developed the doctrine of original sin, lived a wild and sexually promiscuous life during his young adult years. After his conversion to Christianity at age thirty-one, he ended relationships with his mistresses, broke off his engagement to his fiancé, and embraced celibacy. His personal struggles with sexuality no doubt played a role in his determination that sex transmitted original sin to every human generation.

The Protestant Reformation owes its beginning to Martin Luther's guilty conscience. An Augustinian monk, Luther daily confessed his sins in fear of the wrath of God. Years later Luther recalled, "My situation was that, although an impeccable monk, I stood before God as a sinner troubled in conscience, and I had no confidence that my merit would assuage him."[2]

1. Lamott, *Help, Thanks, Wow*, 62.
2. Luther, *Weimar Ausgabe*, vol. LIV, 185; as quoted in Bainton, *Here I Stand*, 49.

Tormented by his conscience, Luther searched for a cure, which he found in Paul's letter to the Romans. His awakening changed his faith and eventually led to the writing and posting of ninety-five theses upon the Wittenburg Church door on October 31, 1517, which began the Protestant break from the Roman Catholic Church.

While not every theologian that transformed Christianity was obsessed with sin, it is a peculiar reoccurrence. Western Christianity has been preoccupied with human sinfulness in ways that Eastern Orthodox churches have not been. Though Western Christianity made salvation from sin the primary purpose of Jesus' atonement, it found a common definition of sin evasive.

Reinhold Niebuhr concluded that sin was rooted in human pride, an idea first voiced by Augustine.[3] Feminist and liberation theologians, however, have shown the inadequacy of this focus on pride, alone, due to the systemic effects of sexism, racism, and classism. "Sin," Rosemary Radford Ruether explains, "has to be seen both in the capacity to set up prideful, antagonistic relations to others and in the passivity of men and women who acquiesce to the group ego."[4] Therefore, sin is also the loss of human potential. Additionally, the church spoke of sin as acts of commission and omission, as individual and corporate. Biblical theologians point to the meaning of the word and define sin as "missing the mark."[5] In such a wide array, Anne Lamott's definition at the opening of this chapter is as good as any. Besides, her past could qualify her as a great sinner, and she is more enjoyable to read than Paul, Augustine, or Luther.

One reason the church is not clear about sin is that the Bible is not clear about sin. From the priests' focus on personal piety and cultic rituals to the prophets' emphasis on social injustice, the Bible's viewpoints change from one voice to another. We examined a couple of related arguments in chapters 3 and 4. In this chapter we will explore one argument about sin between the letters of Paul and John: Can sinners also be saints? In joining this conversation perhaps we could find a healthier pathway to talk about sin.

Sin Dwells Within Saints vs. Saints Do Not Sin

Paul wrote his letter to the Romans as an introduction to Pauline Christianity. His other letters were ongoing conversations with people in churches that

3. Niebuhr, *Nature and Destiny of Man*, 1:186–203.

4. Ruether, *Sexism and God-Talk*, 164. Ruether develops a feminist anthropology on pp. 93–115, 159–92. See also Migliore, *Faith Seeking Understanding*, 130–35.

5. Fitzmyer, *Paul and His Theology*, 71; Wright, *Paul*, 88.

he already knew, but he had never been to Rome. In Romans he compiles his most important ideas about Christianity—many having been developed from previously written letters. He spends the first three chapters of Romans making the case that all human beings are sinners, Jews as well as Gentiles. "For there is no distinction, since all have sinned and fall short of the glory of God" (Rom 3:22b–23). Only then does he shift to speak of God's salvation in Jesus Christ. Paul's assertion that human beings are sinful was not original. He quotes several passages from the Hebrew Bible to build his case. David, Jacob, and Moses' flawed hero stories could testify as well. In the empire almost every religion gave sacrifices to their gods to seek forgiveness for sins. Greek mythology was full of tragedy. Paul develops a theology around the sinfulness of humanity in order to declare that Jesus Christ's death and resurrection had changed the outcome for the human race. "God proves his love for us in that while we still were sinners Christ died for us" (5:8). Where human sin had increased, Paul said, God's grace abounded all the more "leading to eternal life through Jesus Christ our Lord" (5:21).

Paul's reasoning through Romans is straightforward. He presents a problem that all humans are sinners. Then, he declares a solution—Jesus Christ died so that all may be made righteous before God. Finally, he invites people to trust in Jesus so that they may be saved by God's grace (10:9). Unexpectedly, Paul interrupts this rudimentary reasoning with a personal confession: "I do not understand my own actions. For I do not do what I want, but I do the very thing I hate. . . . For I do not do the good I want, but the evil I do not want is what I do. Now if I do what I do not want, it is no longer I that do it, but sin that dwells within me" (7:15–20).

Paul wrote those words two decades after he began following Jesus. He wrote them after he had started countless churches across the Roman Empire and written six of his seven letters in the New Testament. This produces an apparent contradiction. If after all this time of following Jesus Paul still writes, "I do not do what I want, but I do the very thing I hate," and furthermore, "sin . . . dwells within me," in what sense has the problem of human sinfulness been solved by Jesus Christ? Earlier in Romans Paul declared, "Whoever has died is freed from sin . . . so you also must consider yourselves dead to sin and alive to God in Christ Jesus. . . . For sin will have no dominion over you, since you are not under law but under grace" (6:7, 11, 14), only to later confess that sin still dwells in him.

For Paul this is not a contradiction, but a paradox. The sinner made a saint through salvation by faith in Jesus Christ nevertheless remains a sinner. Paul never says that Christians become better people after baptism. He asks, "Should we continue in sin in order that grace may abound?" And answers, "By no means!" (6:1–2). Then pleads, "Therefore, do not let sin

exercise dominion in your mortal bodies, to make you obey their passions"
(6:12). However, his own experience informs him that what we do often
does not match what we want to do. Nevertheless, his confidence in God's
grace persists. At the end of his confession he concludes, "Wretched man
that I am! Who will rescue me from this body of death? Thanks be to God
through Jesus Christ our Lord!" (7:24–25). In Paul's theology the Christian
saint remains a sinner, but this no longer matters. "If Christ is in you, though
the body is dead because of sin, the Spirit is life because of righteousness. . . .
He who raised Christ from the dead will give life to your mortal bodies also
through his Spirit that dwells in you" (8:10–11).

The author of John's letters would not have accepted Paul's confession,
because he admits continuing to sin. This was a sign that you were a child of
the devil, not a child of God. "No one who abides in [God] sins; no one who
sins has either seen him or known him. . . . Everyone who commits sin is a
child of the devil. . . . Those who have been born of God do not sin, because
God's seed abides in them; they cannot sin, because they have been born of
God. The children of God and the children of the devil are revealed in this
way: all who do not do what is right are not from God" (1 John 3:6–10).
John's letters are full of dualistic images: light and dark, love and hate, truth
and falsehood, child of God and child of the devil. They set up only clear
and unambiguous options. People either love or hate; obey the commandments or do not; sin or do not sin.[6] While Paul entertains paradoxical thinking, John does not. John's letters contain no gradations, no nuance. Things
are either one thing or the other.

John did not think about sin in the same way as Paul.[7] Christians
can put sin behind them because Jesus Christ "is the atoning sacrifice for
our sins" (2:2), and God protects them from sin (5:18). Had Paul been
alive and shared his confession in John's church, he would have been cast
aside as a child of the devil, as one who did not know God. Paul did not
confess some sins from his past, which he renounced with remorse. His
confession in Romans 7 was not the conversion story of a sinner who had
found God, repented, and then turned to obeying the commandments of
God. Paul confessed that he continually sins, continually does the evil he
does not wish to do instead of the good he desires, and that sin continues
to exert power over him.

John's views on sin were a direct assault on Paul's theology. John
stated that a person who abided with God would not sin. He said that

6. Donelson, *From Hebrews to Revelation*, 109.

7. Lieu writes, "It would be wrong to read into the letter ideas taken from elsewhere in the New Testament of inherent human sinfulness" (*I, II, & III John*, 56).

everyone who knows God obeys God's commandments. If anyone claims to know God, but does not obey the commandments, then that person is a liar and the truth does not exist in such a person (2:4). Such an idea would have driven Paul mad. He believed that it was impossible to keep the whole Mosaic law and that it was foolishness to believe otherwise. Furthermore, using the commandments as a litmus test for one's faith in God was the very thing Paul fought as he developed a Christian theology that included Gentiles as well as Jews.

Paul understood the struggle with sin to be an inward battle. Sin is within all of us, and therefore within all our congregations and systems. The saints of God are sinners as well. John looked at sin through the lens of dualism. It was a battle with the other. Those outside the community are sinners; those inside the community are saints.

Practicing Midrash

Paul and John's argument about sin affects their judgment of sinners. Although John never uses the term sinner, he prefers other phrases for people who commit sin—children of the devil, liars/deceivers, and antichrists. Even though the word sinner carries its own religious baggage, given John's alternatives, this chapter will stick with the more common term.

The Synoptic Gospels use the word sinner more frequently than other books in the New Testament. The word stuck in the vocabulary of Protestant Christianity through the nineteenth and twentieth centuries. It usually indicates someone not worthy to belong in a religious community, someone that should be excluded by the faithful. When Jesus ate with prostitutes and other sinners, the religious elite scoffed at him, to which he replied, "Those who are well have no need of a physician, but those who are sick; I have come to call not the righteous but sinners" (Mark 2:17). As we explore the way that Paul and John talk about sin, we will watch how they talk about sinners.

(1) Free the Stories to Speak for Themselves

It seems beyond reason that when John wrote that no one who abides in God sins and that those who are born of God do not sin and cannot sin he meant that a Christian disciple would never tell a white lie, fudge on her income taxes, or unwittingly participate in the systemic racism or sexism of the times. Surely, he did not expect Christians to become perfect people with nary a flaw.

Perhaps the intent of John's instructions applied to people who repeatedly committed the same sins—a compulsive liar rather than a child's white lie, a serial thief rather than a bored worker stealing company time, or a violent domestic abuser rather than a spouse that yelled in anger one day. When he said that sin is lawlessness he used the Greek word *anomia*, which might better be translated as iniquity. (Elsewhere in the New Testament this term indicated extreme wickedness.)[8] Unfortunately, John does not talk about sin this way elsewhere in his letter. While it does not take much imagination to conceive a whole continuum of sinfulness—from the most vile and sadistic to simple acts of selfishness that injure little—John's letters do not provide such progressions. From a plain reading, the person who stretches the truth a little is no different from a compulsive liar. This makes applying his words difficult.

Passages earlier in 1 John reveal a contradiction in this all-or-nothing thinking. The writer states that Jesus' death on the cross cleanses believers from all sin. Then he continues, "If we say that we have no sin, we deceive ourselves, and the truth is not in us. If we confess our sins, he who is faithful and just will forgive us our sins and cleanse us from all unrighteousness. If we say that we have not sinned, we make him a liar, and his word is not in us" (1 John 1:8–10). John's words in chapter 1 are hard to reconcile with his words in chapter 3. In the first chapter he says that if we claim not to sin that we make God a liar, while in the third chapter he says those who do not sin are born of God. So which is it? Additionally, if we claim to sin, so that we will not make God a liar, chapter three says that we are children of the devil. It is a no-win situation. We either make God a liar or alternatively become children of the devil.[9]

At the surface these contradictory views should make us suspicious. The Gospel of John defines sin as disbelief in Jesus. This is clearly not the view in at least part of the letter, which speaks of sin as immoral behavior. Could chapter 3, though, talk about sin the way the gospel does—as disbelief in Jesus? If so, by definition those who do not believe are sinners. Unfortunately, there is no way to tell because of John's sweeping language. Could John be quoting opponents who believed Christians were without

8. Culpepper, *1 John, 2 John, 3 John*, 59; Lieu, *I, II, & III John*, 128.

9. Culpepper writes, "Commentators have spared no ingenuity in attempting to resolve the tension between those passages in 1 John which recognize the reality of sin in the life of the Christian (1:8, 10) and those which claim there can be no sin in a Christian's life (3:6, 9; 5:18). Solutions which postulate multiple authors, editors, sources, or opponents do not solve the problem of how the finished product was meant to be understood" (*1 John, 2 John, 3 John*, 63).

sin? The author gives no hint of a citation.[10] It is more likely that John's dualism presents positions as all or nothing when life is much more complicated. If he was responding to different questions or issues in chapters 1 and 3, his dualistic language covers it up.

When John instructed his readers to confess sin in order to receive God's forgiveness and to be cleansed from sin, he admitted that Christians continue to commit sins after baptism. Whatever he means in chapter 3 it does not mean that Christians never sin. According to John not only will believers who confess their sins be forgiven, they will also be cleansed "from all unrighteousness" (1 John 1:9). A few verses later he adds, "If anyone does sin, we have an advocate with the Father, Jesus Christ the righteous; and he is the atoning sacrifice for our sins, and not for ours only but also for the sins of the whole world" (2:1b–2). John does not explain how Jesus made atonement for sins. He simply announces it as if his readers will understand.

John thinks that the saints receive salvation and are cleansed from their sins upon their belief in Jesus Christ. Living as believers in the faith community, however, Christians will eventually sin in daily life. They must not deceive themselves and deny their sin. Instead, they must confess their sins, receive forgiveness and be cleansed once again from all unrighteousness. "In this manner the ideal is maintained," one scholar explains, "and where the ideal is broken through concrete reality, the relationship between God and the believer that is spoiled should be restored."[11] Christians who regularly confess and repent from their sins would not be considered sinners because they have been cleansed from all unrighteousness by Jesus' atoning sacrifice.

John instructs his community to obey the commandments as a way to address sin. All who obey the commandments abide in Jesus and Jesus abides in them (3:24). Those who obey God's commandments know God; but those who do not obey them do not know God (2:3–4). A person's deeds identify them in John. "The children of God and the children of the devil are revealed in this way: all who do not do what is right are not from God" (3:10). Whereas Paul eschewed keeping the law as a means of salvation, John made a new law essential for salvation. "For the love of God is this, that we obey his commandments" (5:3). Unfortunately, other than Jesus' single command in the Gospel of John—to love one another—John's letters do not indicate which commandments to follow. A standard to do what is right, in addition to loving one another, is so flexible that it simply defers to whatever a community says that it means.

10. Lieu, *I, II, & III John*, 131.
11. Van der Watt, "On Ethics in 1 John," 219.

Those who do what is right remain in the good graces of the community. Those who sin must confess and repent in order to be restored to those good graces. Only those who do not comply with the ritual of confession, repentance and forgiveness would be considered sinners. Ultimately, John's dualism creates a dramatic, though undefined contrast. Those who obey the commandments of the community, including confession and repentance when sins are committed, are considered the children of God, while those who break the commandments of the community, and will not submit to confession and repentance are considered children of the devil. In John's community the saints are not sinners and sinners are not saints.

Paul would have been furious if he had been alive to read John's first letter. In Paul's mind to submit to a ritual, any ritual, to gain or maintain your status within the church put the work of your salvation upon your own shoulders instead of trusting in the grace of Jesus Christ. When some un-named teachers tried to convince the Galatians that Gentile male converts would have to be circumcised, Paul wrote with a graphic pun on circumcision, "I wish those who unsettle you would castrate themselves!" (Gal 5:12). John's ritual of confession, which granted the cleansing of sins so that believers could remain as those who did not sin, would have been less painful than circumcision but to Paul would have been no less profane. Perhaps he would have told John to cut off his tongue so he could no longer confess.

Paul provided moral guidelines, but they were not tied to salvation. He sprinkled vice lists throughout his letters in which he catalogs various illicit or unbecoming behaviors and in one case warned the faithful not to associate with those who regularly practiced those behaviors (1 Cor 5:11–13). It is difficult to decipher Paul's thinking in how he constructed these lists. He did not summarize ethical portions from the Mosaic law; neither was he following any collection of Jesus' teachings. There is absolutely nothing Christian about them. Indeed, many Roman sects would be against "fornication, impurity, licentiousness, idolatry, enmities, strife, jealousy, anger, quarrels, dissensions, factions, envy, drunkenness, carousing and things like these" (Gal 5:19–21). Paul's lists were similar to moral guidelines from pagan Rome.[12] In 1 Corinthians and Romans, Paul speaks of an ethic of love, which included phrases reminiscent of the Sermon on the Mount (1 Cor 13; Rom 12–13).

Nevertheless, Paul was also convinced of his own sinfulness. "I am the least of the apostles, unfit to be called an apostle," he wrote the Corinthians,

12. Perrin and Duling write, "Much of Paul's ethical advice is drawn from conventional morality in his time. Christians, like Jews, should settle their disputes outside pagan courts (1 Cor 6); lists of vices and virtues reflect popular Hellenistic morality" (New Testament, 199). See also Seitz, "Lists, Ethical," 3:137–39.

"because I persecuted the church of God" (1 Cor 15:9). According to Acts, Paul participated in the murder of Stephen (Acts 6) and later traveled to Damascus intent on doing further violence against Christians there (9; 22; 26). Rather than condemnation from God, he discovered grace: "By the grace of God I am what I am, and his grace toward me has not been in vain" (1 Cor 15:10). Paul's personal experience informed his theology. He received God's grace even though he persecuted the church. He turned his experience into a universal statement: "While we still were sinners, Christ died for us" (Rom 5:8). This view of salvation never left him. He continued to see himself as a sinner, as well as one thankful for God's grace.

Paul told his congregations to flee from sin, not to conform to this world, and to "discern what is the will of God—what is good and acceptable and perfect" (12:2). However, he did not make behavior a qualifying factor in being part of the church. To require rituals of confessions or codes of conduct to remain in the church community would mean that Christ died for nothing. In Paul's theology God's grace in Christian saints who continue to be sinners has not been in vain.

(2) Listen to the Stories as Contrasting Voices of God

Paul developed his theology as a reaction to what he perceived as problems in Pharisaic Judaism.[13] While other branches of Judaism existed in the first century, Paul writes from his experience, which had been with a group that focused on the law as the emphasis for following the faith.[14] (For instance, he was not a priest that focused on the sacrificial life of the temple.) He would not have thought of this reformation as a new religion, but as a continuation of Judaism, a Messianic or Christian Judaism.[15] In Paul's mind—and it's important to acknowledge that this was his perception, not necessarily the reality—keeping the Mosaic law distorted first-century Judaism and excluded Gentiles.[16] It had become an ineffective burden upon people who could

13. Paul claimed that he had been a Pharisee, but came to regard it as garbage (Phil 3:5).

14. Wright, *Paul*, 108, concedes that there were many Judaisms in Paul's day, but questions how well Paul represented "the wider picture at the time." In addition, "a more variegated attitude to the Law" is undoubtedly due.

15. Borg and Crossan say, "Paul was a Jew and in his own mind never ceased being one. . . . And as a Christ mystic, he saw his Judaism anew in the light of Jesus" (*First Paul*, 26). Their term for Paul is a "Jewish Christ mystic."

16. Wright, *Paul*, 36–37. Paul's problem with Judaism was that it saw its relationship with God as "exclusive privilege," instead of becoming a "worldwide Jew-plus-Gentile people it was always intended to be." See also Hill, "Paul's Problem with Judaism," 317,

never be good enough for God. Paul had failed miserably at this despite his credentials. He had been "circumcised on the eighth day . . . of the tribe of Benjamin . . . as to the law, a Pharisee, as to zeal, a persecutor of the church, as to righteousness under the law, blameless" (Phil 3:5–6). So convinced of his own pious efforts he spoke of them on three more occasions, stating that he was more zealous and advanced in Judaism than his peers (Rom 11:1; 2 Cor 11:21b–29; Gal 1:13–14). As dedicated and righteous as he was, Paul viewed it all as garbage compared to what he found in Christ Jesus.[17]

Think of Paul as the rich young man in Mark's gospel, who asked Jesus how to inherit eternal life. Paul, too, had kept the law from his youth. Paul, too, had done everything humanly possible to inherit eternal life according to his faith, but he did not find it until he found Jesus. Unlike the young man in Mark's gospel, Paul gave up everything to follow Jesus. "For his sake I have suffered the loss of all things, and I regard them as rubbish, in order that I may gain Christ and be found in him, not having a righteousness of my own that comes from the law, but one that comes through faith in Christ, the righteousness from God based on faith" (Phil 3:8–9). Paul's testimony in Philippians reveals a key insight to his theology about sin and salvation. He states that he did not have "a righteousness of my own that comes from the law," but instead had a "righteousness from God based on faith." When he wrote Romans a few years later he returned to this insight,

> Then what becomes of boasting? It is excluded. By what law? By that of works? No, but by the law of faith. For we hold that a person is justified by faith apart from works prescribed by the law. . . . What then are we to say was gained by Abraham, our ancestor according to the flesh? For if Abraham was justified by works, he has something to boast about, but not before God. For what does the scripture say? "Abraham believed God, and it was reckoned to him as righteousness." Now to one who works, wages are not reckoned as a gift but as something due. But to one who without works trusts him who justifies the ungodly, such faith is reckoned as righteousness. (Rom 3:27—4:5)

The failure of the law, according to Paul, was that it made salvation a human achievement instead of God's. The difficulty of keeping the law made most

who said that it was Paul's Christian experience with Gentiles that changed his Jewish theology.

17. Hill contends that Paul had a problem with all of Judaism, not just Pharisaic Judaism. "So long as there was a nonlegalistic (i.e. 'gracious') option available within contemporary Judaism, Paul could sensibly have chosen that option. *So it is not enough to claim that Paul opposed only a particular sort of Judaism.* His argument requires that no alternative might be found apart from Christ" ("Paul's Problem with Judaism," 312).

a failure, while tempting the best to be vain, arrogant, and self-righteous. Paul's confessions that he was the least of the apostles because of his past and that he continued to be a sinner who often did what he hated rather than the good he desired reminded him that God gave him righteousness (or salvation) as a gift. He believed that if salvation "comes through the law, then Christ died for nothing" (Gal 2:21). Ephesians declared, "For by grace you have been saved through faith, and this is not your own doing; it is the gift of God—not the result of works, so that no one may boast" (Eph 2:8–9). Paul's confession that the saints of God remain sinners as well not only expressed Paul's experience; it also reinforced his theology that salvation is received by grace through faith. He guarded against the religious temptation to make good deeds a qualifier for the faith, or an evaluation of the quality of one's faith. He avoided praising the best.

It is likely that Paul's theology of salvation by faith and his rejection of the Mosaic law as a means for salvation gave some the impression that Paul did not think Christians lived by any moral codes. As we covered in chapter 7, there are signs that later writers in the New Testament tried to change Paul's message. Luke wrote a story in Acts that depicts Paul vowing his obedience to the Mosaic law (Acts 21:17–26). Second Peter asserts that Paul's hard-to-understand letters lead to lawlessness (2 Pet 3:15–17). John's strict stand against sin may have been due to an impression that those influenced by Pauline Christianity were lenient about sin.

John warns his community not to love the world or the things of the world (1 John 2:15). Following a theme in John's gospel, he believes the world opposes the church. Sin is out there in the world: "the desire of the flesh, the desire of the eyes, the pride in riches" (2:16). Believers must avoid the world because its sin can infect the church like a virus infects a healthy body. John's words could make a compelling case. Sin spins a web that captures the curious and unsuspecting through the sexual exploitation of women, systemic racism in societies, callus profiteering by multinational corporations, malicious drug cartels, and the many ways the poor or marginalized are exploited for money. Believers cannot open the door to such things. Portraying sin in these terms makes John's insistence that it must be kept out of the community understandable.

"The basic geography is clear," Lewis Donelson notes in charting the theology of John's letters, "if you sin, you are a child of the devil; if you do what is right, you are a child of God. . . . The deeds show who you are. You are who you are in the deed."[18] Such a direct connection between behavior and belonging to the community requires a process for restoration when

18. Donelson, *Hebrews to Revelation*, 125.

human behavior inevitably fails the high standards of the community. Thus confession and repentance become necessary acts for the community.

John's theology about sin, which included the necessity for confession and restoration as well as keeping it outside the community, translated the Priestly theology of the Old Testament into Christian practices. The Priestly writings of the Torah made reconciliation an integral part of God's covenant with Israel. It assumed that Israel would sin and break the Mosaic law. "The possibility of being reconciled with God rather than being destroyed for its sin," Paul Hanson explains, "existed for Israel solely because God had provided a means of atonement."[19] The priests could restore relationships with God through sacrificial rituals, providing a systematic process by which sinners were reconciled to God via atonement for their sins. There is no waiting or wondering about this in the Priestly writings. Do the ritual and you are forgiven, period. John traded one ritual for another. While confession was a better deal for the animals, it brought both the benefits and the problems of the Priests' holiness theology into Christianity. John's theology identifies sin as something in the world that must be kept out of the church, and which requires confession and forgiveness to maintain relationships in the community. Paul could have thought John was restoring the very thing he tried to change from Judaism.

(3) Find Where You Want to Join the Divine Conversation

In her first book, *I Thought It Was Just Me*, Brené Brown defined shame as "the intensely painful feeling or experience of believing we are flawed and therefore unworthy of acceptance and belonging."[20] Brown, who has become a celebrity sociologist through her studies on shame and vulnerability, points out a basic problem the church faces when trying to talk about sin in a healthy manner—connection.

Pauline theology runs the risk of miscommunicating sin as shame by sentencing all human beings as flawed sinners. The first part of Brown's definition is the feeling or experience of believing we are flawed. Classic Pauline theology says just that. "There is no one who is righteous, not even one. . . . All have sinned and fall short of the glory of God" (Rom 3:10, 23). Western Christianity's preoccupation with sin tells its followers to believe that they are flawed human beings. The standard evangelical Christian presentation of the gospel starts with the statement that human beings are sinners.[21]

19. Hanson, *People Called*, 227.

20. Brown, *I Thought It Was Just Me*, 5.

21. McLaren, *New Kind of Christianity*, 33–45. McLaren explains the basic

However, Brown's definition pivots on the words "and therefore." Without the second part of her definition shame does not embody us with its debilitating force. Admitting that you are flawed, that you have issues, even to use the biblical word, that you are a sinner, while not a pleasant thing, is not necessarily a terrible thing. Brown's "and therefore" is what brings us low—"and therefore unworthy of acceptance and belonging." It is here in this second part of her definition that shame joins our divine conversation about sin.

While Paul declares that all human beings are sinners, that in one way or another we have all fallen short of God's glory, he also believes that God's love and grace are more profound than our weaknesses. God loves sinners, he declared to the Romans. "Where sin increased, grace abounded all the more" (5:20). So, Paul sees no problem in identifying himself among sinners. If he is a sinner, then he is loved and rescued by God through Jesus Christ. If the first half of Brown's definition of shame resembles Paul's doctrine that all human beings are flawed, then its similarity stops before "and therefore," because in Paul's theology no human being is unworthy of God's love and of the church's acceptance and belonging. Indeed, Paul passionately announces that nothing will ever be able to separate us from the love of God (8:31–39).

Conversely, John's dualism separates everything. Those who obey the commandments are God's children. Those who commit sin are children of the devil. Even if John's language exaggerates the reality—that all Christians do commit sin, but through confession are made righteous again— his written text promotes an impossible standard. Without understanding the rhetorical language of John's dualism and without a clear definition of sin John's words about sin can be arbitrarily used. When used in a healthy family or community, who generously forgives without judgment, John's words could be used to set high moral standards and through the tight bonds of love discourage behavior that injures self and others. Unfortunately, John's words could also be used by those in power to shame anyone who does not fall in line.

A community with extremely high standards will invariably lead to participants falling short of expectations, which necessitates the need for restoration. John provides that in his first chapter with the promise that confessed sin will be forgiven and the one who confesses will be treated as one who does not sin. In a tight community the pressure to comply, to submit

---

evangelical gospel presentation, then discusses its historical development, which has more to do with Plato than the Bible. Western Christianity, he says, "unwittingly traded its true heritage through Jesus from Judaism for an alien heritage drawn from Greek philosophy and Roman politics" (*New Kind of Christianity*, 41).

to authority over misdeeds can be extremely shaming. John's dualistic language about sin opens the door to Brown's definition of shame—the feeling
of being flawed and therefore unworthy of acceptance and belonging. And
in John's letters we see evidence of this—excluding people because they did
not comply with community standards.

Despite all his talk of loving one another, John's first letter calls some
antichrists, disclosing that "they went out from us, but they did not belong
to us; for if they had belonged to us, they would have remained with us"
(1 John 2:19–20). John's second letter tells readers that if they welcome
someone who teaches falsely they "participate in the evil deeds of such a
person" (2 John 11). Finally, John's third letter reveals a dispute with Diotrephes, a church leader in one of the congregations among John's wider
community. Diotrephes disagrees with John's teachings, does not recognize
John's authority, and expelled those from his congregation who approved of
John. To which John threatens, "If I come, I will call attention to what he is
doing in spreading false charges against us" (3 John 10).

These fractures in John's community are ironic given that he builds
his theology around loving the brothers and sisters of the congregation.
Donelson adds, "His insistence in 2 John that the 'deceivers' should not be
received into the community and not even greeted (10–11) has struck many
readers as contrary to this theology of love. . . . It does not make much
sense to espouse love as the center of the Christian life when love becomes
so circumscribed."[22] Additionally, in each of the conflicts above the sinners
at one time had a relationship with the community. Their sin came from
within, not out in the world. "The author's solution to this dilemma is to declare that any apparent previous common membership was illusory, falsified
by its impermanence," explains Judith Lieu, "had it been genuine belonging,
they would not have separated but would still be secure partners in the common fellowship."[23] If John used ridicule and expulsion against those once re-
spected in the community imagine the chilling affect that had on those who
crossed the line in other ways. Too often this has happened in the church's
history. Imagine for a moment—a pregnant teenager, a gay or lesbian young
adult, an alcoholic disciple, a spouse who had an affair, a strong woman who
will not comply to the congregation's confining rules for women, a transgender believer, and countless others—people that over the course of history
have been branded by the church and shamed because they did not comply
with the community's standards. John's words, "they went out from us, but
they did not belong to us," promote shame and do irreparable harm. Those

22. Donelson, *Hebrews to Revelation*, 118–19.
23. Lieu, *I, II, & III John*, 100.

forced to wear the *Scarlet Letter*, as Nathaniel Hawthorne's novel showed, unduly falls on the vulnerable and the powerless, whereas the powerful, in his case the village pastor, usually remain untouched.

Is John's argument with Paul salvageable? Or has John's dualistic language been so damaging in the church that it is best to declare Paul the winner and muffle John's message?

At the risk of cutting off the reader's own decision about where to join this conversation between Paul and John, I would suggest that John's dualistic language should be dropped from the church's lexicon *in order that* the principles of John's theology about sin may continue to debate Paul. John's bad habit of denigrating his opponents with disparaging names labels them *personae non gratae*. Labeling turns bad actions into bad people. This relates to a major difference between guilt and shame, according to Brown.

> Shame is about who we are and guilt is about our behaviors. . . . Guilt is holding an action or behavior up against our ethics, values and beliefs. We evaluate that behavior (like cheating) and feel guilt when the behavior is inconsistent with who we want to be. Shame is focusing on who we are rather than what we've done. The danger of telling ourselves that we are bad, a cheat, and no good, is that we eventually start to believe it and own it. The person who believes she is "no good" is much more likely to continue to cheat and fulfill that label than the person who feels guilt.[24]

People need the church to talk about guilt in order to help them process it in a healthy way, learn from it, and change behavior through its negative reinforcement. Guilt can motivate change. Shame, however, never has any positive outcomes. It is never redemptive.[25]

Beneath John's damaging language lay some theological concepts that are still worth debating Paul if we can get below the surface of his labels. While Paul's focus on sin is with the internal battle that people wage within themselves, John looks at sin as an external force. Paul might point to his chest and say, "Sin is here, in us." John with his finger pointing away from himself would say, "Sin is out there, in the world." As mentioned earlier there are plenty of forces of sin running rampant in the world. To ignore those forces and to only look internally for the sin within would naïvely let evil run free.

---

24. Brown, *I Thought It Was Just Me*, 13–14.

25. Brown explains, "The idea that there are two types, healthy shame and toxic shame, did not bear out in any of my research" (*I Thought It Was Just Me*, 62).

If John's animosity toward sin could be directed at the actions of people and not by labeling people, it could be productive instead of shame producing. I knew a man who once told me, "Preacher, I've done some bad things in my life. While I appreciate you reminding me of God's love and mercy, I need to hear about God's judgment to keep me on the straight and narrow." Some people require John's dualism of right and wrong as an ethical road map. Making the shift to talk about the destructive nature of sin upon self and others takes John's concern about sin and uses it in productive ways. The church should be uncompromising in condemning the actions of repeated and unremorseful sinners—such as sexual predators, slumlords, and white supremacists—and for calling them into repentance and the larger society to justice.

- As you consider Paul and John's viewpoints about sin which one more closely resembles your own human experience? In what ways?

- What are some positives and negatives in talking about sin as something that dwells within all of us? Do you agree with Paul that saints are sinners? Explain.

- What are some positives and negatives in talking about sin as something that dwells out in the world, which must be avoided at all costs? Do you agree with John that saints cannot be sinners nor can sinners be saints? Explain.

- Do you think congregations should expel or excommunicate persons based on their behavior or beliefs? What would be good or bad about that?

- In what ways can confession and repentance be practiced mercifully and redemptively in the church? In what ways could it be harmfully used?

- How would you like God and Christ's church to handle your own sin? How would you like God and the church to handle the sin of a person who sinned against you?

CHAPTER 10

Who Should Be Leaders in the Church?

First, get the right people on the bus . . . before you figure out
where to drive it.[1]

—JIM COLLINS

ONE OF THE OVERLOOKED aspects of Paul's ministry to churches was his skill at supervising and managing a team of volunteers. In every city where Paul started churches he trained leaders to carry on the work of the congregation while he was gone. We know this because he mentions them so often. He introduces twenty-seven persons by name in Romans 16, beginning with Phoebe, a deacon at the church in Cenchreae. She carried the letter for Paul, and probably preached on his behalf. Teams of people carried out his leadership in his absence; some served as his messengers, or taught the faith, while others were his personal assistants and secretaries.

Timothy, Silvanus, and Sosthenes coauthored of some of Paul's letters. Timothy and Silvanus preached at Corinth. Timothy, Titus, and Epaphroditus visited congregations for Paul. Aquila and Prisca taught the new Christian faith. Congregations had leaders whom Paul trusted, who informed him regarding church ministry: Euodia, Syntyche, and Clement in Philippi; Chloe, Stephanas, Fortunatus, and Achaicus in Corinth; Philemon, Apphia, and Archippus in Colossae. Onesimus, who was the subject of Paul's letter to Philemon, became his personal assistant while in prison. Tertitus was one of Paul's secretaries. Approximately fifty people served as leaders according to his letters. Paul developed this amazing matrix of leaders during a time when transportation meant walking and correspondence was handdelivered. Paul could not call, text, or email his team. He had to train them well; then trust them to faithfully lead in his absence.

The success of Paul's missions depended on solid leadership. If he did not train capable leaders in a church that he founded, when he left for the

---

1. Collins, *Good to Great*, 44.

next town all his work would be left to chance. His letters provided oversight to the churches he started. They allowed him to lead from a distance, but only the leaders in each local congregation or his messengers visiting on his behalf could implement his guidance.

Jim Collins, in such books as *Good to Great* and *Great by Choice*, spent a substantial amount of time researching successful companies. His books attempt to analyze how successful companies continue to improve into truly great companies without falling back from success into mediocrity. He determined that leadership was the single greatest factor in making good companies great, both at the top level of a company's administration and all down the line. Using the metaphor of a bus for a company, Collins determined that getting the right people on the bus was more important than where the CEO was driving it. "If you have the wrong people, it doesn't matter whether you discover the right direction; you *still* won't have a great company. Great vision without great people is irrelevant."[2] Collins is one of many researchers that have studied leadership and written enough books to fill a library. Despite many different approaches and findings, they all agree on one thing—leadership is vitally important to every organization.

Paul recognized this as well and wrote about church leadership in several of his letters. A few decades after Paul's death the Pastoral Letters created an argument within the Pauline tradition about leadership.

EXCURSUS 10.1

Who Wrote Paul's Letters?

Paul wrote the earliest documents in the New Testament. He penned the first letter to the church at Thessalonica around ten to fifteen years after Jesus' death and resurrection. There is no way to know how many letters he wrote to churches and individuals. He mentions letters not in the New Testament, which did not exist when he wrote them. We have what was saved. Thirteen of the twenty-seven books in the New Testament claim Pauline authorship, but they were written over several decades. Most biblical scholars today believe Paul wrote seven of the letters that bear his name. A reasonable chronological order is 1 Thessalonians, 1 Corinthians, 2 Corinthians 10–13, 2 Corinthians 1–9, Galatians,

---

2. Collins, *Good to Great*, 42.

Philippians, and Romans, with Philemon's sequence unknown.[3] Romans was the only letter written to a congregation he had yet to visit. It served as his introduction to them and comprised many ideas from earlier letters.

Colossians and Ephesians contain phrases seen in Paul's authentic letters, leading some scholars to believe Paul wrote them as well.[4] E. P. Sanders thinks that the word-for-word verbatim of the phrases is too perfect and instead suggests that they have been copied.[5] The two are more similar to each other than any other letters. While they sound like Paul in parts, they also contain theological concepts not seen in the undisputed seven. Possibly Paul's assistants first compiled Colossians some time after his death using his notes and former letters, and later wrote Ephesians using Colossians. Colossians claims Timothy as a coauthor.

The Pastoral Letters—1 and 2 Timothy and Titus—are so different from the undisputed letters that scholars think they were written by disciples of the Pauline tradition approximately twenty to thirty years after Paul's death.[6] The writer may have been a "sympathetic commentator on the Pauline heritage," or among those who wanted "to domesticate [Paul's] memory and bring the apostle into the mainstream."[7] They changed some of Paul's beliefs, possibly to move their admired faith hero more in line with changes in the first-century church. However, Borg and Crossan insist that they are anti-Pauline. "They represent . . . a taming of Paul, a domestication of Paul's passion to the normalcy of the Roman imperial world in which he and his followers lived."[8] In doing so, the last letters of the Pauline tradition sound more like Peter's first letter than Paul's first letters. The Pauline disciples may have brought Paul into agreement with church leaders by the end of the first century, but in doing so they created arguments within the Pauline tradition—between Paul's authentic letters and the Pastorals.

---

3. Sanders, *Paul*, 151.

4. Brown, *Introduction*, 600, 621. Brown estimates that about 40 percent of scholars think Paul wrote Colossians, while only 20 percent believe he wrote Ephesians.

5. Sanders, *Paul*, 152.

6. Dunn, "Timothy and Titus," 11:775–82.

7. Brown, *Introduction*, 663.

8. Borg and Crossan, *First Paul*, 15.

Spiritual Gifts vs. Cultural Qualifications

Paul believed that the Holy Spirit empowered those who followed Jesus with spiritual gifts. God gave different talents and abilities to each person for the common good of all: wisdom, knowledge, faith, gifts of healing, miracles, prophecy, discernment, speaking in tongues and discernment of tongues (1 Cor 12:7–10). Note that these are leadership skills, not positions. New churches were starting up across the Roman Empire. There were no offices or positions of leadership. People led in the way they were gifted. Paul described this as the work of the Holy Spirit (12:11).

In Paul's most memorable metaphor, he calls the church the body of Christ and describes it as a human body with eyes, ears, and all the other body parts. Just as a body needs eyes and ears, legs and arms, so the body of Christ needs a variety of leaders. Everyone is essential. Though the Spirit gifts individuals, they are empowered for the good of the whole body.

> Indeed the body does not consist of one member but of many. . . . If the ear would say, "Because I am not an eye, I do not belong to the body," that would not make it any less a part of the body. If the whole body were an eye, where would the hearing be? If the whole body were hearing, where would the sense of smell be? But as it is, God arranged the members of the body, each one of them, as he chose. . . . The members of the body that seem weaker are indispensable, and those members of the body that we think less honorable we clothe with greater honor, and our less respectable members are treated with greater respect; whereas our more respectable members do not need this. (12:14–24)

While Paul believes every person served an essential role in the life of a congregation, he does not think that all leadership gifts are equally important. Apostles, prophets and teachers are most important, while speaking in tongues is least (12:28). The greatest gift, however, is love. Without love prophecy is nothing. Without love speaking in tongues is just a clanging cymbal. Without love sacrificial generosity gains nothing. While prophecy and knowledge come to an end, love never ends (13). Paul's most famous passage originally had nothing to do with romance or weddings. His chapter on love is a commentary about leadership. A congregation properly led is unified in love. They have become one in Christ. The least talented are especially valued. The most talented need no such praise.

Paul believed leadership in the church should be based on spiritual gifts.[9] If God gave someone the talent to preach, then she should preach.

9. Holmberg deduces, "It is obvious that *charismatic authority* is the predominant

If someone had the gift to be an administrator, then he should manage church affairs. If God gave someone the gift of wisdom, then the church should find ways to let that person lead by wisdom. No other qualifications or credentials or status in life mattered, only giftedness. It was a utilitarian approach to leadership. It broke down cultural barriers. "For in the one Spirit we were all baptized into one body—Jews or Greeks, slaves or free—and we were all made to drink of one Spirit" (12:13). It did not matter if someone was male or female, slave or free, old or young, Jewish or Gentile, married, single, or widowed. All were baptized into one body. In the church at least such distinctions would not limit any from using the leadership gifts God had given them.

The Pastoral Letters—1 and 2 Timothy and Titus—were written when Christian congregations had become established. No longer start-ups, they had been growing and thriving for decades. Now, official positions of leadership had been created.[10] There was an "office of bishop," which held some acclaim because people now "aspired" to this "noble task" (1 Tim 3:1). Likewise deacon was an official leadership position in churches. In addition a "council of elders" approved those set apart for leadership by a ritual "laying on of hands" (4:14). The books of 1 Timothy and Titus spend a substantial portion of their letters addressing church leadership and congregational behavior. The difference between Paul's discussion of leadership and the Pastorals is stark. The Pastorals make lists of qualifications concerning bishops, deacons, and elders, but they have little to do with competency. For Paul the only qualification for leadership is giftedness. Now, giftedness is rarely mentioned.

A bishop "must be above reproach, married only once, temperate, sensible, respectable, hospitable, an apt teacher, not a drunkard, not violent but gentle, nor quarrelsome, and not a lover of money." A bishop must not be a recent convert and must manage his household well, "for if someone does not know how to manage his own household, how can he take care of God's church?" Finally, "he must be well thought of by outsiders" (3:2–7). The qualification list for deacons is very similar (3:8–13). In Titus, it mentions that the children of elders must be "believers and not accused of debauchery and not rebellious" (Titus 1:6). Reputation, of the leader and his family,

---

type [of leadership] in the Primitive Church, based mainly as it is on the endowment of divine or extraordinary gifts" (*Paul and Power*, 196).

10. In Paul's undisputed letters, the term bishop is used only once, and deacon twice (Phil 1:1; Rom 16:1). Paul greets the bishops and deacons, plural, of the Philippian church. While those titles later became established offices in the Christian church, there is no way to know what those terms meant in Philippi. Why, for instance, would one small house church have multiple bishops?

became the most important qualification for leadership by the late first century.[11] The only sentence concerning competency refers to bishops, "He must have a firm grasp of the word that is trustworthy in accordance with the teaching, so that he may be able both to preach with sound doctrine and to refute those who contradict it" (1:9).

The contrast between Paul and the Pastoral Letters regarding leadership could hardly be greater. For Paul the qualifications should be based completely on competency as the Spirit gifts each person regardless of credentials or social status in life. For the Pastorals the qualifications one needs to be a leader in the church are almost completely based on cultural respectability with barely a word said about competency. Categorically, women are excluded from nearly all, if not all, positions of leadership. Given that generosity and reputation in the community are required to be a bishop, it is hard to imagine the poor or slaves could become leaders in the churches that received Timothy and Titus's letters.

Practicing Midrash

The extreme positions taken by these writers create an argument about church leadership. Should the qualifications for church leadership solely be based on either competency or cultural norms? If so, how should talent given by the Spirit be judged? Has the Spirit truly gifted a mediocre preacher, or would her less than stellar talent be a sign she has another gift unrealized? Or what behaviors define a good reputation? Are the lists supplied by Timothy and Titus universal for all times, or should they change as society changes? Is such a choice exclusive, or is there some combination of competency and cultural norms, a mixture between these extremes, that could provide principles for selecting good leadership in the church?

Paul and the Pastoral Letters wrote about church leadership from different contexts. The Corinthian church struggled with divisions within its fellowship. It reached the point that when the church gathered for a meal rather than share food together like a potluck dinner each family ate only the food they brought. While some families became drunk, other families barely had enough to eat (1 Cor 11:17–22). Paul initially wrote about church leadership in response to specific problems at the Corinthian church. What he said, though, he later summarized to the Romans. More importantly, he practiced what he said to the Corinthians. Paul wrote about leadership in

---

11. Dunn notes, "The role of overseer as the acceptable public face of the church was evidently of greater importance than his role as instructor in faith!" ("Timothy and Titus," 805).

the mid-fifties of the first century to first-generation churches, but his ideas about leadership exceeded their context. A Pauline disciple wrote 1 Timothy some thirty years after Paul wrote to the Corinthians. By now three generations of believers had come together for worship, study, and fellowship. Timothy's mother, Eunice, and grandmother Lois, like many others nurtured their children and grandchildren in the faith (2 Tim 1:5). No longer could they rely on the charisma of talented individuals. They needed stable leadership. The emerging church at the end of the first century presented another vision for church leadership. For centuries it influenced how the Christian church selected leaders.

From two different contexts Paul and a disciple who admired him wrote about church leadership. To really hear them let each of them speak beyond their context.

(1) Free the Stories to Speak for Themselves

Paul's practice matched his words. He said that only competency as given by the Spirit mattered in regards to leadership. As for social barriers he told the Galatians and Corinthians that the baptized were all one in Christ Jesus. His lists of coworkers include Greeks and Jews as well as women and men. In the letter to Philemon we learn that a runaway slave became one of his closest assistants.

Philemon presents a fascinating look into Paul's mind. Onesimus, a runaway slave, had found his way to Paul, who was in prison. He belonged to Philemon, whose home happened to be the meeting place for the church in Colossae.[12] Onesimus converted to the faith and came to know Paul through his ministry with the Colossians. He must have thought Paul would be a sympathetic ear to his plight. If he had heard Paul preaching what he wrote to the Galatians, "As many of you as were baptized into Christ have clothed yourselves with Christ. There is no longer Jew or Greek, there is no longer slave or free, there is no longer male and female; for all of you are one in Christ Jesus" (Gal 3:27–28), it is understandable that he would trust Paul to help him. Consider the alternative, if we have somehow misunderstood Paul and in fact his teachings had instead reinforced the social strata of the Roman Empire it is unlikely a runaway slave would seek him out.

Paul becomes a father figure to Onesimus and decides to help him. Paul's assistance is consistent with how he wrote about the intersection of faith and social structures. Onesimus broke the law by running away, as did Paul by protecting him. He would have been aware of the social

12. Brown, *Introduction*, 507–8.

injustice of slavery, and that the Roman Empire was economically built on slavery.[13] Paul convinces Onesimus to return to his owner. Onesimus could have kept running, but he trusted Paul's influence upon Philemon. Consequently, he returned carrying the letter with him. It is a personal letter to Philemon. It never discusses criminal or legal matters. It does not speak of the injustices of slavery as a system of labor, or of God's displeasure with it.[14] He speaks to Philemon as a partner and friend. He begins by praising Philemon for his loving and faithful leadership in the church. At the end of the letter he asks Philemon to keep a guest room ready for him for when he is released from prison.

Paul appeals to Philemon to voluntarily release Onesimus from slavery. In convincing Onesimus to return, Paul had already placed his trust in Philemon. "I am bold enough in Christ to command you to do your duty, yet I would rather appeal to you on the basis of love" (Phlm 8–9). Though he hopes Philemon will make a voluntary decision (14), beneath the rhetorical surface, however, the apostle demands. He appeals to Philemon as an elder and as a prisoner for Christ. He shames him by promising to cover any expenses Onesimus has cost him. Finally, he reminds Philemon that he owes him his "own self," concluding, "Yes, brother, let me have this benefit from you in the LORD!" (19–20). Paul's letter, while personal, was not private; he wrote the letter to Philemon's household and "to the church in your house" (2).[15] If Philemon wished to keep his good standing in the Colossian church, he would have to release Onesimus from slavery. As a couple of scholars have noted, "Everyone is watching what he will do."[16]

The letter to Philemon first indicates that Paul believes Onesimus's status as a slave does not limit his standing in the church. Additionally, it shows that Paul attempted to tear down such barriers between believers, and furthermore that he did so as a prophetic voice within the church, but not as a revolutionary prophet in society.[17]

13. Paul would have been aware that the Mosaic law allowed indentured labor for seven years, but prohibited slavery for life (Exod 21:2; Deut 15:12–18).

14. Brown notes that many criticize Paul for not taking a social justice position on slavery. "Tolerating a social evil while gently protesting in the name of Christianity is tantamount to condoning it and ensuring its survival. And indeed through the centuries Paul's failure to condemn slavery was used by some Bible readers as proof that the institution was not evil in itself" (*Introduction*, 507).

15. Borg and Crossan, *First Paul*, 41.

16. Borg and Crossan, *First Paul*, 42.

17. Borg and Crossan suggest that Paul's influence regarding Onesimus did not carry over as a societal response. The book of Colossians, written by his disciples after his death, "addresses Christian slaves and Christian slave-owners and thereby depicts those relationships as perfectly normal" (*First Paul*, 45).

Throughout Paul's letters he mentions numerous women leaders in the churches. Ten of the twenty-seven leaders mentioned in Romans 16 were women.[18] Some had titles, such as Phoebe, who was a deacon in the church at Cenchrae (Rom 16:1), and Junias, whom he recognized as an apostle (16:7). Euodia and Syntyche served as key leaders to the Philippian church. He instructed them to work together and be of the same mind in the Lord (Phil 4:2). Paul made women part of his extended leadership team. Add his thinking in the letter to Philemon and it is easy to imagine Paul treating women as equals in the church. It is also likely that he had to persuade men—husbands and fathers—to receive them as equals, just as he sought to persuade Philemon to accept Onesimus as an equal brother in Christ. Paul practiced what he preached in regards to leadership.

There is no getting around the fact that the role of women was severely restricted in the Pastoral Letters. The subordination of women, however, was not a Christian value created to transform the culture. It was a Roman cultural value that subdued the radical Christian ideals that sprang up in the first generation of the church.[19] First-century philosopher Plutarch sounded similar to the Pastorals when he wrote, "As long as they (the wives) are subordinate to their husbands, they deserve praise. . . . But the husband must not rule over his wife like a despot over his property, but like the soul over the body—full of compassion and growing together with her in love."[20] The movement to restrict women's roles made the church more acceptable as it infiltrated the Roman culture. Bonnie Bowman Thurston reasons that in the first century "Christianity's freedom from normal social patterns (as evidenced by Gal 3:28) threatened [the family], and therefore the whole Roman social order. Thus the writer of the Pastorals wants to orient the church toward a patriarchal order of household duties similar to that of the dominant culture of the Roman empire."[21] To do this the Pastorals, written in Paul's name, pulled the apostle away from his original, more radical, declarations about women in the church. Susan Heine spells out the change from the early ideals of Paul's letters to what became the standard after the Pastorals: "For women to be active in public inside and outside the Christian community is [now] regarded by Christians as shameful. Thus all former activities through which women were of service

18. Borg and Crossan, *First Paul*, 52. Polaski, *Feminist Introduction to Paul*, 45.

19. Polaski suggests that the author of the Pastorals was caught up in the context of his society and taught the status quo: "the hierarchal, patriarchal structures of the Greco-Roman world" (*Feminist Introduction to Paul*, 108).

20. Plutarch; as quoted in Heine, *Women and Early Christianity*, 138 (parenthetical note is Heine's).

21. Thurston, *Widows*, 38–39.

in mission and building up the community were no longer available, indeed forbidden, to them. Only a few decades later it was possible to forget all these services on the part of women and to suppress them. In the name of Paul and with a false appeal to his authority this development was given biblical and Christological support."[22] The author of the Pastorals even declared that women "will be saved through childbearing, provided they continue in faith and love and holiness, with modesty" (1 Tim 2:15). So much for salvation by faith alone![23]

The Pastorals decide to move from spiritual gifts as the major factor in selecting church leaders to cultural qualifications in order to survive as a minority group in an imperial society. Paul was concerned about unwanted notoriety in his day as well. He told the Roman church to "be subject to the governing authorities" (Rom 13:1). Furthermore, while he stressed equality within the church he never spoke of revolutionary social change. Thirty years later, however, equal in the church but not in society would not work. Paul may have thought Jesus was coming soon, but the Pastoral Letters had to plan for the long haul.

It is important to read the Pastoral Letters from their first-century Roman Empire perspective and not judge them by our twenty-first-century eyes. There is no need to fix them, either. Let them speak from their context and hear them, whether we like what they say or not, in order to see if there are principles beneath the surface worth applying for our generation.

(2) Listen to the Stories as Contrasting Voices of God

Paul's position that competency should guide the selection of leaders in the church without regard for societal norms is supported by several passages in his letters. In his discourse on the body of Christ he states that believers are baptized into one body and "all made to drink of one Spirit." Therefore, culturally constructed barriers—between Jews and Greeks, slaves and free—are torn down in the church (1 Cor 12:13). Paul later repeats this statement on baptism to the Galatians, and includes gender barriers (Gal 3:27–28). Colossians repeats the idea, this time juxtaposing the civilized and uncivilized (Col 3:11). Paul did not make his baptism statement in 1 Corinthians to be an exhaustive statement about transcending specific

---

22. Heine, *Women and Early Christianity*, 139.

23. Brown, *Introduction*, 661. Brown believes the verse may have been pointing to Gen 3:16 where Eve is told by God that she will bear children in labor, thus reinforcing the idea of a God-ordained natural order of things.

barriers, but as a living commentary used for whatever cultural barriers mattered in a church's context.[24]

Paul never excludes women from any roles in the church.[25] Earlier in 1 Corinthians, before he spoke about church leadership, Paul made the case for equality of women and men first at home and then in the church. Paul's thinking backtracks more than once making both passages difficult to unwind. One thing is clear in the first passage: he believes marriage to be a mutual relationship (1 Cor 7). The wife has as much say over her husband as the husband has over his wife. There is nothing Paul says of husbands in that passage that he does not also say of wives and vice versa.[26]

In the second discourse Paul states that women should lead worship through prayer and preaching along with men (11). His only stipulation is that women should dress according to local customs as they lead worship. Paul's thesis is a tangled mess.[27] He struggles with two different issues: gender hierarchy and gender difference. He argues for gender equality in the church—no hierarchy—but also for keeping customs that signify the differences between women and men.[28] Paul is not so different from Americans during the past few generations. The struggle for equality of women has often times been as heated regarding clothing as with more substantive issues. Gail Collins opens her book *When Everything Changed: The Amazing Journey of American Women from 1960 to the Present*, with the story of Lois Rabinowitz, who was ejected from a New York City court in 1960 for wearing pants.[29] Paul's dilemma with the Corinthian church should sound

24. Heine, *Women and Early Christianity*, 85.

25. Sampley, "First Letter to the Corinthians," 10:969.

26. Polaski, *Feminist Introduction to Paul*, 51.

27. Heine, *Women and Early Christianity*, 97–98. She has a brief exploration into Paul's arguments about women wearing veils when they led worship. She explains that first Paul appealed to Jewish tradition, then to natural law, and finally just ends the discussion by saying we have no custom of women going without veils. Heine believes Paul had a problem between "theory and praxis, between the knowledge that in Christ men have no advantage over women or *vice versa* (cf. vv. 11, 12), and the inner emotional link with familiar practice—women wear veils. In the light of this contradiction he is not free enough to accept women without veils. Here he might not have found things so difficult had he argued for uncircumcised men. Paul knows the gospel that he preaches to Jew and Gentiles all over the world, but sometimes he had difficulty in acting in accordance with it—a familiar phenomenon to us" (Heine, *Women and Early Christianity*, 98). Elisabeth Schussler Fiorenza writes, "Finally, Paul concludes this mixture of biblical and philosophical arguments with an authoritarian assertion in v. 16, probably because he senses that his theological argument is not very convincing" (Schussler Fiorenza, "I Corinthians," 1183).

28. Crossan and Reed, *In Search of Paul*, 113–14.

29. Gail Collins, *When Everything Changed*, 3.

familiar to anyone involved with the rise of women into the workplace, the boardroom, politics, and the pulpit over the past half century.

Borg and Crossan note what is *not* being questioned in Paul's tortured reasoning, "From the very start of his discussion, it is explicitly clear that Paul presumes . . . that equality is taken for granted—female and male are equal in the communal Christian assembly just as in the private Christian family."[30] In both first-century Roman and Jewish cultures, the husband's authority over his wife was unquestioned and in public spheres there was no hint of gender equality. He bogs down in a convoluted argument in chapter 11 when he attempts to break down barriers in the church without suggesting that societal norms need to be changed as well. While he speaks strongly for equality in the church—including church leadership—Paul never suggests a new social order for the empire. Instead, he advises that new converts in the faith remain in whatever status in life they were when baptized. "Were you a slave when called? Do not be concerned about it. Even if you can gain your freedom, make use of your present condition now more than ever. . . . In whatever condition you were called, brothers and sisters, there remain with God" (7:21–24).

Why did Paul proclaim equality in the church, but not a revolutionary equality for society? I do not think there is a clear answer in his letters. Perhaps it was because he thought Christ's return was pending, therefore his only concern was for the church and being made one in Christ. Perhaps it was because of imperial power, and he feared that if the church brought undue attention upon itself that it would face persecution. Either is plausible, neither is sufficient.

As for his argument that church leadership should be based on competency without regard to status in life, his comments regarding cultural categories, particularly in regards to gender, reinforce this position. Additionally, Paul's actions mirrored his words. We saw in the previous section his practice to involve a wide variety of persons into his circle of leadership. His letters are consistent. When baptized into Christ's body social status no longer matters for all are one in Christ. God chooses leadership for the church based on the gifts that God endows upon followers of Christ. Anyone gifted to preach, should preach; anyone gifted to administer, should manage; anyone gifted to teach, should teach without regard for cultural norms in society.

Conversely, the Pastoral Letters have a great concern about cultural norms. They reinforce the social strata of the Roman Empire within the

---

30. Borg and Crossan, *First Paul*, 51. See also Polaski, *Feminist Introduction to Paul*, 56.

church. A husband's authority is supreme in his household—over wife as husband, children as father, and slaves as master. The leadership role of women is restricted to women's groups in the church. They must remain silent in worship. They cannot have any authority over men (1 Tim 2:8–12). This reverses what Paul preached thirty years earlier. Borg and Crossan propose that the Pastorals are "clearly reacting to what has been happening. There would be no reason to forbid what nobody had ever imagined."[31] Not only did the Pastoral Letters break out in an argument with Paul *in his name*, someone from that group made a late insertion to 1 Corinthians, stating that it is "shameful for a woman to speak in church" (1 Cor 14:34–35).[32] This insertion put the attitude of 1 Timothy into one of Paul's authentic letters. The NRSV of the Bible now puts parentheses around these verses because they were not originally in 1 Corinthians. A footnote for those verses says that some ancient manuscripts place them after v. 40, which is another reason to believe they were later inserted.[33]

Women are told "to love their husbands . . . being submissive to their husbands, so that the word of God may not be discredited" (Titus 2:4–5). These writers cannot imagine gender equality within home and church as expressed by Paul. They do not instruct husbands to love or care for their wives.[34] Leading men in the congregation—bishops and deacons—must "manage" their households well (1 Tim 3:4, 12). That's as close to love and self-sacrifice as you will find in the Pastorals from husband to wife, and father to children. No moral restraint is placed on the behavior of a husband toward his wife and children, as long as he could manage them well. His wife must submit to him, or she would discredit the word of God—which

31. Borg and Crossan, *First Paul*, 56.

32. See Sampley, "First Letter to the Corinthians," 10:968–71. The Pastorals are the background for the insertion, "Women should be silent in the churches. For they are not permitted to speak, but should be subordinate, as the law also says. If there is anything they desire to know, let them ask their husbands at home. For it is shameful for a woman to speak in church" (1 Cor 14:34–35). The text does not fit the 14th chapter of 1 Corinthians and is in direct contradiction to what Paul just wrote in the 11th chapter. It is, however, in perfect agreement with 1 Timothy. Scholars now believe it was inserted into Paul's letter at a later date, most probably during the time period that the Pastorals were written. See also Polaski, *Feminist Introduction*, 56–59.

33. Meeks, *HarperCollins Study Bible*, 2160; Borg and Crossan, *First Paul*, 57.

34. It should be noted that this paradigm is used for slaves and masters as well. Slaves are instructed to be submissive to their masters and not to talk back, not to pilfer. Yet, no instructions are voiced for their masters. Similarly, there is no moral restraint for a husband's authority over wife and children (Titus 2:1–10).

meant her disobedience would offend God. An independent wife is not only singled out for her taboo behavior, but she also becomes a heretic.[35]

The Pastoral Letters' instructions about church leadership matches their behavioral instructions to various groups in the church—older people, women, children, slaves. They all provide order to the churches. They value reputation and respectability more than competency, because the church wants to promote its image in the Roman Empire. If the church selects leaders based on their reputation and cultural qualifications and groups behave according to their social status in Roman life, then the church will be "well thought of by outsiders," and "the name of God and the teaching may not be blasphemed," and "the word of God may not be discredited," so therefore "any opponent will be put to shame, having nothing evil to say of us," and "no occasion to revile us" (1 Tim 3:7; 5:14; 6:1; Titus 2:5, 8). The Pastorals aim to convince Romans that people in the church were just like them; a reaffirmation of Roman social restrictions placed upon many groups was acceptable collateral damage.

Like 1 Peter, the Pastorals spend much of their writing shaping up the church's hierarchy. They have different rules for different people, depending on gender, marital status, citizenship and age. Even salvation is gained through different avenues, depending on status. The editors of the Pastoral Letters save Paul's image as the early church movement became an institution in the Roman world. They clarify his radical ideas. They amend his egalitarian notions for the church. This new Paul is easier to understand; no one should misread him (2 Pet 3:15–16). The Pastorals re-explain any radical notions readers may get from Paul's original letters. Their focus on cultural respectability as a qualification for leadership not only helps churches assimilate into their Roman setting; it also rehabilitates Paul's radical and troublesome sayings.

(3) Find Where You Want to Join the Divine Conversation

There is a cave on the northern edge of ancient Ephesus, which at one point was used by Christians as a gathering place. Near the entrance two life-size figures are painted in the traditional pose of giving a blessing. The person on the left is Paul. The person on the right is Thecla, who is just as tall as Paul and offers the same sign of blessing, indicating that they have equal authority.[36] *The Acts of Paul and Thecla*, a second-century text, tells the story of how Paul converted Thecla to the faith, how she escaped martyrdom, and

35. Heine, *Women and Early Christianity*, 139.
36. Crossan and Reed, *In Search*, xii–xiv.

later joined Paul to preach the gospel.[37] She remains a venerated saint in Eastern Orthodox churches today.

In this fresco, however, her portrait has been defaced. Her raised hand, offering a priestly blessing, and her eyes have been scratched out and the plaster burnt. "An earlier image in which Thecla and Paul were equally authoritative apostolic figures has been replaced by one in which the male is apostolic and authoritative and the female is blinded and silenced."[38] This ancient fresco captures the argument between Paul and the Pastorals about church leadership. Plastered onto the wall of the cave, it first symbolized the story of Paul and Thecla and how her gifts for ministry made her leadership in the church equally valid and valued. Defaced by those who rejected gender equality, it came to represent the choice to let cultural norms determine who could and could not be eligible for church leadership. The fresco represents more than the debate about gender equality; it also speaks to the larger argument between Paul and the Pastorals. Over the centuries when cultural norms have dominated the discussion about church leadership many have been excluded because of them: women, slaves, ethnic and racial outsiders, divorced persons, LGBTQ persons, those without degrees, the poor, convicts, and others. Such discussions continue still. In some church communions only men can serve as pastors or priests. When a congregation is predominantly one racial or ethnic group, it is rare when a person of another racial or ethnic group is selected to serve as the pastor. The consideration to ordain gay, lesbian or transgender persons has split congregations and denominations. Cultural norms—whatever they may be—have been a part of the selection of church leaders for twenty centuries. As you decide where to enter this conversation, it is important to see the discussion beyond any single cultural construction. Paul spoke of how baptism in the church tore down many cultural barriers, and the Pastorals instruct several social groups on how to behave as part of the church. Neither focused on one category.

One thing has largely changed since the first-century debate. The Pastoral Letters limited the leadership pool in order to "be well thought of by outsiders." The disciples of Paul changed the apostle's message in order to make his teachings more acceptable to Roman culture. When social status is used to exclude someone from leadership today, however, it is often made

37. Polaski says that Thecla's story provides "evidence that some of those who understood themselves to stand in the Pauline tradition read Paul very differently than the tradition of the pastorals" (*Feminist Introduction*, 109).

38. Crossan and Reed, *In Search*, xii–xiii. Photographs of the fresco may be found on pp. xii–xiv, as well as in the center photos between pp. 210 and 211. An artistic restoration of the fresco is also on the cover of the book.

counterculturally against the larger society in order to conform to standards of a sub-cultural, church context. Gender and racial equality are the stated norms of American society, today, even if not fully practiced. Acceptance and affirmation of LGBTQ persons is heading in that direction. The decision to exclude persons from church leadership because of gender, race, ethnicity, or sexual orientation is becoming a countercultural decision in the twenty-first-century United States.

This adds another dimension to the argument between Paul and the Pastorals. Who is more true to the intent of the Pastoral Letters regarding church leadership—churches that change the leadership pool based on the changing societal norms of their nation, or churches that retain a fixed idea of cultural qualifications based on the societal norms of first-century Rome? This chapter has shown that Paul's focus on competency, along with his baptismal statement that all are one in Christ, expanded the leadership pool of first-generation churches to include women, slaves, and the uneducated. Yet, Pauline disciples rejected this position within two generations. Instead, they wanted leaders that gave churches respectability in the community, so they excluded groups of persons in the church whose leadership would have conflicted with the cultural norms of Roman society. In early twenty-first-century America, however, to exclude women from church leadership brings contempt upon the church from the larger society. To exclude the poor or uneducated makes the church look elitist. To exclude because of race or ethnicity makes the church look racist. And to exclude gay, lesbian, or transgender persons from church leadership makes the church look judgmental to young adults now and increasingly so to other demographic groups in society. It can be persuasively argued that congregations wishing to "be well thought of by outsiders" should ordain persons for church leadership without regard to gender, race, ethnicity, or sexual orientation. While congregations that exclude persons for leadership based on the fixed categories in the Pastoral Letters must argue that the cultural norms of first-century Rome are universal for all time and that what outsiders think of the church no longer matters.

So, where do you want to join the conversation? How does this argument between Paul and the Pastorals influence your thoughts about leadership in the Christian church?

- Should churches select leadership solely based on a person's competency without regard to any other matters? What could be the rewards and the risks of such a policy?

- Should churches make cultural respectability a priority in selecting leaders—even if that means certain persons would be excluded because of a socially constructed category (gender, race, etc.)? What could be the rewards and the risks of prioritizing respectability and diminishing the importance of competency?

- In what ways could you imagine blending the best ideas from Paul and the Pastoral Letters? Pretend you attend a congregation that is looking for a new pastor. Using the best ideas from Paul and the Pastorals create a pastor profile that could be used to market the open position. What would your ideal pastor or priest look like?

- If you were to argue for Paul's position—that giftedness without regard for social status is the main criterion for leadership—what points would you make to state your case?

- If you were to argue that the Pastoral Letters changed the Pauline position on leadership in order to field church leaders that would reflect positively on congregations in their Roman communities, and that this still had relevance for the church today, what points would you make to state your case? And based on trends of American society, should there be any groups of persons restricted from church leadership because of their social status? If so, whom and why?

- If you were to argue that the qualifications listed in the Pastoral Letters, which restrict top-level leadership to well-connected, married, heterosexual men, are still valid for the church today, what points would you make to state your position? Are there some subcultural contexts (geographic regions, racial or ethnic communities, particular denominations, etc.) in the United States where this approach to leadership may be most fitting? Which ones and why? Are there subcultural contexts where these qualification lists make the church's reputation less respectable today? Which ones and why?

- Consider some ways in which social status may trump simple competency when selecting church leaders—such as a congregation wishing to balance gender and age on the board of deacons or elders. Or if a multiracial congregation would seek a racial or ethnic balance on the church staff to approximate the membership of the church. Or perhaps a welcoming and affirming congregation would seek an LGBTQ candidate to fill a vacant staff position if the rest of the staff is heterosexual and cisgender. Are such examples the same thing if a conservative, evangelical church only considers men for the office of pastor or deacon? If not, how are those examples different? In what ways could such examples be considered a modern parallel to how the Pastoral Letters approached selecting church leaders?

The church still argues about leadership because good leadership is always needed. Getting the right people on the bus—to use Jim Collins's metaphor—means first determining who the right people are. As American society has changed over the past half-century so has leadership across Christian denominations and their churches, and it is likely that both will continue to change for some time. Each time another change is debated Paul and the Pastorals will once again be used to argue the case. As with all these arguments, it is a never-ending conversation.

CONCLUSION

Wrestling with the Bible

The conservative who resists change is as valuable as the
radical who proposes it. . . . It is good that the old should
resist the young, and that the young should prod the old; out
of this tension, as out of the strife of the sexes and the classes,
comes a creative tensile strength, a stimulated development,
a secret and basic unity and movement of the whole.[1]

—WILL AND ARIEL DURANT

A STRANGER ATTACKED HIM under the cover of darkness. Wrestling
throughout the night, neither could defeat the other, nor could they break
free to escape. This is the story of how Jacob became Israel; how the father
of twelve sons became the father of a nation. The attacking stranger wounds
Jacob. The stranger blesses Jacob. It is a curious tale (Gen 32).

Jacob, who had stolen his brother's blessing twenty years earlier, was
now returning to his homeland. Having been told of Jacob's journey home,
Esau set out with four hundred men to greet his return. Jacob assumed the
worst and took precautions. He ensured his safety by sending his entire family, his wives and children, all his livestock and servants across the River
Jabbok, while he camped the night alone on the far side of the river. It was
quintessential Jacob; he would sacrifice his children in order to save his own
skin. He would cowardly slip away, if need be, from Esau's revenge.

After his family had forded the river, and Jacob was alone, a stranger
attacked him and the two wrestled until daybreak. The man's identity is a
mystery. Was it Esau, who somehow surprised Jacob? Or was it a Freudian
dream of Esau? Could it have been an angel from heaven, or God face-to-
face? The ambiguity heightens the suspense of the story. The attacker cannot
defeat Jacob; they battle to a draw after wrestling throughout the night. The
man, though he cannot defeat Jacob, has the power to bless, the authority

1. Durant, *Lessons of History*, 36.

to rename a person. He also has the power to wound, which he does to Jacob's hip, or maybe, as the text euphemistically suggests, his genitals. This stranger did not fight fairly. Of course, neither had Jacob during his life.[2]

The mysterious attacker blessed Jacob, though the words of blessing are a mystery as well. With the blessing, Jacob was renamed Israel, "for you have striven with God and with humans and have prevailed" (32:28). To receive the blessing, Jacob hung on for dear life. In fact, he demanded to be blessed or he would not let go of this mystery.

This was a curious blessing, a cursed blessing. The wrestled blessing permanently injures him, and he limps the rest of his days. Was Jacob's injury a part of the blessing, or simply a consequence of wrestling with mystery? Phyllis Trible describes this as a story of mixed messages: "Jacob gets his blessing, but not on his own terms. . . . As for the stranger in the night, he remains both enemy and friend. He wounds and he blesses; he takes away and he gives. Suddenly and mysteriously he appears; suddenly and mysteriously he disappears, leaving the narrator to contend with Jacob."[3]

This story, about how the father of the Israelites was given the name Israel, stubbornly refuses to give up answers. Despite its importance in Israel's formative mythology, it remains shrouded in mystery. Trible said that the story of Jacob's limp serves as her metaphor for reading the Bible.[4] One wrestles with the Bible and may find blessing or curse, or cursed blessing. There are wounding stories in the Bible as well as healing stories. "We struggle mightily, only to be wounded. But yet we hold on, seeking a blessing."[5]

Hearing the Word of God through Competing Voices

For three thousand years the voices of God have been wrestling in these sacred texts. This study has allowed them to wrestle in the open through the practice of midrash. When we, as students of the Bible, enter the fray we may be caught in this wrestling match and soon blessed or wounded by it. Like Jacob, we may not be sure we are wrestling friend or foe, or both at the same time. Whether one side wins a crippling victory or a magnificent defeat depends on the faith journey of the reader.[6] What we have done in practicing midrash together, you can do on your own when reading the Bible.

2. Trible comments, "This is a dirty contest, not played by civilized rules" ("Strangers and Struggles," 6).

3. Trible, "Strangers and Struggles," 11.

4. Trible, "Jacob's Limp" (sermon reference taken from author's notes).

5. Trible, *Texts of Terror*, 4.

6. The terms are borrowed from Brueggemann, *Genesis*, 270, and Buechner,

The divergent texts in the Bible have revealed significant arguments about God's nature, God's covenant promises, salvation, human sin, church leadership, how inclusive or exclusive is the circle of God's people and what are God's plans for the end of times. Given the number of contrasting passages in the Bible, it is not surprising that Christians disagree on so many matters of faith and practice. More puzzling is the fact that most Christian believers are unaware that the Bible is full of disagreements. Having explored this study you may see the Bible in a new way, as a pluralistic text. For centuries Christians have been trying to smooth over contradictions in the Bible, but the curious reader has always found them. Nine hundred years ago Peter Abelard got in trouble with the pope for pointing out dozens of the Bible's contradictions with his publication of *Yes & No*.[7] Many a preacher and Sunday School teacher has bent over backwards trying to convince sharp youngsters how the obvious contradictions they discovered were not really contradictions at all.

This study begs the reader to stop trying to fix the Bible and just let it speak—contradictions and all. Brian McLaren, in *A New Kind of Christianity*, suggests that we should treat the Bible as "an inspired library,"[8] which has merit since the word *Bible* essentially means library. A library has many voices, many books, many perspectives; some are complementary, some opposing. If we treat the Bible as an inspired library we remove the need to integrate the biblical voices toward an internal consistency, and allow the competing voices to speak their "vigorous internal debate around key questions."[9] A more open understanding of truth will be needed. Absolute truth has no room for competing voices. Rather than imagining truth as a circle with one, singular focal point, let us imagine truth as an oval with foci. God's word has been revealed in this way. Defying conventional wisdom, God speaks a pluralistic truth.

While there are many theological voices in the Bible, this study ran into recurring themes as we moved from the first pages of Genesis through the rest of the Bible. The debates kept resurfacing in part because three major voices influence other sections of the Bible. The Levites from the old

---

Magnificent Defeat, 10–18.

7. Peter Abelard (1079–1142) was one of the great minds of the Middle Ages. The French philosopher's most famous book was *Sic et Non* (Yes & No) in which he took 158 faith statements and showed where in the Bible or in official church teachings each statement was true (Yes) or not true (No). Some statements have as many as fifty references. The whole book was about contradictions of the faith. For an English translation, see Abelard, *Yes & No*.

8. McLaren, *New Kind of Christianity*, 83.

9. McLaren, *New Kind of Christianity*, 82.

northern kingdom of Israel, who wrote Deuteronomy and a companion history of Israel and Judah (Samuel and Kings and possibly Joshua and Judges), developed a justice-based theology that inspired Jeremiah, Micah and Amos. When Matthew and Luke crafted their gospels the theology of Deuteronomy provided a foundation for them. The memory of their enslavement in Egypt was formative for the Deuteronomistic writers. They were to be just as God was just and not do to others as the Egyptians had done to them. Based in their reading of the Mosaic law, the Deuteronomists believed God made a conditional covenant with Israel established by a two-way relationship, which demanded that Israel love the LORD God with all of one's heart, soul and strength and neighbor as self.[10]

The Priests of Judah developed a second influential voice in Scripture. Based in the rituals of Jerusalem's temple, they believed God was holy, set apart, and that God's people had to be holy to keep God's conditional covenant. This tradition spawned a significant portion of the Hebrew Bible from the Priestly writings in the Torah—Leviticus and parts of Genesis, Exodus and Numbers—to Chronicles, Ezra, Nehemiah, Ezekiel, Daniel, Haggai and Zechariah. Their ideas influenced New Testament books such as John's gospel and letters, Peter's letters and the book of Revelation. Like Daniel, believers must operate in the world without defiling themselves by the ways of the world (Dan 1; 3; 6). The holiness-based theology of the Priests aimed to create a sanctuary for the faithful in a dangerous world.

We encountered a third recurring voice in our reading, which did not have a group, like the Priests or the Levites, to carry on its tradition. The self-description of the LORD in Exodus 34:6—"a God merciful and gracious, slow to anger, and abounding in steadfast love and faithfulness"—gave birth to this alternative voice, which believed God's promises were unconditional and everlasting. The Storyteller's tales in Genesis described the world as a wondrous and hazardous place and God as a lover who was always patching things back together. Other writers, such as the Succession Narrative's author, spoke of God and faith in similar ways. Ruth, Jonah, and Isaiah all came to the conclusion that God's steadfast love would be extended to other peoples and nations. These writings influenced Paul and Mark's gospel in the New Testament. Paul declared that God's grace is always greater than human sin (Rom 5). This grace-based theology celebrates life with all its faults. Do not be afraid, it proclaims, have faith.

---

10. Instructions to love or serve God with all your heart and soul are mentioned in Deut 4:29; 10:12; 26:16; Josh 23:14; 2 Kgs 23:3. With all your heart, soul and strength are mentioned in Deut 6:5 and 2 Kgs 23:25. This was picked up by the Synoptic Gospels and paired with love your neighbor as two parts of the greatest commandment.

It is miraculous that these recurring voices were codified into Scripture. The Priests, who wrote competing stories to correct all the problems they had with the Storyteller's tales, when editing the scrolls that became the Hebrew Bible they combined all the stories instead of disposing their rivals. Matthew and Luke erased and changed many of Mark's passages, but they kept more than they altered. Why didn't they shred the other's stories? Walter Brueggemann describes this surviving dialogue as a divine surprise. "The most amazing thing about the Old Testament, and it's not different than the New Testament, is that the canon includes voices to the contrary. . . . J, E, D, and P are competing voices of interpretation and they put them all in. So the D people . . . are all about justice, and the P people are all about purity. But they [both] got in and they're [all] biblical."[11] The pluralistic nature of Scripture might be the best proof of divine inspiration. Humans tend to silence critics, to excommunicate or exclude the divergent voice; God embraces them all. Terence Fretheim in an overview of biblical theology boldly confessed, "Pluralism has been canonized."[12] The seemingly illogical choice of keeping competing and contradictory voices together in Scripture recalls Paul's commentary on Christ and the cross: "God's foolishness is wiser than human wisdom, and God's weakness is stronger than human strength" (1 Cor 1:25).

Recognizing these arguments in the Bible can actually help the believer truly hear the whole word of God. We have seen numerous ways in which the Bible argues with itself. Editors put competing stories side-by-side—such as the creation stories, or the versions of Jacob's blessing. Authors took an earlier text and changed it to alter its meaning, or sometimes omitted stories and chose silence instead—as the Chronicler did with the Historian's work in Samuel and Kings, or the way Matthew and Luke changed Mark's text. Sometimes an author refuted an earlier text and wrote a dissident composition—the way Ruth and Jonah resisted Ezra and Nehemiah's rulings against outsiders, or how the Pastoral letters argued with Paul about leadership. At other times authors wrote from different viewpoints possibly unaware another offered an alternative—such as how the prophets wrote dueling prophecies, or the way John's gospel and the Synoptic Gospels talked about love. Then, we explored the countertestimonies, which argued with the core testimony of Israel's faith (and Christianity's faith to come).

Reading these competing texts, arguing with each other in one form or another, has hopefully shown us the value of each of God's voices. The

11. Brueggemann, "Unity, Purity & Miracle" (lecture transcribed by author from compact disc recording).

12. Fretheim, *Suffering of God*, 19.

last word is not necessarily the better word. The first is not inferior. Often, however, we interpret the first word by the last word, and not the reverse. We allow the Pastorals to comment on original Paul, but not vice versa. We are better served to allow all of God's voices to speak. Let Paul tell the Pastorals, "When I said there is no male nor female in Christ, I did mean that women could serve as deacons and preachers. What did you think that whole convoluted text in 1 Corinthians 11 was all about?" Let Mark tell John, "If I wanted to define faith as belief in Jesus' name, I would have said so! We are saved by faith, not by our deeds, or by orthodox beliefs." When we allow all the voices of God's word to speak on their own behalf, rather than to try to force them into agreement, we bring out the full richness of God's revelation and allow the Bible to correct the church when its stances become skewed.

This study has shown that not all views are equally valid at any one time. At some points in the Bible one argument had the most fitting word over another. At other times separate communities of God's people lived by different words from God, as it best suited them. An example of the latter may be found in Ezekiel's word to the Jewish exiles in Babylon while Jeremiah had a different word to the remnant still living in Jerusalem under King Zedekiah. As the contexts of culture or church change through time, so does the appropriateness of the each message in the Bible. Isaiah argued that the unconditional promises of God for Judah would save Jerusalem. In 701 BC, that word proved correct. But in 609 BC, Jeremiah argued that such words were deceptive. And by 587 BC, his word seemed vindicated. Isaiah's prophecy for 701 BC did not fit for Jeremiah's day. Times had changed. It was a different generation. They faced different problems. So it is true for us today.

The arguments of the Bible force Christians to admit that no one possesses the whole truth of God. They compel me to recognize the divine voice that inspires my Christian adversaries, and to accept their seat at God's table. This recognition could foster more tolerance across ecumenical and ideological divides. Additionally, it frees me to fully embrace the divine word that inspires me. Where Matthew and Luke disagreed on how Jesus told the Parable of the Feast, I am free to fully embrace Luke's more generous version, which ended with the master opening his home and banquet to the poor and outcast, as being true for me, while rejecting Matthew's harsher ending in which the master threw out a homeless man for wearing the wrong clothes to the feast. Ezekiel did not yield to Jeremiah. Second Isaiah did not apologize to Ezra or Nehemiah. Neither should you.

God's word speaks in multiple voices but not all may speak strongly to you. Follow the voice of God that speaks to your heart and soul, though do not go to Thomas Jefferson's extreme and cut out parts of the Bible you do not like.[13] Many Christians live by a canon within the canon. Our strongest beliefs are supported by favorite passages, while we tend to ignore passages that may challenge strongly held beliefs. Biblical writers practiced this when they rewrote older scrolls. I am merely advocating that we consciously, *and with informed awareness*, freely choose some passages over others as more fitting for one's personal faith development.

If Christian rivals are not forced into a true/false, right/wrong dichotomy, then they are free to disagree without the need to convert or condemn. There are enough seats at God's table. Reading about how the holiness theology of the Priests preserved Jewish identity during the dark days of exile and occupation may give you a new admiration for the Amish or for monks and nuns in monastic orders. Reading the justice prophets in the Old Testament may help you hear the calls for social justice today with new ears. Reading about the inclusiveness of the grace-based passages, may help you understand why many Christians openly welcome and affirm gay, lesbian, and transgendered people into the church as God's children made in the image of God.

Practicing midrash with the arguments of the Bible does not deny the divine inspiration of other competing voices. It recognizes them as competing voices and the role they serve as the loyal opposition. A Christian believer does not have to agree with Mark anymore than John did, or with the Storyteller anymore than the Priestly Writers did, but she is confronted by the loyal opposition as a check upon her own biases. You and I are free to live within the voices in the Bible that speak most powerfully to each of us and to wrestle with the other voices in the Bible as Jacob did with his mysterious night visitor. In doing so, we participate in the conversational nature of Scripture.

Practicing Midrash as a Way to Understand God's Revelation

The aim of this study has been to practice midrash with contrasting Scripture passages in order that the reader may wrestle with the Bible in private or in community. As a pastor that has been preaching from and teaching the Bible to congregants for three decades, I must confess a deeper objective. Beyond trying to better understand Scripture, I have approached *Practicing Midrash* as an avenue to wonder about the nature of God's

13. Thomas Jefferson took scissors and cut out all the parts of the Bible that he believed contradicted with reason. See *The Jefferson Bible*.

revelation. Since I choose to encounter the Bible as God's word, I want to consider more than the just the human aspects of these conflicting texts. Beyond how Luke and Matthew decided to adapt and change Mark's gospel because of their theological agendas, I wonder what God was thinking when inspiring these gospel writers. Beyond the ancient politics of the two priestly classes (Priests vs. Levites) vying for power in ancient Israel, I want to ask why did God choose such an incarnational revelation? What purpose does the Bible's pluralism serve?

> I have come to believe that God inspired pluralism within the Bible in order to speak to as many of God's children as possible.

Brian McLaren, in his book *Generous Orthodoxy*, tries to wrap his arms around all the theological diversity of Christianity, claiming to be a "missional, evangelical, post/protestant, liberal/conservative, mystical/poetic, biblical, charismatic/contemplative, fundamentalist/calvinist, anabaptist/anglican, methodist, catholic, green, incarnational, depressed-yet-hopeful, emergent, unfinished Christian." He adds, "To be Christian in a generously orthodox way is not to claim to have the truth captured, stuffed, and mounted on a wall. . . . Orthodoxy isn't a destination. It is a way—a way on which one journeys, and on which one progresses, even if one never (in this life) arrives."[14] While this pluralism may not lead to clear yes-or-no answers, this does not seem to bother God.

The existence of these competing voices calls me to appreciate Christians from other theological camps. I cannot assume another has misinterpreted Scripture, merely because we disagree. She may be accurately interpreting the passages she is quoting. She may simply be a faithful adherent to an opposing argument in the Bible, and we represent a disagreement that is thousands of years old. It is doubtful that we will agree any more than James agreed with Paul, or the Chronicler agreed with the Historian. Nevertheless, God's word speaks to both of us.

Imagine the Christian church without its theological diversity. Could a unified, singular church come anywhere as close to engaging the hundreds of millions of people who profess Jesus Christ as Lord? The pluralism in the Bible has created a multifaceted diversity in the church that has made Jesus Christ far more accessible to the world's population. Imagine the color wheel as a metaphor for the Bible. As three primary colors enable us to see a wide array of colors, so the competing voices in the Bible allow us to see God through a similar prism. That we differ as to our favorite colors does not diminish God's purposes, in fact it shows the wisdom of God's foolishness.

14. McLaren, *Generous Orthodoxy*, 331, 333.

God seems to care more about connecting with her children than in providing absolute answers. Rather than speak with one voice and offer humanity an all-or-nothing choice, God's pluralistic word offers humanity a variety of paths upon which to encounter Jesus Christ.

> *Second, I have come to believe that God inspired pluralism in the Bible to enable the biblical faith to evolve for generations through its competing voices.*

The tension between the arguments in the Bible diminishes their shortcomings. Marcus Borg in *Meeting Jesus Again for the First Time* is particularly critical of the Priestly tradition, but writes, "When the priestly story is understood as one of three ways of imaging the Christian life, rather than the primary way, the problems with it largely disappear."[15] The same could be said of other competing voices. If you realize that the theology that has angered you is only *one* way of encountering God, instead of *the* way, it loses its power to wound because you become aware of *other* ways that bring healing. Just as the opposing forces in a tug-of-war keep each side balanced, so the push and pull of the competing voices balance one another. When one side pulls too far in the extreme the other sides eventually pull back.

These parallel revelations are held together by what Brueggemann calls a "dialogical unity," which "does not seek closure, but hears many voices and attends to many stirrings of the Spirit . . . that refuse closure."[16] The Bible breathes as a living word precisely because there are arguments in it. The dialogical nature of God's word breathes new life into old doctrines, rigid cultural boundaries, and into a church grown stale. Brueggemann insists that God refuses to be trapped by our fixed formulations.[17] By refusing closure these voices speak to each generation as it faces new societal challenges. A self-critical dimension is created by the pluralism of the Bible, according to scholar James Sanders.

15. Borg, *Meeting Jesus Again*, 132. Borg claims that there are three *macro-stories* in the Old Testament—the Priestly story, the Exodus story, and the Return from Exile. He claims that in Jesus' day the Priestly story was the prevailing story in Judaism at the time. Furthermore Borg thinks the three macro-stories influence Christianity today, and finally, that the tension between the stories counterbalance their problems. Borg's insight was useful to this author as one way to see the competing voices I have identified in this study. When one story becomes the primary way to see the Bible its problems become accentuated, whereas if they are held in tension, their problems diminish. For Borg's summary, see *Meeting Jesus Again*, 128–37.

16. Brueggemann, "Unity, Purity & Miracle" (lecture transcribed by author from compact disc recording).

17. Brueggemann, "Unity, Purity & Miracle."

> There is no program that can be constructed on the basis of
> the Bible which can escape the challenge of other portions of
> it: this is an essential part of its pluralism. No one person, no
> denomination, no theology, and certainly no ideology can ex-
> haust the Bible or claim its *unity*. It bears with it its own redeem-
> ing contradictions, and this is the major reason it has lasted so
> long and has spoken effectively to so many different historical
> contexts and communities. Once a theme or strain or thread
> rightly perceived in the Bible has been isolated and absolutized,
> it simply becomes available for challenge from another theme or
> strain also there. The whole Bible . . . can never be stuffed into
> one theological box, as classically recognized by the term *bibli-
> cal paradox*: the canon always contains the seed of redemption
> of any abuse of it.[18]

The disagreements push for new ways to understand God. Biblical theolo-
gies must continually reform to address new cultural situations, because if
one does not, another will and gain an upper hand. Without a voice of justice in the Bible to counter what was taught in the churches of slave-owners,
African American slaves may never have come to believe in what Frederick
Douglass called the Christianity of Christ. Without a voice of grace, Martin
Luther may have died futilely trying to appease a demanding God and the
Reformation may never have happened. The pluralism of the Bible creates
the dynamics for reform. The arguments of the Bible constantly provide a
counterbalance to all movements of church and society.

> *I have come to believe that a third reason God inspired pluralism
> in the Bible was to create a living dialogue, an indirect communi-
> cation, which invites persons to faith in God by tuning to the voice
> that speaks most powerfully to them.*

Richard Niebuhr in *Christ and Culture* came to the conclusion that
the conversational dialogue of competing ideas develops faith in believers.
Here, the faithful, introduced to competing truth claims, discover the truth
that speaks to the heart.

> It is not in lonely internal debate but in the living dialogue of
> the self with other selves that we can come to the point where
> we can make a decision and say, "Whatever may be the duty of
> other[s], this is my duty," or "Whatever others do, this is what
> I must do." Were it not for that first clause—"Whatever others
> think or do"—the second could not follow. So it is with the
> confrontation by Christ. If after the long dialogue with Mark,

18. Sanders, *Canon and Community*, 37.

Matthew, John and Paul, and Harnack, Schweitzer, Bultmann, and Dodd, I come to the conclusion that whatever Christ means to others and requires of others this is what he means to me and requires of me.[19]

The Bible's arguments help believers to say, "This is what Christ means to me." By giving believers and the church multiple voices to hear, the Bible provides a comparison of belief from which to say, "Yes, I believe that," or "No, I do not believe that." Sometimes it is only when you acknowledge what you are against that you can see what you are for. This is what Niebuhr called the living dialogue that makes faith personally real. Like the crowd that heard Hananiah and Jeremiah's prophetic duel that day in the Jerusalem temple courtyard, each person must decide whom to believe as he reads Scripture.

Soren Kierkegaard, a nineteenth-century Danish philosopher, spent years observing and evaluating the communication of faith in a society where nearly everyone was Christian. He became convinced that indirect communication was the only possible way to create true relationships with God.[20] Since God is illusive, God must be encountered through metaphors and intangible spiritual experiences. Kierkegaard said that attempts at direct communication with and about God amounted to paganism.[21]

He rejected the idea that to become Christian a person simply endorsed a list of doctrines, as someone might agree with the Boy Scout pledge or the mission statement of the Rotary Club. "Being a Christian is defined not by the 'what' of Christianity but by the 'how' of the Christian."[22] Endorsement is based on gathering information and then a decision to agree or not. Instead, he described faith as an inward expression of one's being to God. Faith, like love, is something that must be practiced to be real. This must be caught through indirect communication instead of being taught by the direct communication of instruction.[23] It is in the act of

---

19. Niebuhr, *Christ and Culture*, 245.

20. Kierkegaard, *Concluding Unscientific Postscript*, 1:239–45.

21. Kierkegaard, *Concluding Unscientific Postscript*, 1:243, 245.

22. Kierkegaard, *Concluding Unscientific Postscript*, 1:610.

23. Kierkegaard explained the difference by imagining a mother admonishing her child about to attend a party. "'Now, mind your manners and watch the other polite children and behave as they do,' so he, too, could live on and behave as he saw others behave. He would never do anything first and would never have any opinion unless he first knew that others had it, because 'the others' would be his very first. On special occasions he would act like someone who does not know how to eat a course that is served at a banquet; he would reconnoiter until he saw how the others did it, etc. Such a person could perhaps know ever so much, perhaps even know the system by rote; he could perhaps live in a Christian country, know how to bow his head every time God's

observing the communication of others—such as attending a play, watching the interaction of others, reading multiple philosophical or theological points of view—that allows us to internalize those debates and create a living dialogue within our own souls.

The arguments of the Bible marvelously provide a reader's theatre of God's word. The competing voices of God speak and we overhear their conversation, their arguments, much like an audience at a play. As Paul and James argue about salvation by faith or by faithful actions we have our own internal dialogue. As the Storyteller and the Priestly Writers debate whether to reveal a hero's flaws and sins we decide what leaders we want to follow—those as flawed as us or those who are shining role models to which we aspire. The indirect communication of God's pluralistic word makes the illusive God of Abraham, Isaac and Jacob perceptible.

This opportunity to hear different biblical arguments, different beliefs about God and our relationship to God offers believers the chance to personally develop their faith. In James Fowler's classic study of faith development, *Stages of Faith*, he proposes that the ability to reflect on your own beliefs and to observe and recognize the value in other belief systems is a necessary exercise to develop your faith beyond the cultural instruction of your childhood.[24] The Bible's pluralism provides a text for the formation of faith and the reformation of faith as believers test the teachings from their childhood.

The conversation of the competing voices in the Bible invites rather than excludes. It allows for the kind of generous orthodoxy McLaren promotes, which "will welcome others into the passionate pursuit of truth, not exclude them for failing to possess it already."[25] The conversational nature of the Bible invites Christ to enter into the human heart. Each unique child of God listening to the conversation of God's voices in Scripture gravitates to

---

name is mentioned, perhaps also see God in nature if he was in the company of others who saw God; in short, well, he could be a congenial partygoer—and yet he would be deceived by the direct relation to truth, to the ethical, to God. . . . At the end of his life, one would have to say that one thing had escaped him: he had not become aware of God" (*Concluding Unscientific Postscript*, 1:244–45).

24. Fowler, *Stages of Faith*, 174–83. See chapter 19, "Stage 4—Individuative-Reflective Faith." The transition to fourth stage of faith development includes a "critical distancing from one's previous assumptive value system and the emergence of an executive ego" (*Stages of Faith*, 179). Earlier in the book Fowler points out that an adolescent's ability to understand that another person can have an entirely different perspective about an independent object or issue from himself or herself, and can reflect about both perspectives moves an individual from childhood toward adulthood (*Stages of Faith*, 68–75).

25. McLaren, *Generous Orthodoxy*, 335.

the ones that most powerfully speak to her soul. The word of God invites an individual to observe this divine conversation and then allows her to follow the way to God that is most true to her.

The circumstances of the disagreements in the Bible, the arguments one set of writers had with another set, their corrections of each other, died with them long ago. Yet, their inspired writings continue to speak across time and culture. They have impacted the church for two thousand years (and the Jewish faith far longer) during formation and reformation, prophecy and order, as each generation interpreted those testimonies for their own times. While their testimony is a human word born from the conflicts and challenges of their own context, the sacred text they all share makes the Bible a living word for the conflicts and challenges of other generations. By practicing midrash with these competing texts we hear the dialogue of voices that allows God's word to speak to a wide diversity of human beings, more deeply to the individual believer, and to evolve the faith and the church for a new day. For these purposes I believe God created a pluralistic Bible.

The genius of God's foolishness is that the competing voices in the Bible make God's revelation highly adaptable. Rather than inspire a mono-chromatic word that is black and white, God inspired a trichromatic word that is able to produce an unfathomable array of beliefs and practices on a wide spectrum of understanding God. The word of God fits every context, every culture, and every challenge because one of these competing voices, or a combination of them, will speak to the situation at hand. And wher-ever a biblical idea gets misconstrued the other voices in time will inspire a self-correction. The arguments in the Bible testify that God's word is not carved in stone, but is a living word renewed every time God's competing voices are allowed to grapple with a new situation. Through these wrestling testimonies, God still speaks.

A Pluralistic Word for a Pluralistic Age

It is perhaps too convenient that this study should conclude that the Bible is pluralistic in nature, given that we are living in a pluralistic age. American society in the early twenty-first century is awash in competing voices, each professing a claim to truth. Like the search for the historical Jesus in Albert Schweitzer's day, one could conclude that this study has more likely over-laid the present age upon the Bible than discovered something essential in the Bible.[26] Such a conclusion, however, would also have to raise questions

26. In his 1906 study, Schweitzer examined four decades of late nineteenth-century

about biblical interpretation in the past. The perceived unity of the Bible, so long preached by the church, has been the product of the hegemony of the Christian West more than the actual text of the Bible. Context does not change the Bible, but it does change what we see in the Bible and what we do not see. Walter Brueggemann believes biblical interpretation is now moving away from a unified "hegemonic interpretation" toward a "pluralistic interpretive context." This shift, he believes, is reflected both in the biblical texts and now in our culture at large.[27]

The growing pluralism of our day is much more like the great writing periods of the Bible—740–580 BC (leading to exile), 525–400 BC (return from exile), and AD 50–100 (after Jesus)—than the relatively stable period of American Protestantism during the nineteenth and twentieth centuries. The pluralism of our day is enabling us to see that pluralism has been in the Bible for all these years. The church laid a veneer upon the Bible, promoting an orthodox and catholic faith that pretended such contradictions and debates did not exist. The present age grants us permission to pull back the veneer.

The postmodern age is dismantling centuries-in-the-making central ideas about human life, the world, meaning, politics, faith, God and much more. In the vacuum created by this void, a rush of competing values and stories and truths are creating a pluralistic terrain where everything feels relative. As unsettling as these times are, they are not as severe as what the Hebrew people experienced when Assyrian and Babylonian armies came crashing down upon their land, or what the first Christians encountered on a roller-coaster ride of Jesus' experience, followed by the destruction of Jerusalem, and persecution from the Roman Empire. The pluralism of belief erupted in the Bible precisely because the chaotic turmoil of the day diminished the old stories and values and made everything up for grabs.

The fact that everything is up for grabs again is preciously why it is important for people of faith to hear all the competing voices in the Bible. At a time when our society seems to be losing our ability to talk to one another, the pluralism of the Bible is one way to help Christians (and maybe all

---

exploration for the historical Jesus and concluded that scholars had conformed Jesus into the "human standards and human psychology" of the day. "We have made Jesus hold another language with our time from that which He really held" (*Quest of the Historical Jesus*, 400). Schweitzer's study is a warning to all would-be scholars seeking some discovery in Scripture. Rather than discovering something out of the Bible, you may just be implanting something into the Bible. See also Ehrman *Apocalyptic Prophet*, ix–xi. He suggests that a hundred years of additional scholarship has merely proven Schweitzer's conclusion. While this study's task has not been a quest for the historical Jesus, it has certainly been written under the same contextual constraints.

27. Brueggemann, *Theology of the Old Testament*, 710.

citizens)—with opposing viewpoints—to begin conversations again. These contrasting stories call us out from our echo chambers and back into the town square for civil discussion. When we recognize that God has inspired all these competing voices, it forces us to recognize the Spirit of God working in those with whom we disagree, and it rightly makes us skeptical of the one who claims to have a monopoly on God's truth.

The answers that Christians seek in the Bible—about God, humanity, faith, life, a life to follow—are not *in* the Bible such as a recipe is in a cookbook. They rise to the surface through the practice of midrash, which encourages the competing voices in the Bible to debate and argue and invite the rest of us to join the conversation. They are in a constant flux as new generations of believers try to face the challenges of their times. The Bible is a living word not because of the words on its pages but through the conversations its words stimulate.

The evidence that the genius of God's conversational revelation thrived in chaotic and unsettling times should be received as good news. The competing voices of God's word enabled both Jews and early Christians to find God working in their lives during perilous days and chaotic times. So, the multiple voices of God's word will also inspire today's faithful in a myriad of situations to faithfully respond in this pluralistic age. Those who choose to separate from culture, or who are already being disenfranchised in society, may gravitate to the holiness theology of Priests of Judah, or the stories in the book of Daniel, or the Gospel of John. Those who see the injustice of the world and long to redeem it may be inspired by Deuteronomy's justice-based theology, or the voice of the justice prophets, or Luke's gospel and will actively work to bring God's justice and peace to the world against all odds. Those who long to break down barriers and make the church an avenue for accepting and receiving all those who are hurting and need God's love may be moved by the Storyteller's tales in Genesis or Jesus' emphasis on faith in Mark's gospel, or by Paul's words that in Christ there are no longer barriers between us. In the complex and diverse world ahead of us, the church will have to minister in countless ways. The competing voices of God's word offer hope for this age.

So, like Jacob let us wrestle with God's word by the way we practice midrash. In mystery we encounter it and hold on for dear life. The push and pull of wrestling will be both blessing and curse. We will find blessing in one of the arguments, divine words that speak most profoundly to us. We may be cursed by other arguments, fighting with divine words that feel adversarial to us. We may insist or demand to know the truth and the whole truth from this mysterious wrestler. But as Jacob found out, God's messenger does not yield answers so easily. Maybe, it is not for us to figure out the paradox of God's word. Maybe we are simply to hold on for its blessing, even if it is a wounding blessing.

Elie Wiesel recalled a comment made by Martin Buber, the great twentieth-century Jewish philosopher and author of *I And Thou*, in a speech to a group of Catholic priests:

> What is the difference between Jews and Christians? We all await the Messiah. You believe He has already come and gone, while we do not. I therefore propose that we await Him together. And when He appears, we can ask Him: "Were You here before?" Then he paused and added: "And I hope that at that moment I will be close enough to whisper in his ear, 'For the love of heaven, don't answer.'"[28]

Amen. And may the conversations continue.

---

28. Wiesel, *All Rivers Run to the Sea*, 354–55.

Bibliography

Abelard, Peter. *Yes & No: The Complete English Translation of Peter Abelard's Sic et Non*. Translated by Priscilla Throop. Charlotte, VT: MedievalMS, 2007.

Anderson, Bernhard. *From Creation to New Creation*. Minneapolis: Fortress, 1994.

———. "Names of God." In *IDB* 2:407–17.

Armstrong, Karen. *The Bible*. New York: Grove, 2007.

Auld, A. Graeme. *Life in Kings: Reshaping the Royal Story in the Hebrew Bible*. Atlanta: SBL, 2017.

Bainton, Roland. *Here I Stand: A Life of Martin Luther*. Nashville: Abingdon, 1978.

The Barna Group. "Meet the 'Spiritual but Not Religious.'" Research Releases, Faith & Christianity. April 6, 2017. https://www.barna.com/research/meet-spiritual-not-religious/.

———. "A New Generation Expresses Its Skepticism and Frustration with Christianity." Research Releases, Millennials & Generations. September 21, 2007. https://www.barna.com/research/a-new-generation-expresses-its-skepticism-and-frustration-with-christianity/.

———. "Six Reasons Young Christians Leave Church." Research Releases, Millennials & Generations. September 27, 2011. https://www.barna.com/research/six-reasons-young-christians-leave-church/.

Bird, Michael, and Joel Willitts, eds. *Paul and the Gospels: Christologies, Conflicts and Convergenes*. New York: T. & T. Clark, 2011.

Black, Clifton. "First, Second, and Third Letters of John." In *NIB*, edited by Leander Keck et al., 12:363–469. Nashville: Abingdon, 1998.

Bloom, Harold, and David Rosenburg. *The Book of J*. New York: Grove, 1990.

The Book of Common Prayer: According to the Use of the Episcopal Church. New York: Seabury, 1979.

The Book of Common Worship. Louisville: Westminster John Knox, 1993.

Boorer, Suzanne. "The Envisioning of the Land in the Priestly Material: Fulfilled Promise or Future Hope?" In Dozeman et al., *Pentateuch, Hexateuch, or Enneateuch?*, 99–125.

Borg, Marcus, ed. *The Lost Gospel Q*. Berkeley, CA: Ulysses, 1996.

———. *Meeting Jesus Again for the First Time*. San Francisco: HarperCollins, 1994.

Borg, Marcus, and John Dominic Crossan. *The First Paul: Reclaiming the Radical Visionary behind the Church's Conservative Icon*. New York: HarperOne, 2009.

Bourgel, Jonathan. "The Destruction of the Samaritan Temple by John Hyrcanus: A Reconsideration." *JBL* 135 (2016) 505–23.

Bright, John. *History of Israel*. Philadelphia: Westminster, 1972.

Brown, Brené. *I Thought It Was Just Me (But It Isn't)*. Paperback. New York: Gotham, 2008.

Brown, Dan. *The Da Vinci Code*. New York: Knopf Doubleday, 2003.

Brown, Raymond. *An Introduction to the New Testament*. New York: Doubleday, 1997.

Bruce, F. F. *The Gospel of John*. Grand Rapids: Eerdmans, 1983.

Brueggemann, Walter. *David's Truth*. Philadelphia: Fortress, 1985.

———. *Genesis*. Interpretation. Atlanta: John Knox, 1982.

———. *The Land*. Overtures to Biblical Theology. Philadelphia: Fortress, 1977.

———. *Texts That Linger, Words That Explode*. Minneapolis: Fortress, 2000.

———. *Theology of the Old Testament*. Philadelphia: Fortress, 1997.

———. "Unity, Purity & Miracle." Lecture delivered at the Festival of Homiletics, Wieuca Road Baptist Church, Atlanta, GA, May 21, 2009. Transcribed from compact disc recording.

Buechner, Frederick. *The Faces of Jesus*. New York: Harper & Row, 1989.

———. *Magnificent Defeat*. New York: Seabury, 1966.

———. *The Son of Laughter*. San Francisco: HarperSanFrancisco, 1993.

Bultmann, Rudolph. *Theology of the New Testament*. Translated by Kendrick Grobel. 2 volumes in 1. New York: Scribner, 1955.

Butler Bass, Diane. *Christianity After Religion*. New York: HarperOne, 2012.

Buttrick, George Arthur, gen. ed. *The Interpreter's Dictionary of the Bible*. 4 volumes. Nashville: Abingdon, 1962.

Camus, Albert. *Lettres À Un Ami Allemand*. Paris: Gallimard, 1948.

Collins, Gail. *When Everything Changed: The Amazing Journey of American Women from 1960 to the Present*. New York: Little, Brown, 2009.

Collins, Jim. *Good to Great: Why Some Companies Make the Leap . . . and Others Don't*. New York: HarperCollins, 2001.

Collins, Jim, and Morten Hansen. *Great by Choice: Uncertainty, Chaos, and Luck—Why Some Thrive Despite Them All*. New York: HarperCollins, 2011.

Colwell, Ernest. *New or Old? The Christian Struggle with Change and Tradition*. Philadelphia: Westminster, 1970.

Conrad, Edgar. *Reading Isaiah*. Minneapolis: Fortress, 1991.

Cox, Harvey. *The Future of Faith*. New York: HarperOne, 2009.

Crenshaw, James. *Old Testament Wisdom: An Introduction*. Atlanta: John Knox, 1981.

———. *A Whirlpool of Torment: Israelite Traditions of God as an Oppressive Presence*. Overtures to Biblical Theology. Philadelphia: Fortress, 1984.

Crossan, John Dominic, ed. *Sayings Parallels: A Workbook for the Jesus Tradition*. Philadelphia: Fortress, 1986.

Crossan, John Dominic, and Brian Reed. *In Search of Paul*. San Francisco: HarperCollins, 2004.

Culpepper, Alan. *1 John, 2 John, 3 John*. Knox Preaching Guides. Atlanta: John Knox, 1985.

———. "The Relationship between the Gospel of John and 1 John." In Culpepper and Anderson, *Communities in Dispute*, 95–121.

Culpepper, Alan, and Paul Anderson, eds. *Communities in Dispute: Current Scholarship on the Johannine Epistles*. Early Christianity and Its Literature. Atlanta: SBL, 2014.

Darr, Katheryn Pfisterer. "The Book of Ezekiel." In *NIB*, edited by Leander Keck et al., 6:1073–607. Nashville: Abingdon, 2001.

De Pury, Albert. "The Jacob Story and the Beginning of the Formation of the Pentateuch." In Dozeman and Schmid, *A Farewell to the Yahwist?*, 51–72.

Dinkler, Michael Beth. "Building Character on the Road to Emmaus: Lukan Characterization in Contemporary Literary Perspective." *JBL* 136 (2017) 687–706.

Dodd, C. H. *The Historical Tradition in the Fourth Gospel*. Cambridge: Cambridge University Press, 1965.

Donelson, Lewis. *From Hebrews to Revelation*. Louisville: Westminster John Knox, 2001.

Dozeman, Thomas, and Konrad Schmid, eds. *A Farewell to the Yahwist?* Atlanta: SBL, 2006.

Dozeman, Thomas, et al., eds. *Pentateuch, Hexateuch, or Enneateuch? Identifying Literary Works in Genesis through Kings*. Atlanta: SBL, 2011.

Dunn, James D. G. "The First and Second Letters to Timothy and the Letter to Titus." In *NIB*, edited by Leander Keck et al., 11:773–880. Nashville: Abingdon, 2000.

Durant, Will, and Ariel Durant. *The Lessons of History*. New York: Simon & Schuster, 1968.

Edenburg, Cynthia. "From Eden to Babylon: Reading Genesis 2–4 as a Paradigmatic Narrative." In Dozeman et al., *Pentateuch, Hexateuch, or Enneateuch?*, 155–67.

Ehrman, Bart. *Apocalyptic Prophet of the New Millennium*. New York: Oxford University Press, 1999.

———. *Jesus Before the Gospels*. New York: HarperCollins, 2016.

Eisenbaum, Pamela. *Paul Was Not a Christian: The Original Message of a Misunderstood Apostle*. New York: HarperOne, 2009.

Fitzgerald, F. Scott. "The Crack Up: A Desolately Frank Document from One for Whom the Salt of Life Has Lost Its Savor." *Esquire*, February 1936, 41, 164.

Fitzmyer, Joseph. *Paul and His Theology*. Englewood Cliffs, NJ: Prentice Hall, 1989.

Fowler, James. *Stages of Faith*. New York: HarperCollins, 1981.

Fox, Michael V. "Wisdom in Qoheleth." In *In Search of Wisdom: Essays in Memory of John G. Gammie*, edited by Leo G. Perdue et al., 115–31. Louisville: Westminster John Knox, 1993.

Fretheim, Terence. *Deuteronomic History*. Third printing. Nashville: Abingdon, 1989.

———. *The Suffering of God: An Old Testament Perspective*. Overtures to Biblical Theology. Philadelphia: Fortress, 1984.

Friedman, Richard Elliot. *The Bible with Sources Revealed*. New York: HarperSanFrancisco, 2003.

———. "The Deuteronomistic School." In *Fortunate the Eyes That See: Essays in Honor of David Noel Freedman in Celebration of His Seventieth Birthday*, edited by Astrid Beck et al., 70–80. Grand Rapids: Eerdmans, 1995.

———. *The Hidden Book in the Bible*. New York: HarperSanFrancisco, 1998.

———. *Who Wrote the Bible?* New York: Simon & Schuster, 1987. Reprint, San Francisco: HarperCollins, 1997. Citations refer to the HarperCollins edition.

Gammie, John. *Holiness in Israel*. Overtures to Biblical Theology. Minneapolis: Fortress, 1989.

Garland, David. *A Theology of Mark's Gospel*. Grand Rapids: Zondervan, 2015.

Gaster, T. H. "Samaritans." In *IDB*, 4:190–97.

Geoghegan, Jeffrey. "The Redaction of Kings and Priestly Authority in Jerusalem." In Leuchter and Adam, *Soundings in Kings*, 109–18.

Gerhardsson, Birger. *The Testing of God's Son: An Analysis of an Early Christian Midrash.* Translated by John Toy. Lund: CWK Gleerup, 1966. Reprint, Eugene, OR: Wipf & Stock, 2009. Citations refer to the Wipf & Stock edition.

Goodacre, Mark. *The Case against Q: Studies in Markan Priority and Synoptic Problem.* Harrisburg, PA: Trinity, 2002.

Goswell, Gregory. "Jonah among the Twelve Prophets." *JBL* 135 (2016) 283–99.

Gray, John. *I & II Kings.* Philadelphia: Westminster, 1970.

Griffith-Jones, Robin. *The Four Witnesses: The Rebel, the Rabbi, the Chronicler, and the Mystic.* San Francisco: HarperCollins, 2000.

Grobel, Kendrick. "Harmony of the Gospels." In *IDB* 2:525.

Ham, T. C. "The Gentle Voice of God in Job." *JBL* 132 (2013) 527–41.

Hammer, Reuven. *The Classic Midrash: Tannaitic Commentaries on the Bible.* New York: Paulist, 1995.

Hanson, Paul. *The Diversity of Scripture: A Theological Interpretation.* Overtures to Biblical Theology. Philadelphia: Fortress, 1982.

———. *The People Called: The Growth of Community in the Bible.* San Francisco: Harper & Row, 1986.

Harrelson, Walter. *The Ten Commandments and Human Rights.* Overtures to Biblical Theology. Philadelphia: Fortress, 1980.

Hays, Richard. *Echoes of Scripture in the Gospels.* Waco, TX: Baylor University Press, 2016.

———. *Echoes of Scripture in the Letters of Paul.* New Haven: Yale University Press, 1989.

———. "What Is 'Real Participation in Christ'? A Dialogue with E. P. Sanders in Pauline Soteriology." In Udoh et al., *Redefining First-Century Jewish and Christian Identities,* 336–51.

Heine, Susan. *Women and Early Christianity.* Minneapolis: Augsburg, 1988.

Hicks, Richard. "Markan Discipleship according to Malachi." *JBL* 132 (2013) 179–99.

Hiebert, Theodore. "The Book of Habakkuk." In *NIB,* edited by Leander Keck et al., 7:621–55. Nashville: Abingdon, 1996.

Hill, Craig. "On the Source of Paul's Problem with Judaism." In Udoh et al., *Redefining First-Century Jewish and Christian Identities,* 311–18.

Hillerbrand, Hans, ed. *The Reformation: A Narrative History Related by Contemporary Observers and Participants.* Grand Rapids: Baker, 1978.

Holladay, William. *Isaiah: Scroll of a Prophetic Heritage.* Grand Rapids: Eerdmans, 1978.

———. *Jeremiah.* Hermeneia. 2 vols. Minneapolis: Fortress, 1989.

———. *Jeremiah: A Fresh Reading.* New York: Pilgrim, 1990.

———. *Jeremiah: Spokesman out of Time.* New York: Pilgrim, 1974.

Holmberg, Bengt. *Paul and Power: The Structure of Authority in the Primitive Church as Reflected in the Pauline Epistles.* Lund: CWK Gleerup, 1978. Reprint, Philadelphia: Fortress, 1980. Citations refer to the Fortress edition.

Horne, Milton. *Proverbs-Ecclesiastes.* Smyth & Helwys Bible Commentary. Macon, GA: Smyth & Helwys, 2003.

Humphreys, W. Lee. *The Tragic Vision and the Hebrew Tradition.* Overtures to Biblical Theology. Philadelphia: Fortress, 1985.

Iverson, Kelly. "A Centurion's 'Confession': A Performance-Critical Analysis of Mark 15:39." *JBL* 130 (2011) 329–50.

Jefferson, Thomas. *The Jefferson Bible: The Life and Morals of Jesus of Nazareth*. Radford, VA: Wilder, 2007.

Johnson, Luke Timothy. "The Letter of James." In *NIB*, edited by Leander Keck et al., 12:175–225. Nashville: Abingdon, 1998.

Jones, Peter Rhea. *1, 2, & 3 John*. Smyth & Helwys Bible Commentary. Macon, GA: Smyth & Helwys, 2009.

Joseph, Simon. "'Why Do You Call Me "Master". . . ?' Q 6:46, the Inaugural Sermon, and the Demands of Discipleship." *JBL* 132 (2013) 955–72.

Kelley, Dean. *Why Conservative Churches Are Growing: A Study in Sociology of Religion with a New Preface for the ROSE edition*. Macon, GA: Mercer University Press, 1986.

Kierkegaard, Soren. *Concluding Unscientific Postscript to Philosophical Fragments*. Vol. 1. Translated and edited by Howard Hong and Edna Hong. Princeton: Princeton University Press, 1992.

Kindlon, Dan. *Too Much of a Good Thing: Raising Children of Character in an Indulgent Age*. New York: Hyperion, 2001.

King, Martin Luther, Jr. *A Testament of Hope: The Essential Writings of Martin Luther King, Jr*. Edited by James Washington. San Francisco: Harper & Row, 1986.

Kingsmill, Edmee. *The Song of Songs and the Eros of God: A Study in Biblical Intertextuality*. Oxford: Oxford University Press, 2010.

Kinnaman, David. *UnChristian: What a New Generation Really Thinks about Christianity . . . and Why It Matters*. Grand Rapids: Baker, 2007.

———. *You Lost Me: Why Young People Are Leaving the Church . . . and Rethinking Faith*. Grand Rapids: Baker, 2011.

Klein, Ralph. "The Books of Ezra & Nehemiah." In *NIB*, edited by Leander Keck et al., 3:661–851. Nashville: Abingdon, 1999.

Kruse, Colin. "Paul and John: Two Witnesses, One Gospel." In Bird and Willitts, *Paul and the Gospels*, 197–219.

Kunst, Judith. *The Burning Word: A Christian Encounter with Jewish Midrash*. Brewster, MA: Paraclete, 2006.

Kusher, Harold. *When Bad Things Happen to Good People*. New York: Avon, 1981.

Lamott, Anne. *Help, Thanks, Wow: The Three Essential Prayers*. New York: Riverhead, 2012.

———. *Small Victories: Spotting Improbable Moments of Grace*. New York: Riverhead, 2014.

Landy, Frances. *Paradoxes of Paradise: Identity and Difference in the Song of Songs*. Rev. ed. Sheffield, UK: Sheffield Phoenix, 2011.

Leuchter, Mark. "The Sociolinguistic and Rhetorical Implications of the Source Citations in Kings." In Leuchter and Adam, *Soundings in Kings*, 119–34.

Leuchter, Mark, and Klaus-Peter Adam, eds. *Soundings in Kings: Perspectives and Methods in Contemporary Scholarship*. Minneapolis: Fortress, 2010.

Lieu, Judith. "The Audience of the Johannine Epistles." In Culpepper and Anderson, *Communities in Dispute*, 123–40.

———. *I, II, & III John*. New Testament Library. Louisville: Westminster John Knox, 2008.

Lincoln, Abraham. *Abraham Lincoln: His Speeches and Writings*. Edited by Roy Basler. Cleveland: World, 1946. Reprint, New York: Da Capo, 1990. Citations refer to the Da Capo edition.

Lohfink, Norbert. *The Theology of the Pentateuch: Themes of the Priestly Narrative and Deuteronomy*. Translated by Linda Maloney. Minneapolis: Fortress, 1994.

Lutheran Book of Worship. Minneapolis: Augsburg, 1978.

McLaren, Brian. *Finding Our Way Again*. Nashville: Nelson, 2008.

———. *Generous Orthodoxy*. Grand Rapids: Zondervan, 2004.

———. *A New Kind of Christianity*. New York: HarperOne, 2010.

Meeks, Wayne, gen. ed. *The HarperCollins Study Bible*. New York: HarperCollins, 1993.

Mendenhall, George. "Covenant." In *IDB*, 1:714–23.

Migliore, Daniel. *Faith Seeking Understanding*. Grand Rapids: Eerdmans, 1991.

Miller, Robert, ed. *The Complete Gospels*. Sonoma, CA: Polebridge, 1992.

Moberly, R. W. L. *The Old Testament of the Old Testament: Patriarchal Narratives and Mosaic Yahwism*. Overtures to Biblical Theology. Philadelphia: Fortress, 1992.

Mosbo, Thomas. *Luke the Composer*. Minneapolis: Fortress, 2017.

Murphy, Cullen. *The Word according to Eve: Women and the Bible in Ancient Times and Our Own*. New York: Houghton Mifflin, 1998.

Neville, Richard. "Differentiation in Genesis 1: An Exegetical Creation *ex nihilo*." *JBL* 130 (2011) 209–26.

Newsom, Carol. "The Book of Job." In *NIB*, edited by Leander Keck et al., 4:317–637. Nashville: Abingdon, 1996.

Niebuhr, Reinhold. *The Nature and Destiny of Man: Human Nature*. Vol. 1. New York: Scribner, 1964.

Niebuhr, Richard. *Christ and Culture*. New York: Harper & Row, 1951.

O'Day, Gail. "The Gospel of John." In *NIB*, edited by Leander Keck et al., 9:491–865. Nashville: Abingdon, 1995.

Odell, Margaret. *Ezekiel*. Smyth & Helwys Bible Commentary. Macon, GA: Smyth & Helwys, 2005.

Pagels, Elaine. *Beyond Belief: The Secret Gospel of Thomas*. New York: Random House, 2003.

———. *The Gnostic Gospels*. New York: Random House, 1979. Reprint, New York: Vintage, 1989. Citations refer to the Vintage edition.

Pajunen, Mika. "The Saga of Judah's Kings Continues: The Reception of Chronicles in the Late Second Temple Period." *JBL* 136 (2017) 565–84.

Perkins, Pheme. "The Gospel of Mark." In *NIB*, edited by Leander Keck et al., 8:507–733. Nashville: Abingdon, 1995.

Perrin, Norman, and Dennis Duling. *The New Testament: An Introduction*. 2nd ed. New York: Harcourt Brace Jovanovich, 1982.

Peterson, Brian Neil. *John's Use of Ezekiel: Understanding the Unique Perspective of the Fourth Gospel*. Minneapolis: Fortress, 2015.

Polaski, Sandra Hack. *A Feminist Introduction to Paul*. St. Louis: Chalice, 2005.

Radford Ruether, Rosemary. *Sexism and God-Talk: Toward a Feminist Theology*. Boston: Beacon, 1983.

Rast, Walter. "Joshua." In *Harper's Bible Commentary*, edited by James Mays et al., 235–44. New York: Harper & Row, 1988.

Riley, Gregory. *One Jesus, Many Christs*. Minneapolis: Fortress, 2000.

Robertson, A. T. *A Harmony of the Gospels*. New York: Harper & Row, 1922.

Robinson, James. *The Gospel of Jesus: In Search of the Original Good News*. San Francisco: HarperCollins, 2005.

Rowley, Harold. *Moses and the Decalogue*. Manchester, UK: Manchester University Press, 1951.

Russell, Bertrand. *Mortals and Others*: Vol. 2, *American Essays 1931–1935*. Edited by Harry Ruja. New York: Routledge, 1998.

Sampley, J. Paul. "The First Letter to the Corinthians." In *NIB*, edited by Leander Keck et al., 10:771–1003. Nashville: Abingdon, 2002.

Sanders, E. P. *Paul: The Apostle's Life, Letters, and Thought*. Minneapolis: Fortress, 2015.

Sanders, James. *Canon and Community: A Guide to Canonical Criticism*. Guides to Biblical Scholarship. Philadelphia: Fortress, 1984.

———. *From Sacred Story to Sacred Text*. Philadelphia: Fortress, 1987.

Scholtes, Peter. *They'll Know We Are Christians*. Los Angeles: F.E.L., 1966; assigned to Lorenz (administered by Music Services), 1991.

Schussler Fiorenza, Elisabeth. "I Corinthians." In *Harper's Bible Commentary*, edited by James Mays et al., 1168–89. San Francisco: Harper & Row, 1988.

Schweitzer, Albert. *The Quest of the Historical Jesus*. Translated by W. Montgomery. UK ed., 1910. Reprint, with introduction by James Robinson, New York: Macmillan, 1968. Citations refer to the Macmillan edition.

Schwiebert, Jonathan. "Jesus's Question to Pilate in Mark 15:2." *JBL* 136 (2017) 937–47.

Seitz, Oscar. "Lists, Ethical." In *IDB*, 3:137–39.

Simpson, Cuthbert. "The Growth of the Hexateuch." In *IDB*, 2:188–200.

Skinner, Christopher. "Virtue in the New Testament: The Legacies of Paul and John in Comparative Perspective." In Skinner and Iverson, *Unity and Diversity*, 301–24.

Skinner, Christopher, and Kelly Iverson, eds. *Unity and Diversity in the Gospels and Paul*. Atlanta: SBL, 2012.

Snicket, Lemony [Daniel Handler]. *The Vile Village*. A Series of Unfortunate Events 7. New York: Scholastic, 2001.

St. John of the Cross. *Dark Night of the Soul*. Translated and edited by Allison Peers. First Image edition, 1959, by arrangement with Newman Press. Reprint, New York: Doubleday, 1990. Citations refer to the Doubleday edition.

Thompson, Marianne Meye. *The God of the Gospel of John*. Grand Rapids: Eerdmans, 2001.

Thurston, Bonnie Bowman. *The Widows: A Women's Ministry in the Early Church*. Minneapolis: Fortress, 1989.

Tickle, Phyllis. *The Great Emergence*. Grand Rapids: Baker, 2008.

Towner, W. Sibley. "The Book of Ecclesiastes." In *NIB*, edited by Leander Keck et al., 5:265–360. Nashville: Abingdon, 1997.

Trible, Phyllis. "The Book of Jonah." In *NIB*, edited by Leander Keck et al., 7:463–529. Nashville: Abingdon, 1996.

———. *God and the Rhetoric of Sexuality*. Philadelphia: Fortress, 1978.

———. "Jacob's Limp." Sermon delivered at Sardis Baptist Meetinghouse, Charlotte, NC, 2010.

———. *Rhetorical Criticism: Context, Method, and the Book of Jonah*. Guides to Biblical Scholarship. Minneapolis: Fortress, 1994.

———. *Strangers and Struggles*. Wake Forest Divinity School convocation booklet. Winston-Salem, NC: Wake Forest Divinity School, 2001.

———. *Texts of Terror*. Philadelphia: Fortress, 1984.

Tuckett, Christopher. "Jesus and the Gospels." In *NIB*, edited by Leander Keck et al., 8:71–86. Nashville: Abingdon, 1995.

Udoh, Fabian, et al., eds. *Redefining First-Century Jewish and Christian Identities: Essays in Honor of Ed Parish Sanders*. Notre Dame: University of Notre Dame Press, 2008.

Van Beek, G. W. "Samaria." In *IDB*, 4:182–88.

Van der Watt, Jan. "On Ethics in 1 John." In Culpepper and Anderson, *Communities in Dispute*, 197–222.

Van Seters, John. *Abraham in History and Tradition*. New Haven: Yale University Press, 1975.

———. *The Life of Moses: The Yahwist as Historian in Exodus-Numbers*. Louisville: Westminster John Knox, 1994.

———. *Prologue to History: The Yahwist as Historian in Genesis*. Louisville: Westminster John Knox, 1992.

———. "The Report of the Yahwist's Demise Has Been Greatly Exaggerated!" In Dozeman and Schmid, *A Farewell to the Yahwist?*, 143–57.

Von Rad, Gerhard. *Old Testament Theology*. Translated by D. M. G. Stalker. 2 vols. Edinburgh: Oliver and Boyd, 1962, 1965; San Francisco: Harper & Row, 1962, 1965. Citations refer to the Harper & Row editions.

Walsh, Carey. *Exquisite Desire: Religion, the Erotic and the Song of Songs*. Minneapolis: Fortress, 2000.

Weems, Renita. "The Song of Songs." In *NIB*, edited by Leander Keck et al., 5:361–434. Nashville: Abingdon, 1997.

Westermann, Claus. *Genesis: An Introduction*. Minneapolis: Fortress, 1992.

Wiesel, Elie. *All Rivers Run to the Sea: Memoirs*. New York: Knopf, 1995.

Wright, N. T. *Paul*. Minneapolis: Fortress, 2005.

Scripture Index

Genesis

Exodus